Editor
Walter Kelly, M.A.

Editorial Project Manager
Ina Massler Levin, M.A.

Editor-in-Chief
Sharon Coan, M.S. Ed.

Illustrator
José Tapia

Cover Artist
Larry Bauer

Associate Designer
Denise Bauer

Art Director
Elayne Roberts

Imaging
Hillary Merriman

Product Manager
Phil Garcia

Publishers
Rachelle Cracchiolo, M.S. Ed.
Mary Dupuy Smith, M.S. Ed.

HOW TO MANAGE YOUR
Middle School Classroom

Author

Jeff Williams

Teacher Created Materials, Inc.
6421 Industry Way
Westminster, CA 92683
www.teachercreated.com

©1996 Teacher Created Materials, Inc.
Reprinted, 2000
Made in U.S.A.
ISBN-1-55734-548-1

Table of Contents

Table of Contents *(cont.)*

Introduction

Once we stop learning, we stop teaching.

—teaching credo

This book was written with one purpose in mind: to improve the quality of middle school education. It is not a philosophical treatise filled with theory and speculation. Neither is it a research effort chronicling the procedures and practices of random teachers. This book is foremost a hands-on, nuts-and-bolts, bare-bones guide to what works in middle school—real knowledge gained through real experience. Many of the methods are timeless in their application, and many reflect the new demands of our changing society.

❑

Historically, middle school has been thought of as a time when youngsters create havoc for parents and teachers. Middle school teachers have seen little respect; their job has been just to get the student to high school in one piece, where "real" teachers could take over. Consequently, for many teachers the middle school has become merely a purgatory until a really nice spot in high school or elementary school opens up. Thus, in some middle schools, teachers may come and go like the wind. Unfortunately for the students, however, these transitional years may be the most impressionable and vulnerable of their young lives. At this time and this place they desperately need the stability of strong, effective teachers. Teaching middle school has its own intricacies; thus, the need continues for serious intermediate training.

❑

Meanwhile, this book will shed a few points of light on practical aspects of being a middle school teacher and the joy and success that can accompany it. This book is for the young and green, as well as the old and gray. In teaching excellence, there is no age indicator. Appropriate to this truism are the words of John F. Kennedy:

Youth is not an indicator of vitality, just as age is not an indicator of wisdom . . . .

Again, it all comes down to the quality of the individual.

The Micro/Macro Worlds of Middle School

In the micro-world of biology, understanding the basic forces which govern the early adolescent makes a big difference to teaching success. In the macro-world, teachers need to be aware of large issues concerning new ideas in teaching. All these factors combine for one clear goal—a better world for the students.

The middle years can be roughly defined as those between the ages of 10 and 14. When seen from a physiological and psychological framework, this is a unique stage in everyone's life. During this period, moreover, students' cognitive abilities are rising to new heights.

In many ways, middle school students are small children. When given the opportunity, however, middle schoolers show complex, adult-like thought. It is this basic contradiction which presents the greatest challenge to the middle school teacher. If the physiological and psychological framework of these students is understood, however, the teacher can recognize and adjust to their behavioral patterns.

Outline of Chapter 1

I. Biochemistry, Psychology, and Cognitive Growth
  A. Biochemistry
  B. Psychology
  C. Cognitive Growth

II. Megatrends in Education
  A. Teaming
  B. Block Scheduling
  C. Authentic Assessment

D. Mastery Learning
E. Interdisciplinary Instruction
F. Year-Around School
G. Site-Based Management
H. Learning Styles
I. Real-World Skills
J. Cooperative Learning
K. Technology Gap

The middle school student experiences these distinct biochemical changes:
1. puberty (growth spurt)
2. sexual maturation

Emotionally, the young adolescents experience the following:
1. identity crisis
2. peer pressure
3. family stability (or breakdown) and other factors which contribute to early adolescent experiences

Finally, the preadolescent reaches a stage of mental development characterized by the following:
1. expanding brain power
2. moral thought
3. problem-solving skills

The Micro/Macro Worlds of Middle School *(cont.)*

I. Biochemistry, Psychology, and Cognitive Growth

A. Biochemistry

Puberty

Puberty is the growth period which ends childhood and forms adolescents into their adult bodies. The first signals of puberty are undetectable, usually occurring around age 9 or 10.

This is the stage when hormones increase their concentration. For females, this means a dramatic increase in estrogen. Testosterone increases in males at this point. However, both hormones—testosterone and estrogen—are present in both males and females. About a year after hormonal deployment, the body shows its first visual signs of puberty—breast enlargement for the girls and testes enlargement for the boys.

Once the body has signaled puberty, it prepares itself for the last great biological miracle—the growth spurt. Around 10 to 12 years of age, children get noticeably heavier. The growth spurt is usually preceded by an accumulation of fat. This layer of fat creates a storehouse of energy needed to complete the growth spurt.

From ages 10 to 14, a young person can grow up to 10 inches. (There are many trips to clothing and shoe stores during these years.) In addition to height, adolescents experience rapid increase in muscle development.

This is a point where middle schoolers can make great strides in athletics, sometimes outperforming adults in many activities. The need to exercise and be physical is a part of all healthy adolescents' lives. Their bodies call out to be exercised. This is one reason middle school students cannot sit at a desk for long periods of time. As the muscular frame of the body becomes more pronounced, the body becomes more coordinated in general, losing the awkwardness sometimes associated with the preadolescent.

Along with weight, height, and muscle increase, young people experience minor increases in their oil, sweat, and odor glands. This is the reason for the most dreaded of all middle school afflictions—acne. Millions of dollars are spent on acne medicines, perhaps the largest segment of the medical industry targeted specifically to adolescents.

Also, the pubescent will probably take showers more seriously (to the relief of the parents) because shampoo, soap, and deodorant become essential to fight sweat and odor.

A Note About Nutrition

It is essential that young persons receive proper nutrition. Specifically, pubescents need calories and protein, calcium, iron, zinc, and vitamin D. Teachers who suspect malnutrition indicated by low energy levels, skin and hair problems, serious weight problems, or other signs should consult the school counselors for help for these children.

The Micro/Macro Worlds of Middle School *(cont.)*

A. Biochemistry *(cont.)*

Sexual Maturation

While puberty is making youngsters taller, heavier, and more muscular, the body is getting ready to make reproduction possible. This is revealed in two ways. For males, this means the capability of ejaculation, or sperm discharge. For females, this will result in the first menstrual period, called the *menarche.*

The menarche ushers in a new stage of life for all young women. Unfortunately, this can be a time of much pain and discomfort because of premenstrual cramps.

Moodiness, lack of effort, daydreaming, inattention, needing to go to the bathroom frequently, and other behaviors are sometimes caused by the menstrual cycle. Males are likewise affected by their new and somewhat awesome capability. It is only humane that teachers understand these signals and provide support for this difficult time. Again, nutrition plays an important part in this cycle as well. Iron deficiency, for example, will complicate menstrual activity greatly.

Apart from these two life-changing events, ejaculation and menstruation, the pubescent also experiences changes in what are known as the secondary sex characteristics. These changes mostly affect the appearance. For both sexes, hair growth develops under the arms, on the legs and arms, on the face, and around the pubic area. In addition, hair becomes coarser and darker. The voice changes, getting lower as the larynx grows larger. Body shapes tend to become more gender-specific, with females "curving out" around the hips and chest, and males developing wider shoulders.

With all these physiological changes taking place, it is easy to see how an early adolescent can be confused and self-conscious.

B. Psychology

Identity Crises

Along with many biochemical changes taking place in the middle schooler, there are a host of psychological concerns which confront the child and spill over into the classroom on a daily basis. Among the most important are identity crises, peer pressures, and influences from the family.

Throughout the early years, kids tend to understand their place in the world, worrying little about creating a self-identity. Starting in the middle school, however, a number of factors come together to give students a whole new concern in life—the search for identity. This search is the cause for a great majority of the early adolescents' behavior and attitudes. Such identity concerns can sometimes consume the time and energy of middle schoolers, blurring the importance of academics.

The Micro/Ma of Middle S

(handwritten note on page:)
Good questions –
Speak / Silent to the Bone
fitting in / cliques

The Girls
Breakfast Club
Bria's lesson

B. Psychology *(cont.)*

Questions which seem irrelevant to adults but are

- "Who will I hang around with? Who are my
- "Where in the cafeteria will I eat lunch?"
- "How do I fit into the social circle? Am I jock, prep,
- "When will I have my first romance (go with someone)?"

These questions of identity are usually much more important than anything else to middle schoolers. The good teacher knows how to work with these factors, not against them. Part of being a middle school teacher is understanding the context of the students' world, channeling their concerns and energies into productive results.

Peer Pressure

Peer pressure is closely linked with identity crises. The conventional wisdom of the family can seem outdated as the young person turns more and more to friends for ideas, values, and suggestions about life. Some even rebel blatantly against authority, causing complications in the home and classroom as well.

However, not all young people reject their old notions and values. For some, the connection to the family is strengthened even more during these years. The search for identity in such cases usually results in rejection of radical values.

Unfortunately, many children are influenced by newly acquired friends to break their bonds of home life and respect for teachers. Frequently parents are surprised and concerned when their children come home with new and different styles of clothing, haircut, or attitude. Sometimes, this is done simply to test the limits, to see how far they can push. In most cases, students' rebellious attitudes, clothing, and hair styles fade away as they mature.

The dark side of peer pressure emerges when students are tempted to try things they have been told never to do. In an alarming number of cases, this means experimentation with alcohol and other illegal drugs. This occurs at all socioeconomic levels; moreover, a growing number of drug users seem to be getting younger each year. This is evidenced by the need for elementary school anti-drug campaigns.

The Stability of the American Family

One of the prime destructive influences on our youth today is the breakdown of the family. Since almost half of all students come from single-parent or broken homes, the teacher is filling in as a parent. Complaining about the state of affairs is useless and inefficient. Teachers would do well to find ways to incorporate a family atmosphere into their classrooms, where a child can have a warm family environment for a part of his or her day.

The Micro/Macro Worlds of Middle School *(cont.)*

Compare + contrast
- lesson comparing two unrelated things

B. Psychology *(cont.)*

Other Factors

Other factors in the psychology of the young person are embarrassment, feelings of awkwardness, depression, feelings of isolation, confusion, anger, love, and disappointment. These stormy feelings blow through our lives like the wind, becoming especially erratic in the middle school years. For a teacher, this will manifest itself in a number of interesting interludes throughout the year. Dealing with sobbing girls (and sometimes boys) is not uncommon. Boys at this age, for instance, usually fight over romantic affairs more than anything else. In general, the middle school years are times of emotional swings.

C. Cognitive Growth

Besides the emotional and physical states of the early adolescent, the third domain of living is their cognitive, or mental, development. There are three areas of cognitive growth which every middle school teacher needs to know: expanding brain power, moral thought, problem solving.

Expanding Brain Power

The puberty cycle of young people affects all parts of their bodies, even their brains. By age 10, most children can start reasoning logically. Through trial and error, they begin to hypothesize about general principles.

An example of high-level thought processes is found in the ability of sixth graders to do complex algebraic equations. Before this, most students used their brain power to memorize multiplication tables. A fourth grader can tell you the answer to this question: $2 + 2 = ?$

But a fourth grader will probably not give you the answer to this: $2x + 3 = 11$.

This kind of operation is done by sixth graders all over the country.

Still another example of high-level thinking can appear in the English class. Middle school students are able to chart and diagram intricate comparisons and contrasts. Seeing similarities and differences is not easy for the brain. For instance, an elementary student can probably tell you the difference between a cop and a robber:

> *"The cop is good, and the robber is bad."*

But, if asked what is the same between a cop and a robber, the student might well have trouble understanding. If middle schoolers were asked this same question, they would be able to give various high level answers, perhaps like these:

> *"They are both people."*
> *"They both have a goal in mind."*
> *"They both wear their own types of uniforms."*
> *"One is a result of the other."*

The Micro/Macro Worlds of Middle School *(cont.)*

C. Cognitive Growth *(cont.)*

All in all, the brain power of the young person is quite formidable, capable of complex operations and scientific reasoning. Teachers have a big hand in this development, providing practice in high-level skills and encouraging complex thought processes, both inside and outside the classroom.

The most effective way a teacher can encourage the continuous growth of the brain is by encouraging reading. It is common knowledge that regular readers do better on spelling tests, are better writers, and show more general intelligence than infrequent readers; moreover, they are not prone to vegetate in front of TV. Reading helps children in all areas and in all subjects. The best part of reading, however, is that it is fun! How else can one be carried off into new worlds and exciting situations on a daily basis? The necessity of reading for the early adolescent cannot be overemphasized. Children who do not read during these years of brain growth may well fall far behind the cognitive growth of those who do.

Moral Thought

An exciting cognitive development, that of complex moral thought, begins in the middle school period. Many scholars tell us that the highest levels of thought are those of evaluation and judgment from reasoning. If this is true, then moral thought achieves the highest levels of thinking.

Students share different values, and some students are almost "anti-moral," meaning their code of ethics is to have none. However, large numbers of students can be preoccupied with moralizing about such issues as endangered species, saving the rain forest, abortion, religion, drugs, crime, welfare, racism, and other such topics.

The middle school teacher can build on this natural desire to argue what is right by providing fair treatment for all sides of an issue. The middle school classroom is an excellent forum for the exchange of opinions on moral issues. This enhances the students' rhetorical and speaking skills, as well as their insight into other opinions. As always, the teachers should stimulate thought processes by asking questions and giving feedback, exercising care in being judgmental.

Problem Solving

One cognitive skill that requires high-level critical thinking is problem solving. This skill becomes extremely important to the middle schooler who is faced with more and more complex problems every day, from math puzzles to the Valentine's Day Dance. If students are not equipped with problem-solving techniques (like the "four-step process"), they may well become frustrated and make poor choices. Problem solving is a critical real-world skill that should be transferred from the school to the outer world.

The Micro/Macro Worlds of Middle School *(cont.)*

C. Cognitive Growth *(cont.)*

The most basic problem-solving technique is the age old four-step process:

The Four-Step Process

1. Define the Problem
2. List the Options/Solutions

3. Try the "Best" Solution
4. If You Fail, Go Back to Step 2

Let's take a simple example. You are driving down the street one day, and you hear the explosive noise of a blowout. You get out of your car, and you see that your rear tire is flat. According to the four-step process, you could solve the problem as follows:

1. The problem is a flat tire.

2. The options/solutions are to . . .
   - get a jack and change the old tire for the spare.
   - leave the car and walk.

3. Solution #1 works.

4. The problem is solved.

Unfortunately, many problems are not as clear-cut as the this one. Let's take a scary, but all-too-typical, middle school problem.

✉ Showdown with Big Jake ✉

Theodore is a seventh grader at Rosa Parks Middle School. He is constantly picked on by an eighth grader everybody calls "Big Jake."

One day, Big Jake slams Theodore's locker and announces that Theodore is the biggest "sucker" that Big Jake has ever seen. Then he announces that if Theodore had any guts at all, he would meet him to fight on Friday after school at the "cornfields."

What should Theodore do to solve this problem? He remembers from Mrs. Clay's class about what to do when you have a problem. If Theodore uses the four-step process, he might come up with the following:

1. The problem is that Big Jake wants to fight me.

2. Some solutions are these:
   - Stand up for myself and fight him.
   - Not fight him and be called a "sissy."
   - Find someone else to fight him for me.
   - Tell parents or teachers and be called a "snitch."

The Micro/Macro World
of Middle School (cont.)

(handwritten note overlapping text:) Problem Solving — 4 step process — be creative → cleverly

3. O_____ ...
   c_____ ...
   kn_____ ... be called
   "sissy" or "sai_____ he is a very
   proud y_____. His decision is a
   compromi_____ by choosing options 1 and
   3 together, _____ will show up for the fight
   with his older _____ to protect him.

4. As the sand whir_____ into the air at the
   cornfields on that h_____ [-]day afternoon,
   Theodore waits nerv_____ g Jake.
   He hopes his solution w_____ ork. Here
   comes the bully, kicking sand and
   sneering wildly. Big Jake cannot even
   start to fight Theodore with Theodore's
   big brother right there.

"So, you going to fight like a man, or let your brother do the fighting for you—you little wuss," snarls Jake.

"Fighting you wouldn't solve anything, Jake. You just like to pick on people who are smaller than you," shouts Theodore, with a new wind of courage. The others start saying the same thing, too. The crowd turns on Jake, and he is suddenly surrounded. So Big Jake just curses him and goes home.

In this example, Theodore knew all his options and knew the direct consequences of them. By listing the parts of his problem, he was able to resolve the situation cleverly. Putting together your options and thinking on a new level is what problem solving is all about. As Theodore grows older, he will build on his problem-solving techniques. Who knows, he might find the cure for cancer or the common cold.

Teachers can encourage students to use their problem-solving skills by giving them a challenge and saying "Now you figure it out." In today's information age when new problems are continually being created, problem-solving abilities are crucial. The early adolescent needs rich experience with problem-solving activities. Teachers should plan many opportunities for them to engage in such activities.

The biochemistry of middle schoolers is a complex web of developmental change. These physiologically changing youngsters also face a maze of psychological concerns. Their most dramatic development, however, is in sheer brain power and capacity for complex thinking. This is the micro-world of hormones, neurons, and super egos which will have direct effect on the teacher's life. In a directly opposite orientation, the teacher feels the pull of the macro-world. These influences combine to comprise the megatrends in education.

The Micro/Macro Worlds of Middle School *(cont.)*

II. Megatrends in Education

Try something, and if it doesn't work, then try something else, but above all, try something!

—Winston Churchill

Along with the complications of adolescent development within, the teacher is also faced with complications of the educational world without. Some say there is a coming educational revolution. Some say that we are just at a point in the ever-turning cycle of reform and revision. In the famous federal analysis of education in 1983, a "rising tide of mediocrity" in our educational system was cited as choking our nation. While we watch Japan, Germany, and other countries surpass us in academic competencies and economic power, it is clear that schools are changing and trying different approaches to learning. Some of the most important reforms, like teaming, have already rooted and flowered. Some reforms, like block scheduling, are edging their way in, and some are still just ideas on the drawing table.

A middle school teacher needs to understand what is happening in the greater educational context and what is on the "cutting edge." Following is a brief list of some reforms gaining wide acceptance, two or three of which may already have affected your campus.

A. Teaming

The process of formal teaming is discussed in detail in Chapter 7. In general, teaming provides for a core group of teachers in different academic areas to share a pool or team together. This provides greater structure over large groups of students and gives teachers an efficient administration vehicle. A major improvement that teaming allows for is curriculum lining.

B. Block Scheduling

The need to give teachers more quality time with students has resulted in block scheduling, a term for throwing out the seven-to eight-subject daily schedule. Most block schedules double the time of the old 50-minute class. This, in turn, creates a two-day schedule, still composed of eight classes. Most educators greet block scheduling with open arms. Who would argue that we do not need more time to teach?

Some schools have even gone further with the block scheduling idea, combining disciplines into a "liberal arts" block (English and history) and a "science" block (science, technology, and math). The next day would be a "fine arts" block (music, dance, art), and then an "elective" block. Educators have found that approaches like this create more in-depth learning, more quality teaching in general, and better motivated students.

The negative aspects of block scheduling are that students and teachers sometimes have problems getting used to seeing each other every other day, instead of on a daily basis. Another problem is that teachers may have a hard time at first preparing longer lessons.

The Micro/Macro Worlds
of Middle School *(cont.)*

C. Authentic Assessment

A catchy buzz phrase in educational circles is "authentic assessment." This refers to a reevaluation of how we grade students. The procedure runs contrary to reliance upon traditional pencil-and-paper tests. To make your assessment of students' work authentic, more personal observation, mastery learning, peer and self-evaluations, and, above all, portfolios of students' work are needed. The theory is that this will help students prepare for the real world where workers are assessed on performance, as well as products. Furthermore, workers are asked to identify their own weaknesses so they can improve themselves through further training. Authentic assessment techniques are outlined in Chapter 5.

D. Mastery Learning

A genuine common-sense reform idea is the concept of mastery learning. It relies upon a simple rule: a student cannot go any further in a class until he or she has mastered the present content. So instead of giving an "F" on a paper, a teacher should give a "Do over until it is done right." Master teachers employ this technique frequently when they see that students have not grasped the purpose of an assignment. The mastery learning concept lends itself especially to self-paced units or modular units.

The main drawback of the mastery learning process is that it is extremely inefficient. A teacher simply does not have the time to address every student's individual needs which are all on separate calendars. Until class sizes go down or mastery learning is made more efficient, it cannot be fully realized. However, most teachers incorporate mastery learning principles into their teaching systems.

E. Interdisciplinary Instruction

Seeing learning as a whole process and not little isolated bits is the idea behind interdisciplinary instruction. More and more, teachers are being asked to team with other teachers to create units which act in conjunction with one another. Because they offer a certain theme, they are often called *thematic units*. The preparation for this type of teaching is more intense and involved, but the rewards are great. Students come to see learning as continuing from class to class, rather than as separate disciplines.

The drawbacks of thematic units can be political struggles within the teacher team, the time needed for preparation, and the shortage of good materials and resources. There are publishers, however, who put out excellent thematic units written by teachers (see back cover).

F. Year-Around School

Many reformists point out that a summer vacation has lost its relevance in today's information age. Many schools around the country are switching to a year-around schedule with the same amount of vacation, but it is just spread over more of the year. Such schedules work particularly well for students who cannot afford summer camps and vacations, for the year-around schedule provides them with guidance and positive supervision for closely connected periods of time.

The Micro/Macro Worlds of Middle School *(cont.)*

G. Site-Based Management

Probably the most exciting and powerful movement within education has been a power shift. The recognition that each campus is different and should be able to govern itself, try new things, and balance its own budget is long overdue. The transfer of power and administration from state and district to the campus itself is the essence of site-based management. In this context, a humble teacher can have a powerful voice in school, city, and community affairs.

H. Learning Styles

This idea reflects the common sense that we all learn differently. If a student cannot conform to the style of the teacher, the teacher must make some effort to conform to the style of the student. Proponents of the learning-styles theory assert that teachers should have two or three options to connect with the student for maximum comprehension.

I. Real-World Skills

There seems to be a widening gap between the school room and the work room. What is valued traditionally in our schools has been memorization of data, following directions, completing assignments, and studying for tests. The real world is seen as valuing a range of other skills, like problem solving, technical expertise, and social skills. The recognition that we should teach students skills that will help them in the real world has a rising tide of support.

J. Cooperative Learning

Having students team up for shared goals is coming back strongly. The need for social skills training is apparent today. On a broader level, the need for teamwork in the real world requires that we produce students who are ready to sacrifice for the greater good of society.

K. Technology Gap

Students in the United States are lagging in math and science. We need to educate our children about the scientific forces shaping the modern world, and many teachers are calling for immediate improvement.

The most important aspect of teaching remains as constant as the North Star—the special relationship of love and learning between the teacher and student. To encourage in every student a love of learning and moral character is the prime directive. Everything else is really on the periphery.

Creating Order in the Classroom

All battles are won before they are fought.

—Sun Tzu

The number one goal in all classrooms is first to create order. This does not happen all at once but in stages. The middle school classroom has its own unique challenges. Handling discipline problems is a part of every middle school teacher's life. However, these problems can be kept to an acceptable minimum if mutual respect is achieved.

What follows is a "nuts-and-bolts" how-to guide to achieving an ordered classroom.

Outline of Chapter 2

I. The First Week of School
   A. Creating the Environment: Preparing the Classroom
   B. First Day Activities
   C. Names/ID Cards
   D. Seating

II. Making Rules

III. Establishing Routines
   A. Warm-Ups
   B. Student Helpers
   C. Weekly Routines
   D. Making a Syllabus/Keeping a Calendar
   E. Keeping a Notebook

IV. Discipline
   A. Common Discipline Problems and Techniques to Stop Them
   B. Serious Discipline Problems and Their Solutions
   C. Violence in the Classroom
   D. Conflict Resolution
   E. Achieving Mutual Respect

Reproducibles for Chapter 2 (See pages 233–244.)

1. Matching Game

2. Personary Activity Sheet

3. Personal ID Sheet

4. Student Helpers Form

5. Syllabus Unit Planner

6. Mediators (5)

7. Conflict Resolution Form

Creating Order in the Classroom *(cont.)*

I. The First Week of School

Nothing is more dreadful and exciting at the same time than the anticipation of the first day of school. The summer vacation is over, and it's back to the mill. At the same time, the creative possibilities of a whole new group of young people are endless. In a greater sense, the obligation to society is a positive motivator for us all.

A. Creating the Environment: Preparing the Classroom

It is essential that you take some time to create your own atmosphere in a classroom.

Students like unique and colorful rooms. They are turned off by bare walls and blank areas. A room needs character, especially in middle school. A young person needs to feel at home. Sometimes, teachers see more of these youngsters than their parents do. Creating comfort zones is a tremendous help for all involved. Here are a few suggestions:

1. Provide a reading center with pillows or couches. Every subject involves reading, and students appreciate being able to lounge comfortably and read. After all, how would you feel if you had to sit in those stiff desks all day?

2. Make a technology center where students can have access to tape players, typewriters, or computers. Students can experience "books on tape," listen to instructional audio tape, practice typing, or use computers for various purposes.

3. Provide for tutoring corners where students who need to catch up or work alone can have the privacy to do so.

4. Bring plants and animals into the classroom. Plants can really enhance learning by relaxing the classroom. Small pets like gerbils are incredibly popular in the classroom and build a class spirit. For some, taking care of the class pet provides a duty and sense of self-worth. As has been documented from their use in hospitals, pets can even be therapeutic.

5. Eventually, put up pictures of the students. Photographs provide a real sense of identity, and students love to see themselves in pictures.

6. Hang attractive and informative posters from which students can learn.

7. Eventually hang student work and projects in and outside the classroom.

B. First Day Activities

Before any warm bodies come through the door, have all your paperwork ready. This usually includes class roster/attendance form, scheduling/head count forms, and your own activity with plenty of materials at hand. Place clear instructions on the board. Take a careful look at all schedules to make sure each student is in the right class. Late students might need to get schedules from the office. Be firm with students about discipline from the very start. This will send a message across the class that you mean business. After you have taken roll and checked schedules, begin your activity.

Creating Order in the Classroom *(cont.)*

B. First Day Activities *(cont.)*

All teachers have their own way to start the year. If you plan to get up in front of class and lecture students about class rules, you may not find much success. Many master teachers suggest that you have an active exercise which lets people introduce themselves and get to know one another. These "get to know you" activities come in myriad varieties. Some effective ones are the following:

1. *Pair Shares.* Have students pair up. Assign pairs that show variety. Next have them copy a question set and quiz each other on this personal information. They have to learn each other's answers and try to repeat them to the class. Questions like the following will stimulate interesting and informative discussion.

   • What is your name and birthday?
   • What is your favorite hobby?
   • What is your favorite subject, color, movie?
   • Do you have any pets?
   • How big is your family?
   • What are your plans for the future?

   This activity will create a lively atmosphere which you can monitor and support for about 15 minutes. After most students have finished, tell them that now they will share the information about their partners. They can look at the answers but should try to tell the class as much as they have memorized. This adds another 15 minutes of quality time.

   One advantage of this activity is that it shifts to another person the embarrassment of having to talk about oneself. It can be fun and silly, but it also utilizes memory, speaking, and cooperative skills.

2. *Matching Game.* There are many varieties of this activity. Basically, it calls for students to record personal information as in pair shares. They can write on paper, but if you are really prepared, you will provide preprinted activity sheets with picture boxes. For a ready-to-copy Matching Game form, see page 233. In these picture boxes, have students write their answers.

   Next, students must get up and search for classmates with the same answers in the picture boxes. When they find a match, have the students write their names in the box and move on to other students. Call time in 15 to 20 minutes. Now have volunteers recount how many matches they have found. Try to call upon everybody and announce each name. Other particulars about each one will be revealed in the students' presentations.

   This activity encourages students to meet one another, surprising many with their shared similarities. It would also be a nice touch if you had prizes like bookmarks or posters to give to those students who matched the most.

Creating Order in the Classroom *(cont.)*

3. *Personaries.* In this exercise, students create dictionary definitions of themselves and display them. Individually, or in pairs, have students write their definitions on the Personary Activity Sheet (page 234). If working in pairs, they can dictate to each other. The personary must include name, pronunciation key, part of speech, three-part definition, synonym, antonym, and picture, if desired. In their definitions, they need to include personality traits, physical characteristics, hobbies, etc. Once everybody is finished, have each person get up and read his/her personary to the class.

   Then have them tape all personaries together and string them across the class. This will provide a festival atmosphere as well as interesting and informative reading material. Students usually enjoy looking at everybody's personaries, especially if you have a large number of students. One-hundred fifty personaries can keep them busy for a month.

4. *Drawing Activity.* A simple and easy activity that can be fun for the students is making a map of the classroom from first-hand observation. Also, they can make a symbol of themselves to display. Another idea is to have them all write their names and symbols on a big piece of butcher paper for display.

5. *Writing Activity.* Give students an interesting set of questions to answer on paper. Questions like these will keep students writing for a good 15–20 minutes.

   • What did you do in the summer?
   • How do you feel about coming back to school?
   • What is your favorite subject and why?
   • What would you like to see more of in school?
   • What is your idea of a good teacher?
   • What do you like to do after school or on the weekends?

   After you call time, have a discussion to talk about the answers. You can learn much about the students this way, and it utilizes writing and speaking skills.

6. *Reading Activity.* Some teachers start their first days with a story, reading aloud or silently. The story is always interesting and related somehow to school. This will generate a discussion session where students voice opinions and thoughts. An activity like this provides a low-stress solution to what is often a very tense day, relieving anxieties and providing a relaxing atmosphere.

   Whatever activity you select, remember to have plenty of supplies and leave time to go over important matters, such as these: materials for the course, student notebooks, school policies, rules, bell schedules, and fire drill procedures.

Creating Order in the Classroom *(cont.)*

C. Names/ID Cards

An essential task for every teacher the first week of school is to get a list of all students with their personal information and class schedules. This will serve as a quick fingertip reference for addresses, phone numbers, and the locations of students at any given time of day. The list gives you immediate student access.

Most teachers like the ease of index cards for this information. However, some teachers prefer a form that they organize alphabetically and put into a student notebook. (Such a notebook can also store student records.) For a copy of Personal ID sheets, see page 235.

By the first week of school, you should also know everybody's name. Students appreciate being called by name, instead of "young man," "you there," or "young lady." A teacher will never get respect without knowing the names of the students. Also, be sure that students respect your name. Let your students know right from the beginning that you have a name and that they are expected to address you properly.

D. Seating

Seating arrangements make a big difference in the middle school classroom. The first week it is easy to use alphabetical order until you make an official seating chart.

In general, students have a possessive feeling about their desks. They want to know where they will be sitting every day. Without a seating chart, valuable class time will be wasted settling seating disputes. It is important that seating be enforced and standardized.

Remember also that seating is functional, changing according to instruction. There is no need to keep one seating pattern all year. Following are some varieties of seating patterns:

1. *Traditional Rows*

   Desks lined in straight rows facing the front of class work well for lectures, tests, individual work, or direct instructions. The traditional manner tends to keep the class well focused.

2. *Group Seating*

   The next most common form of seating is desks pushed together to form groups. The benefit of group seating is obvious—it allows students to focus together on work. Some teachers have permanent group seating, seeing the benefits of teamwork on a daily basis.

3. *Divided Rows*

   In this variation on long rows, desks are formed in two wings, facing each other. This allows for a middle area which the teacher can use for various purposes.

4. *Circular Seating*

   In this pattern, desks are formed into a circle. This allows for a "round table" effect, which is good for readings and discussions. Also, this pattern might be a good idea for class quiz shows and games, where contestants are in the middle. The teacher can sit or circulate around the room.

Creating Order in the Classroom *(cont.)*

II. Making Rules

Once you have established names and seating, the time is ripe to "lay down the law." Many teachers will tell you that it is best to have students cooperate in the legislative process. These ground rules will let students know exactly what to expect, especially since they have a hand in making them.

The process of making rules should take at least 30 minutes or more. Specifically, you should do these things:

- Ask your students, "What behaviors do you think are unacceptable in the classroom?"
- List all their answers on the board or screen.
- Go over each one and distill the best rules. Mark these on a poster board in large legible writing.
- Next, provide for a discussion of what happens after the rules have been broken or what the consequences should be. List the appropriate consequences below the rules on the poster board.

Let's step in now to Pine Oaks Middle School, in Cricket County Unified School District. Mrs. Eloise Agrippa is a seasoned English teacher. She goes through the rule-making process each year. Let's see how she did this year . . .

✉ Mrs. Agrippa Makes Rules ✉

Mrs. Agrippa is a sixth grade math teacher at Pine Oaks Middle School. On the second day of class, she decides it is time to make class rules. With students' participation, she lists the behaviors that are not acceptable.

One student suggests, "Well, I don't like it when people are talking all around me and I'm trying to listen."

"That's a good point, Andrea. I'll list 'Raise your hand before your speak,'" answers Mrs. Agrippa.

Paul puts in "You shouldn't be able just to get up when you feel like it."

"OK," replies Mrs. Agrippa, "How about . . . 'Do not get up without permission.'"

Cynthia cries, "How about if you bring candy to class, you have to bring enough for everybody!"

This results in murmurs of agreement that spread throughout the classroom.

"I'm sorry," replies Mrs. Agrippa, "School rules forbid food in the classroom, but good try. I'll write 'No candy or gum in the classroom.'"

Chrystina says "I'm sick of boys bothering us and messing with our things."

"That's a good point, Chrystina," answers Mrs. Agrippa, "but that will also apply to all girls as well. I'll put 'Have respect for each other's space and property.'"

Creating Order in the Classroom *(cont.)*

After a time in this fashion, Mrs. Agrippa's class has made a set of excellent rules. "You did a great job with the rules," Mrs. Agrippa tells her students, "and now let's go over the consequences of breaking those rules."

Mrs. Agrippa tells her class that she wants to be fair and that if anybody breaks these rules, she will give them the benefit of the doubt by giving them a warning. If the behavior happens a second time, she will administer classroom discipline, and if anyone is so foolish as to repeat for a third time, she will send him or her to the office with a referral and call the parents that night.

With a serious look, Mrs. Agrippa asks the class "Does everyone understand the consequences?" The students, impressed with images of the office and parental phone calls, nod their heads.

"Good," says Mrs. Agrippa, "then we are all in agreement. Let's put these rules up for everybody to see."

Mrs. Agrippa's Class Rules

1. Raise your hand before talking.
2. Do not get out of your seat without permission.
3. Respect each other's space and property.
4. Do not bring gum or candy to class.
5. Do not throw things in the classroom.

Consequences:

1st offense—warning
2nd offense—classroom discipline
3rd offense—referral to office

After everyone has surveyed the rules, Mrs. Agrippa says, "I will enforce these rules strictly, fairly, and consistently. You will know exactly what to expect in my classroom. I know we all slip up every now and then, but the important thing is to learn from our mistakes."

Making class rules with consequences is the foundation of an ordered classroom. These common misbehaviors can infect a class if not dealt with promptly and consistently. Mrs. Agrippa did a good job of bringing in student concerns, but in the end, she had final say. In fact, Mrs. Agrippa's rules stay pretty much the same over the years. Most middle school classrooms have rules like Mrs. Agrippa's. Handling the circumstances in which students break those rules is called *discipline*. We will discuss discipline later in the chapter.

Creating Order in the Classroom *(cont.)*

III. Establishing Routines

In the middle school classroom, it is extremely important that you establish some sort of routine. This increases efficiency because students know what materials to bring to class and what to expect. Successful middle school teachers tend to incorporate a number of routines:

A. Warm-Ups

A routine which gets students on task before the bell even rings is a pre-class exercise or warm-up. Warm-ups literally get the brain ready for the day's lesson, just like stretching exercises before an athletic game. Warm-ups allow time for the teacher to take attendance, get materials ready, and monitor student behavior. As students work on their warm-ups, walk around and see how they are doing. This will ensure accountability.

Warm-ups may be different and suited to each teaching style, but here is a set of common denominators:

- They do not take longer than 10–15 minutes (20–25 in a block schedule).
- They are challenging exercises that have relevance to past or future lessons.
- They are not "busy work" but quality thinking exercises.
- They usually are not graded, but answers are discussed in class.

Some common examples of warm-up exercises are the following:

1. Questions and Answers

A stimulating and challenging set of questions is given to the student from the overhead screen or blackboard. Students might have to use their textbooks to find answers.

2. Journals

Students are given a topic to write about, allowing expression of inner feelings and attitudes. Journals are kept private.

3. Vocabulary

Through various word games, students test their knowledge of the week's vocabulary words. Writing definitions, creating synonyms and antonyms, and drawing symbols are a few ideas.

4. Creative Writing

A good way to warm up and increase thinking skills is to have students write about a topic or a picture on screen. Students then read these out loud.

5. Problem Solving

Letting students solve a certain complex problem related to the class is a favorite warm-up among science and math teachers. For example, a long word problem can be fun and challenging.

Creating Order in the Classroom *(cont.)*

B. Student Helpers

Another routine to establish is the use of student helpers. This not only increases efficiency but teaches responsibility as well. Student helpers work best with the following activities:

1. Attendance

Find students with an eye for detail and a desire for accuracy and let them take attendance. However, it is not recommended that students mark on attendance cards. Have them tell you the names of absent or tardy students so you can verify and enter them.

2. Scribes/Recorders

Have students with good handwriting frequently do the listing and writing on blackboards or overheads. Have a date monitor who changes the date every day on the board.

3. Paper Passers/Homework Collectors

Select responsible students to collect homework and pass out papers.

4. Organizers

Have volunteers organize book shelves, racks, or areas as needed.

5. Messengers

For across-school correspondence, select a handful of messengers to deliver it.

6. Transparency Washers

The task of cleaning transparencies can be transferred to the volunteer. Some students love to work together cleaning transparencies—one washing and one drying.

Make a chart in class which lists jobs. "Change the guard" every now and then to include everybody and share responsibility. Middle schoolers have a lot of energy they can channel into productive activity. It is important to stress a shared community of workers where everyone feels needed and productive. Spread these jobs around to increase the motivation of "slacker" students by giving them a sense of self-worth. For a Student Helpers form, see page 236.

C. Weekly Routines

It is good sense to develop a weekly routine. No one routine is best for everyone. Let's go back to Pine Oaks Middle School and profile Mrs. Linda Clay, an English teacher.

✉ Mrs. Clay's Week ✉

Linda has been teaching English for 10 years in middle school and has developed a successful weekly schedule. It looks like this:

Monday—spelling pre-test, writing
      workshop
Tuesday—reading, grammar

Wednesday—authors, cooperative learning
Thursday—reading, speaking workshop
Friday—spelling test, enrichment

Creating Order in the Classroom *(cont.)*

Students know generally what to expect in Mrs. Clay's classroom. For instance, Billy knows that today is Tuesday, so he should bring his novel to class. Tomorrow, Billy will probably remember to bring his pencils for the authors' map lesson. And on Thursday night, Billy will study for his weekly spelling test on Friday. However, once the spelling test is over, Billy knows that he can turn to other enrichment activities. Billy loves Fridays in Mrs. Clay's class.

Setting a weekly routine can help students find security in the confused world of middle school.

D. Making a Syllabus/Keeping a Calendar

Most teachers are required to make detailed lesson plans for each day of teaching. Sometimes these can be so time consuming that one loses sight of the big picture. All teachers should take time to reflect on the big picture and plan their objectives for at least a six-week period. Keep in mind that a syllabus is flexible and can change.

However, students do appreciate being handed a syllabus every six weeks or so because it increases their awareness and confidence in the course. It gives them a road map to see where they are going and how to get there. In addition, a syllabus functions as a calendar on which to make important notes. A syllabus should provide the following information:

1. list of projects, readings, special units, events
2. important due dates
3. calendar with activity/lesson indicated
4. special notes about the planning period

For specifics on planning units, see Chapter 4. A Syllabus Unit Planner ready for you to copy and use is on pages 237–238.

E. Keeping a Notebook

Another good routine to establish is good organization. As a teacher, you will have to answer the fundamental question, "How will students organize and retain information in my class?" For most teachers, this means a three-ring notebook.

The notebook is probably the best tool for students because it keeps work in sections, has pockets, and can hold spirals and supply bags. The common supply list given by most teachers is as follows:

1. 2" notebook with pockets
2. sectional dividers
3. supply bag, with "the works"
4. warm-up spiral notebook

Let's again turn to Pine Oak Middle School. It is time to meet Mr. Hamad, the sixth grade science teacher. Mr. Hamad is doing the right thing by trying to get his students organized early in the course.

Creating Order in the Classroom *(cont.)*

✉ Mr. Hamad's Notebook ✉

Mr. Hamad likes his science students to be very organized. In their science notebooks, he requires them to have the following sections:

   I. Vocabulary

  II. Labs/Classwork

 III. Collateral Readings

 IV. Homework/Home Experiments

  V. Extra-Credit

 VI. Warm-Up Spiral

Mr. Hamad explains to the class early on that organization is very important in his class, as well as in the real world. In real jobs, your boss will expect you to have organized files and systems.

In fact, organization is so important that it will be part of their grade. Their notebooks will be checked and recorded by the binder monitors (student helpers) every Friday. All that the students have to do is put their papers in the proper place in their notebooks, and they will get a "100." However, if they do not have their binders organized, they will get no credit and have to make it up in an after-school organization workshop. In this example, Mr. Hamad is not only creating rules of organization but enforcing them weekly by the efficient use of student helpers.

Unfortunately, the notebook system is not flawless. The drawbacks to using notebooks are the following:

1. *Paper Damage:* The advantage of notebooks—transferability of paper—is also their biggest weakness. Paper will get stretched, ripped, and torn from the metal rings which keep it. One way to solve this problem is through reinforcers. These small white circles adhere to the paper and mend the rip.

2. *Binder Crisis:* It is going to happen; somebody will drop a binder and the contents will bleed all over the floor. What look like a million papers go flying everywhere, and the student must hurry to the next class. The best thing to do is to take time to carefully put the papers back in order. You can always write the student a pass to go to class.

3. *Ring Damage:* Sometimes the metal rings on a binder get bent. Unless you can bend them back, that binder is useless and will only be a problem for the student.

4. *Binder Bulk:* Binders tend to be heavy and big, hard to carry, and a burden on the locker. It is usually a good idea to have one binder for several classes.

Some effective ways to establish routines are to provide warm-ups, assign student helpers, establish a weekly pattern, give students a syllabus, and require notebooks for class organization. However, do not let routines stifle your spontaneity. Change things around every now and then and provide for variety.

Creating Order in the Classroom *(cont.)*

IV. Discipline

If you work with large numbers of students, you will have to administer discipline. More and more, teachers are being asked to handle their own discipline problems. Sending kids to the office is considered a last resort and suggests that the teacher cannot handle the problem. Many teachers will tell you that discipline problems have been getting steadily worse over the years. Quite certainly they have changed, requiring new methods to deal with them. For instance, corporal punishment has been rejected, seen as archaic, cruel, and useless. It does not matter where you teach—at an elite private school or the poorest inner-city school—you will encounter behavior problems. So how do teachers deal with behavior problems in this modern world?

The best defense against behavioral problems is an exciting curriculum. When students are interested in their classes and their minds are being challenged, they do not have time for misbehavior. Unfortunately, the most exciting curriculum in the world cannot stop all misbehavior. In all cases the teacher's aim should be to deal with discipline quickly and efficiently, without cutting into class time. Good teachers practice preventive discipline, redirecting behavior to avoid problems. The last resort is corrective discipline where behavior must be stopped immediately.

What follows is a guide to . . .

- common discipline problems and techniques to stop them.
- serious behavioral problems and their solutions.
- conflict resolution.

A. Common Discipline Problems and Techniques to Stop Them

If you ask any experienced middle school teacher "What's the most common form of misbehavior?" the probable answer is "talking." This means talking out of turn, discussions with neighbors, or interrupting. Other common misbehaviors are inappropriate silliness, blurting out, rudeness, chewing gum, and fidgeting in a seat. Depending on the dynamics of your class, you will deal with this type of problem 10–15 times a day. How can a teacher take care of these problems without wasting valuable class time? Here are some valued techniques:

1. Physical Proximity

By standing or walking near the student who is talking, a teacher can usually snuff out extraneous chatter. Proximity is a powerful weapon to defeat most misbehaviors in the classroom. A teacher needs to be physically omnipresent—walking up and down aisles, around the back of the room, on the sides, and in front. Using physical proximity, a teacher can stop talking problems without missing a beat of the lesson.

2. Signaling a Student

By writing their names on the board or tagging their desks with a self-sticking note, a teacher can send a signal that offending students will suffer consequences from their misbehavior. Again, this technique will not interrupt a lesson.

Creating Order in the Classroom *(cont.)*

3. Hand/Eye Signals

Making eye contact, waving a hand, or other obvious gestures can be effective in some cases to stop misbehavior. Unfortunately, this also gives the student undue attention.

4. Polite Requests

Some teachers command such respect from their students they can ask them politely to stop a given behavior and the students will. "Could you please stop talking? It's very rude and it bothers other people around you." This technique is effective because it places the burden of decision on the student. Also, students are more likely to respect teachers they feel respect their intelligence enough to ask politely.

A firmer form of this technique is "I'm going to ask you politely once, please stop taking." The politeness is edged with a strong signal that the next time the teacher will not be polite at all.

5. Role Reversal

An effective technique for some students is to make them see how rude they are being by putting them in the teacher's shoes. Ask the student "How would you feel if you were the teacher and I was interrupting you?" Sometimes, kids have simply never looked at their behavior from another's point of view.

6. Feelings

For some teachers, an effective strategy is to point out that teachers have feelings, too. Students feel ashamed that they hurt someone's feelings. If a teacher sadly announces that it hurts her feelings when students interrupt her, students usually think twice. This is also effective for male teachers, breaking societal stereotypes that males do not show their feelings.

7. Irony/Humor

Some teachers can make effective use of humor and irony to stop spontaneous chatter. "Oh, I'm sorry, did I interrupt you? I'm just trying to teach a class. Would you mind if I continued?" or "Do I have your permission to continue?" are questions which send a clear message to the students and require intelligence to fully understand.

8. Merit System

Some teachers do very well with the merit system, also called a token economy. In this system, students are rewarded with a merit or other positive reinforcement for behaving themselves properly. At certain times, those who have collected enough merits are given extra privileges. On the other hand, misbehavior warrants demerits, with certain consequences.

Creating Order in the Classroom *(cont.)*

B. Serious Discipline Problems and Their Solutions

If a student ignores your warning or reprimand and continues misbehaving or talking, it should be considered a serious problem. Besides talking, the other two common problems in the middle school classroom are tardiness and not preparing homework. For these graver discipline problems, you might try this:

1. Isolation/Time Out

If talking is a constant problem, you may have to isolate students by moving them away from tempting conversations. When isolating, always move students nearer to you so you can keep an eye on them. Moving students to the back of the class is counterproductive. Some chronic discipline problems need long term or permanent isolation. Remember that isolation is not a punishment; it is used to help the student do better in school.

Some teachers prefer to have a "time out station." This is a good idea for two reasons. First, students are likely already to be trained on what a "time out" is from elementary school, where it is a standard discipline procedure. Second, "time out" gives a psychological break for the students and lets them think about their actions. Making time out a comfortable place is an interesting ploy that makes it possible for the students to relax and reflect on why they have to be separated from the group.

2. Mediator/Discipline Responses

If students are particularly offensive, administer a mediator immediately. Mediators are plays on the old "writing sentences" punishment. However, they are more advanced and effective. Instead of copying "I will not talk in class" one hundred times, students must copy a set of questions and answers which tell them exactly what they did wrong and how it affects the class. Questions like "What did I do wrong?" and "What should I have done?" also have compete answers which must be copied in full. A mediator usually comes out to about a page. Mediators are commonly used for talking, tardiness, rudeness, not following directions, not having homework, and inappropriate silliness. It is easy to make your own mediator; just type out specific behaviors which you find inappropriate and word the mediator so that the students get the full import of what they did wrong. Then laminate it and keep in a handy place. For mediator forms on Tardiness, Rudeness, Silliness, Not Following Directions, and Talking, see pages 239–243.

3. Teacher-Student Conference

A time-honored technique for stopping misbehaviors is the old "hallway chat." (Note: Keep an eye on the class at the same time, perhaps propping the door open.) The advantages of this technique are that it confronts the students immediately and seriously. Without their peers as an audience, some students can be made to feel the gravity of the situation. In Mr. Rockler's eighth grade history class, students are preparing for the school day . . .

Creating Order in the Classroom *(cont.)*

✉ Jimmy's Deal ✉

"Everybody take out your lines, please," announced Mr. Rockler to his eighth grade history students who still had the morning grumps. "Now," continued Mr. Rockler, "we will see how far Spain moved up the continent—Jimmy, put that up. Please stop talking and take out your time line, please . . . Thank you." As the teacher continued his exercise, Jimmy was laughing and being annoying.

"Jimmy, I'll give you one last chance to join the class," said Mr. Rockler, who had no patience for class clowns. Jimmy stopped at that direct comment.

"Man, I'm not doing nothin'! Why you pickin, on me, Mister?" blurted out Jimmy. Mr. Rockler wheeled around and faced Jimmy directly.

"Number one," said Mr. Rockler, "my name is Mr. Rockler, not *Mister,* and number two, you can get up and follow me out into the hallway."

At this point, Mr. Rockler could write a referral on Jimmy for disrespect, but he decides to use the teacher-student conference option. Out in the hallway, Mr. Rockler confronts Jimmy.

"Jimmy, you are showing me no respect, and I don't appreciate it. You know that I don't put up with people cutting up in my class, don't you . . ."

"Yeah, I guess, . . ." Jimmy mumbles as he stares at the floor.

"Jimmy, what's the problem? Is there something I should be aware of?"

"Well . . ."

"What is it? Maybe I can help?"

"You wouldn't understand, Man," Jimmy sneers.

"Try me; at least I can let you back into my class."

"My girlfriend broke up with me, okay, Man? Are you happy?"

After a pause, Mr. Rockler says, "I understand, Jimmy, but you can't let that interfere with your own success. Now, come back into class. I want you to use the reading center to read your novel, and if you feel like it, you can join the rest of the class, okay?"

"Yeah, okay."

Creating Order in the Classroom *(cont.)*

In this example, Mr. Rockler is able to diffuse a potentially explosive situation. Mr. Rockler's clever compromise with Jimmy to use the reading center achieves two things: (1) Jimmy will have more time to think out his "life-threatening" problem and will feel as if Mr. Rockler's room is safe, and (2) Jimmy will spend time improving his brain by reading, although he will have to make up the time line activity.

Another, less dramatic, way to conduct a teacher-student conference is to talk to the child after class, at lunch, or after school. This gives a private, low-stress environment to what can become a productive discussion.

4. Assigning Detention

Some teachers find it productive in many ways to assign detention for misbehavior. This works especially well if students are missing assignments or behind on school work. An efficient way to structure detention hall is for your team to organize team d-halls, where one teacher stays after school with d-hall students once a week (see Chapter 7 "Teaming").

Lunch detention can be an effective strategy for those less serious offenses, especially effective for the more social of the species because they cannot stand to miss out on lunch-time gossip.

Check your school policy on this, for some school districts will not allow students' lunch time to be used for this purpose.

5. Calling Parents

From your students' records, you can get the phone numbers of the parents. Some parents appreciate being called at work, while others like to discuss personal matters in the home only. All you have to do is ask. Parents usually make a tremendous difference in the discipline process (see Chapter 11, Parental Involvement).

6. Giving a Referral

Your last resort as a teacher is to remove the offending student. Every school has its own discipline referral form. At this stage, the student becomes the responsibility of the administrator of discipline and will be assigned in-school suspension or other measures, depending on the nature of the problem. Parents may also be called at work to notify them immediately of their child's problem.

The following list of behaviors will commonly result in a referral:

- vocally arguing with a teacher/extreme disrespect
- cursing
- hitting/fighting
- defacing property/graffiti
- refusing to do school work

When administering a referral, you may wish to send the student immediately or wait to give the referral to your administrator later.

Creating Order in the Classroom *(cont.)*

7. **Calling for an Administrator**

   In middle school the two maximum offenses are these:

   - drugs and/or alcohol
   - weapons

   If you suspect or hear about either of these two offenses, never confront the student personally. Call for an administrator to get the student to a safe area before attempting any inventories. Dealing with drugs and weapons is not your job, so do not make it your job; let a trained professional handle it. Students with drugs or weapons should be handed over to the local law enforcement agencies. Children with a history of these types of problems need professional counseling. They still can turn their lives around if somebody cares enough to help.

C. Violence in the Classroom

Very rarely, violence may erupt in the classroom. The most common occurrence is fighting. Although it happens more in the hallways and outside, fighting is still a potentiality in the classroom. Fighting is more common in middle school than during any other time of life. This fact crosses cultures and economic classes, probably owing to the biochemical and psychological changes that color the middle years. Fighting also crosses gender lines. Girls are almost as likely to be victims or perpetrators of violence as are boys in middle school.

It is important to distinguish between violence and "play" fighting. In particular, boys are prone to running, chasing, dodging, wrestling, and "ninja" fighting, if given the chance. Such activities express their need for exercise and the imaginative adventure world that most young boys slip in and out of.

However, if and when a real fight does break out, you need immediately to do the following:

1. Shout "Break it up now!" Sometimes, a strong, loud, authoritative voice actually works.
2. Call for an administrator immediately, by messenger or intercom.
3. Learn your district policy. Some districts want teachers to physically break up fights.
4. If you break the fight up, put fighters on separate sides of the room.
5. Wait for an administrator to arrive to collect the students.
6. After a fight, a teacher may approach the class in two ways. First, you can act as if nothing has happened and speed right along with the day's activities. Second, you may stop and talk about the fight with the class and develop a spontaneous lesson on violence. Either way, make sure you document the fight immediately and write up all students involved.

Creating Order
in the Classroom *(cont.)*

D. Conflict Resolution

Teachers can help decrease violence in schools and society by teaching conflict resolution. The techniques may be used for just about any disagreement. In conflict resolution, students generally follow these steps:

1. Both parties sit down and explain their sides of the story.
2. A trained mediator (either student or adult) is present to make sure both sides are equally represented.
3. An attempt is made to see each other's viewpoint.
4. Options and compromises are put on the table.
5. Some sort of agreement is made, even it it is "an agreement to disagree."

Many schools have peer mediation groups trained by counselors to mediate conflicts and find resolution. The idea here is to become more tolerant of others. At the very least, participants in conflict resolution sessions go home with much to think about.

If you want to try to mediate a session, find a good time during or after school and have students fill out conflict resolution forms. For a Conflict Resolution form, see page 244.

E. Achieving Mutual Respect

Above all, achieving an ordered classroom involves adherence to the principle of mutual respect. Many master teachers tell their students "If you respect me, then I'll respect you." By handling minor discipline problems efficiently and serious problems correctly, as well as having routines and a clear set of class rules, teachers generally receive a healthy level of respect from their students.

We have seen how Mrs. Clay handled her weekly routines, how Mr. Hamad made use of student helpers, how Mrs. Agrippa developed her class rules, and how Mr. Rockler administered discipline efficiently. Discipline will not be a major problem in these classrooms. Experienced middle school teachers have their system in place and continuously improve it. Achieving mutual respect usually means walking a fine line between being a student's friend and being a student's authority. Other practices that seem to help students gain respect are *fairness, consistency, humor,* and *apologies.*

Fairness is a big factor in achieving respect. If students see the teacher give favor to some students but come down on others for minor offenses, then they will probably not trust that teacher. Consistency, which is related to fairness, is another practice which middle schoolers are quick to detect. If a teacher does not provide the same consequences for misbehaviors, he or she will not be respected. Turning confrontational situations into humorous ones can diffuse a discipline problem and add to class morale. Apologizing is another good leadership technique. We all lose our tempers sometimes. You might turn this around for the better. If you were to come right out and explain to kids that you were out of line and should not have told Adam that he "whines like a baby," they would tend to respect you for it. Apologizing to students also gives a model for the rest of the class to follow.

Teaching the Basics

When you have created order in your classroom, you must attend to what tax payers are paying you for—teaching the basics. This includes state and district mandates. You will also have to decide how you will use the textbook. In addition, the basics are expanding to include many other special considerations that you must weave into your curriculum.

Outline of Chapter 3

I. Staying in Tune with the Essential Elements
    A. State Requirements
    B. District Guidelines

II. How to Make Effective Use of the Textbook
    A. Background/Purpose
    B. Textbooks in the Classroom
    C. Keeping Tabs on the Textbooks

III. How to Make the "Boring" Fun
    A. Quiz Show
    B. Dramatic Interpretation
    C. Costumes
    D. Audio-Visuals
    E. Manipulatives
    F. Simulations
    G. Oral Readings
    H. Word Games/Puzzles

IV. High-Level Thinking
    A. Literal
    B. Interpretive/Applied
    C. Analytical/Critical/Creative
    D. Evaluative/Moral

V. Learning Styles
    A. Cognitive Maps
    B. Allowing Options

VI. Special Needs Students
    A. ADD (Attention Deficit Disorder)
    B. "Slow Learners"/General Learning Disability
    C. Dyslexia
    D. Wheelchair Bound
    E. Hearing/Visually Impaired
    F. Emotionally Disturbed
    G. Bilingual
    H. Gifted
    I. Special Classrooms

VII. Reading in the Content Area

Reproducibles for Chapter 3 (See pages 245–247.)

1. *Book Check-Out List*
2. *Textbook Record Sheet*
3. *Cognitive Map Form*

Teaching the Basics *(cont.)*

I. Staying in Tune with the Essential Elements

A. State Requirements

Not just anyone can be a classroom teacher. The training for teachers is generally intense, and many candidates are refused a teaching license for legitimate reasons. Every teacher carries a certification that lists appropriate grade levels and subjects which that teacher is licensed to teach. Each state, working with colleges and universities, handles the licensing procedures. When you are hired by a public school, you sign a contract with that district. Your ultimate boss is actually the governor, representing the people of your state. (Incidentally, the highest level of power in education in the country is the state, according to the United States Constitution, since all powers not mentioned therein automatically belong to the state.)

As a servant of your state, you are charged with a vital task: to ensure the preservation of our culture, to instill good values, and to spark the fires of success, curiosity, and achievement. However, the state realizes that this must be done in an organized fashion. They have developed, therefore, a detailed list of objectives which every student should master according to grade level and content area. This list, often called the Essential Elements of Education, is combined with all the other state administrative guidelines and comes in a stack of paperwork and notebooks about a mile high.

However, the Essential Elements (EE's) are easy to find and reference. *It is important that you make a copy of these if you are not provided with one.* The EE's spell out specifically what they expect from the schools in terms of curriculum. It is your job to know and achieve these goals because that is what you are paid for. Even in private schools, state EE's are a fundamental part of being an effective teacher.

Teachers need to take a second look at their state's EE's because they are changing. Formerly, state EE's concentrated only on cognitive goals, which are specific in nature. For instance, an eighth grade history objective in the state of Nebraska might read as follows:

Students will learn the specific geographical areas of Nebraska and be able to explain their significance.

Today, EE's are reflecting reformist ideas by adding new dimensions, such as emotional (sometimes called *affective*) objectives. An emotional objective in the same history class might read as follows:

Students will appreciate native American culture by analyzing their native language, art, dance, habitation, and religion.

Notice, the objective is to "appreciate" and not just "learn." This is a new way of thinking about education.

Whatever type of EE's your state has, you are expected to teach them. In fact, the core of your course should reflect the EE's.

In essence, the states are trying to speed reform. Teachers can help this process by knowing and supporting their state's EE's.

Teaching the Basics *(cont.)*

B. District Guidelines

District guidelines are based on the EE's but provide a much more specific list of objectives. For instance, each district usually has a reading list for each grade level. If you are a reading teacher, you must stick to that list. For science, specific labs are listed, and so on for each subject and grade level. Guidelines are essential to follow for these reasons:

1. To Eliminate Redundancy

It can be very frustrating if you plan to read a book for a class and, as you are introducing it, students pipe up "We've already read that in fifth grade." Keeping teaching materials grade-specific can eliminate redundancy. Curriculum would be a mess without guidelines on major teaching materials like books and science labs. Also, bad feelings are avoided between teachers who might "intrude on another's curriculum." This process of streamlining the district curriculum is also known as curriculum lining.

2. To Provide Course Structure

Especially for the teacher new to a district, guidelines can give an automatic outline for the year. If you do not know what you are going to teach, at least you can get a good idea from the guidelines. This might sound like an Orwellian nightmare, with Big Brother looking over your shoulder and telling you what to do. However, guidelines usually have built-in flexibility and are not as rigid as they seem. The guidelines will not teach the course. It is your job to come up with ways to meet those guidelines.

Most teachers use the guidelines for reference and ideas. For example, let's return to Pine Oaks Middle School and meet Loretta Orangetree. Mrs. Orangetree is a sixth grade language arts (LA) teacher. She is getting ready to plan a 12 week instructional period . . .

✉ Mrs. Orangetree Plans a Semester ✉

As Mrs. Orangetree fumbles for her notebook, referred to as "the red one that says 'guidelines' on it," she is apprehensive about the coming year. "What should I teach this year? What can I do better this year? What kinds of things should I do in the classroom?"

"Now, where did I put the new guidelines?" she mumbles.

"Ah!" she says as she takes it off the shelf. Looking in the table of contents, she sees the title "Grade 6: Language Arts."

Turning to the appropriate page, Loretta scans the section until she finds what she wants—"instructional units." The pages report: Cricket County 6th Grade Language Arts Units:

I.	Folklore	V.	Science Fiction
II.	Mystery	VI.	Poetry
III.	Historical Fiction	VII.	Novel
IV.	Theater/Play		

Teaching the Basics *(cont.)*

As she turns the pages, Mrs. Orangetree gets lots of good ideas that she can build on or attach to her already advanced curriculum. She decides to start out on the folklore unit, then move to poetry, and end up with a mystery unit in the winter.

Her district, moreover, provides a multitude of extra resources and activities from the top teachers of the district. Loretta will make copies of these for her classes.

She also notices that the mythology unit she wanted to do is found only in 7th grade. She will have to find another unit or talk to the 7th grade teachers to work out a compromise. Now, Mrs. Orangetree can start the fun—planning.

In this example, the teacher not only found many ideas and materials for her unit, but also she avoided a major conflict with the 7th grade English teachers. Giving teachers areas of curriculum to work within is not meant to restrict the creative freedom of the teacher but to eliminate redundancy.

Staying in tune with state and district guidelines is imperative for an effective teacher.

II. How to Make Effective Use of the Textbook

A. Background/Purpose

The textbook has been the basic tool of teaching since the first Roman grammar schools. The efficiency and consistency of textbooks were recognized by the Romans who were on their way to reeducate the known world. During the Middle Ages, monks were busy copying manuscripts of Greco-Roman authors, as well as writing books of their own. These would become the textbooks of the first universities. As society became more advanced in literature, science, business, and culture, the printing press was developed and books flooded cities and villages.

In America, the first real textbook was the Bible. This was used for grammar, moral lessons, and storytelling for small children as well as older youths. In 1837, Horace Mann put the first public school system in place in Massachusetts. His ideas of uniform teacher training and public schools open to all children became the model for the present American education. This system also demanded a full textbook industry.

Today the textbook industry is privately managed, making millions of dollars each year in lucrative state contracts. Textbooks are the most expensive part of many state budgets. The state education board sets the standards for textbooks. These books are loaned to students and used for approximately three to five years. Throughout the years, the purpose of textbooks has remained the same:

1. Provide Content Basis for the Class

All the information that you are expected to teach is contained in the textbook. In most cases, the teachers cannot remember the detailed facts and exact figures that a textbook has. It is a giant bank of knowledge for the whole course, contained in a portable package that fits neatly into a backpack.

Teaching the Basics *(cont.)*

2. Evaluation/Testing

Also, the text has excellent tests and other evaluative questions that come right from the readings. This increases teacher efficiency and gives instant feedback to the students.

3. Activities

Frequently textbooks have interesting, preplanned activities appropriate for the grade level which they serve. Recent textbooks reflect many reform ideas, like adding cooperative learning exercises, portfolio ideas, interdisciplinary formats, and critical thinking skills.

B. Textbooks in the Classroom

Many teachers find textbooks to be useful and effective tools. For instance, most math teachers would not dream of discarding the textbook. However, some advanced teachers will not even crack open a textbook the whole year because they have gathered their own materials. Essentially, they have made their own textbooks. Most teachers will find it useful to use textbooks some of the time.

To complicate matters, texts vary in quality and individual style. A great text to one teacher might be useless to another. In addition, the actual content in texts changes with each new edition. The textbook companies usually try to reflect the state Essential Elements, which are constantly changing. In your school's book vault, you might find a 1985 world history text which chronicles the history of Western Europe. However, the updated text is called *The Eastern Hemisphere*. The same case can be found in most subjects where emphasis has shifted or new information has been added. Finding the right textbook for your style is a worthy endeavor.

If you are a teacher who does not use the textbook often, you will at least need to provide a class set of texts. Class sets are only to be used in the classroom. However, if students need to take a text home, have them check it out on the Book Check-Out List (page 245). The Book Check-Out List, designed to be used with all class books or materials, is essential to keep tabs on your texts or other books that you give students.

C. Keeping Tabs on the Textbooks

The state lends textbooks to students, and it is the teachers' responsibility to be the custodian of those books. Think of the textbook as a financial resource worth up to 50 dollars. If you have 150 students, this could equal $7,500, a substantial amount of money to put in the hands of children on a daily basis. Therefore, it is essential that you keep tabs on the textbooks. The best way to do this is the following:

1. Identifying the book

First, a teacher needs to have each student write his or her name in the textbook in the appropriate place. Names as well as other identifying information like school, class, and date should be written in ink. Some teachers stamp their names in the text with a personalized stamp. Every book needs to be checked for accuracy, a task easily done with student helpers.

Teaching the Basics *(cont.)*

2. Textbook rules

Make sure students know that they are responsible for keeping up with their texts. Any damage to the text will be considered vandalism and dealt with appropriately. Tell them that texts will be checked periodically throughout the year. A damaged or vandalized textbook is a financial loss for the taxpayers. Our students deserve the best but should be expected to care for these materials.

3. Textbook records

Carefully record textbook numbers with the corresponding student name on your Textbook Records Sheet (page 246). If a student has lost a textbook, have a loaner ready until it shows up or is replaced. Record lost textbooks immediately on your records sheet. The office handles the routine for replacing textbooks.

Also, be careful to record damage or gross negligence to textbooks. Typical middle school textbook problems are the following:

- pen marks on pages
- crossing out words, lines
- ripped, torn pages
- writing bad language in text
- doodling, drawing on pictures
- water, food, drink damage
- defaced cover

4. Book covers

Keep textbooks healthy by providing a cover. Many book covers are large, sturdy paper with the names and logos of companies from which they were donated. (However, a cut up brown paper grocery bag will work equally as well.) Have all students cover their texts correctly. One good method to cover a textbook follows:

a. *Sizing*

   Lay book on cover. Indicate where top and bottom folds will go with a pencil or crease. Make sure the creases or marks are parallel with the cover edges. Next, to size the side flaps, open the textbook completely. Indicate where the cover needs to fold on the side by a pencil or crease. It is important that you open the textbook all the way to expand it completely. Again, make sure the folds on both sides are equal in length.

b. *Folding*

   Now, remove the book and fold over the top and bottom flaps. It should match the height of the book. Next, fold the side flaps in. These flaps will be pockets to hold the sides of the book.

c. *Covering*

   Simply place the book sides into the side flaps, and the book is properly covered. To add extra strength, tape the side flaps directly to the front cover so they stay in place.

Teaching the Basics *(cont.)*

III. How to Make the "Boring" Fun

Middle school textbooks have been criticized by teachers as being dry, useless, confusing, and ill-suited to the needs of students in various developmental stages. From the students' point of view, the most frequent criticism by far is that the textbook is "boring." In a text-driven classroom, students generally perceive that class as boring as well. Interestingly, classes without textbooks, like gym, art, and music, are consistently ranked as the most popular classes by the students.

Successful teachers learn how to go beyond the textbook and distill the core elements or objectives of the lesson. The master teacher knows that the text does not teach the class—the teacher does. Teachers have developed a variety of techniques to engage the students' interests. These techniques tend to drive home information and get students excited about school. Here are some examples:

A. Quiz Show

Have students team up to compete for prizes. Taking information from the text or other sources, come up with questions and answers. Contestants will answer the questions given by the announcer. Additional roles for the quiz show format are time keeper, judge, and scorer. Stress proper audience behavior, where any talking could penalize the team's score.

TV game show formats are easily adaptable to the classroom. The benefits of the quiz show format are immediate. Students poring over their texts, using all the vocabulary you never thought they would use, and becoming excited about the class in general are just a few of the benefits from this popular technique.

B. Dramatic Interpretation

Have students team up to present dramatic skits based on stories or information developed in class. This technique can be used for any subject. Young people love play acting, and if channeled to incorporate class information, this process is very rewarding. Here are some examples of how different subjects can use the dramatic skits:

English: Act out plays or other literature ("*Julius Caesar* for Kids").

History: Act out historical scenes ("The Landing of Captain John Smith").

Science: Act out scientific phenomena ("A Day in the Life of an Amoeba").

Math: Act out situations that involve math ("Going to the Store with $20"), or math operations ("The Fraction Family").

Foreign Language: Act out scenes spoken with the appropriate language ("Our Visit to Spain").

When assigning dramatic interpretations, always give a clear set of criteria for each group to follow. You can assign a specific situation, or you can let the groups choose. Either way, make sure the learning objective is attained. Your students will have fun and appreciate your class more when given these opportunities.

Teaching the Basics *(cont.)*

C. Costumes

Spice up student interest as well as faculty surprise by wearing content-related costumes. This can be appropriate for all subjects. Teachers can come up with original ideas to stimulate student interest. For example, a bumblebee costume for science, togas for history, a fractionally painted face for math, or knightly armor for a King Arthur unit in literature.

Whatever the costume, kids are likely never to forget it. They will perceive your class as fun and interesting. Even when they have to do "boring" work, looking up and seeing a giant bee walk down the aisle is sure to stimulate curiosity and positive feelings. In general, costuming leaves a big impression on students and increases motivation.

The other side of the coin on costuming is having students dress up for activities such as a "Medieval Festival," "Colonial Town Meeting," etc. These must be planned in advance and are usually connected with a thematic celebration (page 82). Things like "Pirate Day" or "Greek Philosopher's Day" are sure to spice up a classroom.

D. Audio-Visuals

A popular option to enhancing dry text is to provide video or audio supplements. This can make a text come alive with graphic pictures or sounds.

Also, most schools today have media centers where video cameras and tape recorders can be used. Making student generated videos or tapes will create a buzz of excitement among your students. You can create skits to teach a lesson, or you can be very bold and actually work toward a video with script and set designs. This is a guaranteed crowd pleaser. Your biggest problem with this scenario is controlling the level of excitement that will invade your class every day. "Are we going to film today?" "When are we going to watch the video," and "I've got a great idea about the film . . ." are common comments that children will bombard you with.

Along with video, do not underestimate the power of audio tapes. Kids really love music. Many teachers keep stereos in their rooms to play during appropriate times. Classical music can be soothing for individual exercises, while popular music may be appropriate for some activities. It is important, of course, not to let the music distract students from the overall lesson.

Audio tapes made for teachers, like *Hymns from the American Revolution, Songs of the Mountain Men, Folk Songs of the Cowboys,* and *Indian Tribal Chants,* are powerful learning tools. Also, some teachers like to play self-help tapes made for kids, like *Learning for Success* or *How to Be Your Own Best Friend.* Inspirational tapes such as these can have a huge impact on some students' lives.

Tapes made for teachers can be purchased at bookstores or through teacher catalogs. If the prices are daunting, realize that this is an investment for a lifetime.

Teaching the Basics *(cont.)*

E. Manipulatives

A fancy word for "things kids can touch" is the term "manipulatives." Manipulatives are especially useful in science and math, where models and diagrams are important. Applicable to other subjects as well, manipulatives let the students handle and feel objects, instead of just reading or hearing about them.

Common manipulatives in math are tangrams or other geometric shapes. For science, three-dimensional models of a cell, DNA, or the solar system let students learn by seeing and feeling how everything fits together. A famous manipulative for science is the human skeleton model. Taking apart bones and putting them back together has inspired many future doctors.

Passing around objects like Revolutionary money or Indian arrowheads helps students focus on content as a real, living thing.

F. Simulations

Simulation activities are used like the dramatic presentations, except they conform to specific data. For instance, common simulations are these:

- mock trials
- political conventions
- historical conferences/meetings
- famous situations/events

G. Oral Readings

Add life to a text by having students read out loud. Then ask students to use their listening skills to put the readings into their own words to practice speaking skills.

H. Word Games/Puzzles

From the text, have students create word searches or crossword puzzles from vocabulary words. Have them create synonyms from words they find in the text. In a word game called a "cloze activity," teachers blank out every seventh word and have students predict what it should be. These successful techniques produce fulfillment of learning objectives and excitement from students. Another consequence is the reduction of discipline problems. Keep in mind, however, that learning cannot be exciting all the time, and that it is beneficial for the student to learn the value of hard work.

IV. High-Level Thinking

It is not enough to teach just the basics. Society demands more emphasis on high-level thinking. The idea behind high level thinking was best articulated by Benjamin Bloom in his system of classification, or taxonomy, that charts the levels of thinking and their appropriate actions. As a certified teacher, you are probably familiar with Bloom's Taxonomy, a standard for many school systems and college education courses.

According to Bloom, learning takes place on different levels. Memorizing the capitals of every state in the Union is considered to be low-level thinking. Students need to apply knowledge, analyze data for accuracy, synthesize, and bring together information and evaluate it.

Teaching the Basics *(cont.)*

IV. High-Level Thinking *(cont.)*

Broken down into the most basic form, the levels of thinking can be seen as the following:

A. Literal: memorization of facts—*Example: "What is the date of American independence?"*

B. Interpretive/Applied: reading between the lines, making inferences, applying old knowledge to a new context—*Example: "From what you have read so far, what do you think will happen next?"*

C. Analytical/Critical/Creative: breaking down the whole into parts, making generalizations, finding meaning, creating personal expressions—Example: "Compare and contrast the life of Robinson Crusoe with that of Edgar Allan Poe."

D. Evaluative/Moral: making judgments to form personal identity—*Example: "Was Julius Caesar a hero or mere tyrant—why?"*

Extending questions by students into larger issues, demanding reasoning skills, asking for judgments, and creating high-level projects are part of every successful teacher's curriculum.

Let's go back to Pine Oaks Middle School and check on Mr. Hamad. He will try to hit high-level thinking in a new assignment.

✉ Mr. Hamad Finds the Fountain of Youth ✉

"In our study of body processes," says Mr. Hamad to his 7th period class, "we have learned how the body operates. Now, who knows what happens to the body when a person dies?"
Hands shoot up.

"Like, the blood congeals or something. I saw it on a special," answered Jamail.

"That's semi-correct," replied Mr. Hamad, "and what if I told you that you have the power to suspend life and never die?"

The class was aroused, trying to picture infinite life.

"I don't know about that," said Luis. "I think it's probably better just to die. Why would you want to be walking around like a mummy?"

"That's a good point, Luis," commented Mr. Hamad. "In this assignment, you will not only construct a complete body system, but you will analyze how body systems can be suspended and evaluate whether that is good or bad for society."

"Oh, Mr. H," said Bryon, "I saw a whole special on cryogenics, where they freeze your brain when you die and put you in space or something. Then, in like a thousand years, when they found the cure for cancer or whatever, they put your brain back on."

"Mr. Hamad," shouted Vanessa, "we are studying about that in English too. The myths we are reading talk about the Fountain of Youth and if you drink it, you will live forever."

"Good," replied Mr. Hamad, "and you can certainly use that in your evaluation. Now, get in your groups and get to work!"

In this example, Mr. Hamad turns a typical biology assignment into a search for the age-old Fountain of Youth. Students are not just learning facts but applying those facts, synthesizing those facts, and evaluating important questions for our society.

Teaching the Basics *(cont.)*

V. Learning Styles

This theory is rooted in common sense, but recently it has been armored with research from educational psychologists. The theory of learning styles can be generally summarized as follows:

- All students have the capacity to learn.
- Students can learn the same things by different methods.
- Recognizing how a student learns is critical to success.

Associated with learning styles is the idea of multiple intelligences, developed fully by Howard Gardner. Gardner notes that the measure of IQ has long been taken by a standard series of tests. He suggests that intelligence cannot be measured this way because the brain is too complex, containing many different kinds of intelligences or abilities. For instance, some people have truly amazing athletic abilities. Gardner would call this *kinesthetic* intelligence. Some might be gifted in music, while some people have a natural talent for making friends and networking. Other types of intelligences are *linguistic, intrapersonal, spatial,* and *logical-mathematical.* In *Frames of Mind,* he asserts a new definition of intelligence.

> *An intelligence is the ability to solve problems or to create products that are valued within one or more cultural settings—a definition that says nothing about either the sources of these abilities or the proper means of "testing" them.*

The implications for the teacher are that one must be able to recognize how a student learns best and adjust to that style. Visual learners, for example, need to see pictures, graphs, and charts in order to make things real. Have them draw their notes next to the information to symbolize knowledge. Many teachers use note-taking devices which are visual. Among the most successful is the cognitive map. For an effective Cognitive Map Form, see page 247.

A. Cognitive Maps

Cognitive maps are note-taking devices which allow the student to see relationships and draw symbols, as well as taking written notes. Using colors or map pencils enhances interest and activates memory. Cognitive maps can be taught by transparency or the chalkboard.

The first step in making a cognitive map is to create a central symbol for the lesson or lecture. For instance, a lecture on pioneers might have the symbol of a covered wagon. Next, main ideas of the lecture are listed and explained with supporting details, enlivened by images and symbols representing those ideas. Students will remember more from graphic organizers like these than simply from line-by-line notes.

B. Allowing Options

Some students are able to express themselves better in different modes. For instance, a student could make a dance routine to show the migrations of the Pilgrims rather than a diagram on a poster board (kinesthetic learners).

In general, teachers need to appreciate the different types of intelligences that students exhibit. Giving options is the best way to teach the same material for different learning styles.

Teaching the Basics *(cont.)*

VI. Special Needs Students

Traditionally kept out of regular classrooms, students with special needs are making an impact on the regular teacher. The concept of mainstreaming (recently retitled "inclusion") means that special students should be in a regular setting as much as possible. This is not only a theory but federal law.

A. ADD (Attention Deficit Disorder)

Often called hyperactivity, ADD incorporates many learning disabilities. Historically, these children were considered "slow," or having "ants in their pants," or being the "class clowns." Now these students are often treated with medications which help them adjust. The characteristics of this disorder are as follows:

- excessive activity, far beyond normal levels
- short attention span
- impulsive behavior

- easily distracted
- continually loud or disruptive
- susceptible to daydreaming/wandering

Help and support for these special students can be given first by understanding that in most cases they cannot help their behavior. Monitor these students carefully and use preventive discipline techniques as much as possible. Talk to the parents, former teachers, and counselors of the students to get ideas that work. It is also very important to be aware of the medications used by these students and their possible side effects.

B. "Slow Learners"/General Learning Disability

These students have been tested and identified with general learning disability, sometimes diagnosed as LD (learning disabled). No one quite knows the causes for this condition. The characteristics usually are these:

- shows uneven pattern of intellectual development
- lags behind peers in normal class exercises

- shows erratic attention and focus
- has trouble in reading and language skills

Recent recognition that these students are able to think on high levels has been influencing teachers. Many of these special students you will find have not been properly diagnosed. Sometimes, these students show remarkable gifts of certain skills but in other areas are extremely underdeveloped. Suggestions are to adapt instruction to the students' individual levels, reinforce language and reading development as much as possible, and attempt to develop internal motivation.

C. Dyslexia

Dyslexia is a problem with reading. It may be hard to detect and sometimes take years to diagnose. In the meantime, these students are seen as dumb or slow. For some reason, this condition affects part of the brain that processes written information. Dyslexic students are often very bright in other areas. Dyslexia is also a blanket term for dyslexia-related problems, especially dysgraphia, where handwriting is confused and out of order. Dyslexics need audio-visual support to grasp learning objectives. However, they should continue to practice reading and writing.

Teaching the Basics *(cont.)*

D. Wheelchair Bound

Teachers are saddened to see students bound to wheelchairs, unable to do all the things other kids do. However, feeling sorry for people will not advance them. As a teacher, you must rid yourself of any misconceptions about the abilities of these special students. Some are able to participate in all normal classroom experiences, while others benefit from the experience and environment. Do not underestimate the wheelchair students. Treat them just like anyone else. Call on them with questions if applicable. Involve them as much as possible in class activities, field trips, etc. Above all, be "wheelchair blind" just as you are "color blind" to different races and ethnicities.

Make contact with the special education staff, become as familiar as you can with the students' medical conditions, and nurture their sense of self-concept.

E Hearing/Visually Impaired

This population of students goes from extreme (blind/deaf) to mild. Most of these students have obvious resources to aid them in learning. In addition, many are gifted and talented in other areas. A good example of what one blind and deaf person could accomplish is seen in the life of Helen Keller. It is essential that we realize the potential of these students is great. They can go to college and get degrees just like others in your classroom. Modifying learning exercises is necessary to aid in comprehension. Preferential seating, tape recorders, typewriters, and individual care work best for these students.

F. Emotionally Disturbed

A potential nightmare for teachers is the emotionally disturbed student. These students usually display the following traits:

- hostile aggressiveness
- impulsive and disruptive activity
- anti-social, isolate tendencies
- inability to interact normally with peers
- self-injuriousness

- unrealistic fears and phobias
- continual desire for attention despite consequences
- depression
- creation of a fantasy world

With these students, behavior should be checked rigidly. They need strong consequences and firm action. Sometimes these students are classified under the label "behavior disorder." Whatever the case, these students can make life miserable for the teacher if not effectively dealt with. To complicate matters, they are often very intelligent.

Emotional disturbances can be genetic but are often are seen as environmental. The upbringing and home life of these kids frequently involves abuse, neglect, and broken families. Many times, they lack good adult role models. In these cases, getting psychological help and counseling might make a big difference. Above all, do not let these students disrupt your class. Draw a "line in the sand" and take appropriate actions.

Teaching the Basics *(cont.)*

G. Bilingual

You may have to teach students who are not competent in English. The greatest number of bilingual students in the United States speak Spanish. Other languages common in our public schools are French, German, Vietnamese, and Chinese.

Bilingual students do best with classes like math and science, usually taking ESL (English as a Second Language) classes as they adjust. Many are new to our culture, so give them opportunities to speak about where they live and share their cultural values. These students can pick up English quickly and be productive students and citizens.

H. Gifted

The term "gifted" is loosely applied to those students who go beyond the normal thinking levels of the average student. In one sense of the word, many teachers think all their students are gifted. However, some are more academically gifted than others. Some schools pool these students according to their test scores and performance into special classes. Names for these classes range from "Gifted and Talented," to "Honors," to "Aim High," to "AP" (advanced placement), and a host of others.

As a teacher you need to challenge them to think on the highest levels of learning. Other suggestions are these:

- Curriculum compacting—Go over information faster.
- In-depth learning—Dive deep into topics with research and support.
- Options—Let these students follow their interests.
- Extra-credit—Give quality extra-credit assignments.
- cooperative learning—give opportunities to learn with peers.
- Leadership roles—Have these students be peer mentors or tutors to help others.
- Imagination—Give opportunities to show creative expression.

These suggestions go for all your students but especially the gifted. It is truly amazing what middle school children can accomplish if given the opportunity.

I. Special Classrooms

The typical middle school has a three-layer organization for special students. The first layer is the special education classroom. Because of the range of needs associated with special students, the job is not easy. These professionals are thoroughly trained and make a big difference in the quality of your school. Observe such classes for ideas of how to teach special students.

The second layer of special education is the regular classroom, recently the site for more and more special education.

The third layer is the special education support room, frequently called the "resource room." The idea is to provide support to the teachers by giving students one-on-one attention when they are behind. Also the directors of these programs help with special problems of individual students. The student is put back in the regular classroom when ready. In essence, this program serves as a support or buffer for the student and teaching aid for the teacher.

Teaching the Basics *(cont.)*

VII. Reading in the Content Area

In middle school, every teacher is a reading teacher. It is impossible to overstate the importance of reading on the adolescent brain. Recently, teacher certification programs are incorporating reading classes into their curriculum. Sometimes called "Content Area Literacy," these courses teach means and strategies to nurture good reading skills. A leading pundit of this movement is Dr. Robin Eanes of St. Edwards University, Austin, Texas. Reading, she asserts, is the responsibility of all teachers. In her recent textbook for college teaching candidates, she writes,

> *"Since each content area has its own vocabulary, conceptional frameworks, learning methods and resource materials, one reading class cannot adequately prepare students for meeting the learning demands they will face in all their other classes." (Content Area Literacy, page 5)*

To motivate students to read in the middle school, educators have come up with many ideas. A favorite is Sustained Silent Reading (SSR). Not as formidable as its name, SSR is designed for the entire school to heed, even the coaches and PE classes. The idea is to practice reading a book, magazine, or newspaper as a constant hobby.

Some schools have a "drop-everything-and-read" period built into their week. The idea is to get every child into the habit of reading.

You can develop literacy skills by being aware of how students read and encouraging good reading habits. Reading centers, reading contests, book fairs, book swaps, and other reading related activities can foster a lifelong love of learning. Dr. Eanes' book, *Content Area Literacy: Teaching for the 21st Century,* is a great source for teaching strategies.

Book Swap!

A reading exercise that many teachers love is the book swap.

Rules:

1. All students must bring a book they are reading.
2. If students do not have a book, one will be provided for them.
3. All students must have their names in their books or have the library card.
4. The teacher will give the signal to swap books. Conditions of swapping (change it each time): same T-shirt color, same hair color, same shoe color, same eye color, boys switch with girls, free swap, etc.
5. After swapping, read for seven minutes.
6. After reading, you may recommend or not recommend a book. Continue until out of time (usually about 5–10 swaps).
7. When finished, return all books to the owners.

Curriculum Development

If he has not the concern for humanity, the love of living creatures,
the vision of the priest and the artist, he must not teach.

—Pearl Buck

Outline of Chapter 4

I. The Psycho-Motor Domain: The Need for Movement
   A. Background
   B. Integration

II. Creating Instructional Units
   A. Planning an Instructional Unit
   B. Lesson Planning
   C. The Learning Cycle

III. Cooperative Learning
   A. Background
   B. Informal Cooperative Learning
   C. Formal Cooperative Learning
   D. Heterogeneous Grouping
   E. Group Size
   F. Managing Cooperative Learning
   G. Planning Cooperative Learning Exercises
      Sample Project: Magazine Makers
   H. Conclusion/Mrs. Orangetree Strikes Gold!

IV. Projects
   A. Conception
   B. Resource Accumulation
   C. Writing/Typing
      Sample Project: Medieval Diary
   D. Management
   E. Presentation

V. Guest Speakers

VI. Field Trips
   A. Ten Steps to a Successful Field Trip
   B. Liability Factors
   C. Ways to Make Trips Safe
   D. Conclusion

VII. Thematic Celebrations

VIII. Organizing Your Curriculum

Reproducibles for Chapter 4 (See pages 248–258.)

1. *IU Planning Sheet*
2. *Lesson Plan Form*
3. *Cooperative Learning Home Groups*
4. *Cooperative Learning Lesson Plan*
5. *Presentation Evaluation Form*
6. *Guest Speakers Matrix*
7. *Field Trip Form*
8. *Field Trip Checklist*
9. *Field Trip Letter to Parents Form*
10. *Field Trip Nonparticipant Form*
11. *Student Award Form*

Curriculum Development

(cont.)

As one masters teaching the basics, the task of creating and implementing exciting curriculum begins. Providing a variety of methodology, such as cooperative learning, projects, guest speakers, field trips, and thematic celebrations, ensures a rewarding state of mind and increased learning. Exciting curriculum is the best deterrent to discipline problems, and integrating movement into your curriculum is a primary consideration.

I. The Psycho-Motor Domain: The Need for Movement

A. Background

All effective middle school teachers integrate physical movement into their basic curriculum structure. Remember the middle schooler's brain is experiencing a growth spurt, and the body is too. This translates into a need to get up and move around to gain experience and practice. Most new teachers, especially if trained for secondary schools, assume that their job is mainly one of cognitive teaching—how to think and what to think. They are less prepared to teach the emotional side (affective domain) of life, but they usually do understand that psychological health is a prerequisite for any learning. Teachers new to middle school are rarely prepared to teach the third domain—the psycho-motor or physical.

Middle schoolers can rarely sit quietly for more than 30 minutes, depending on the lesson. Traditional lecture methods are hard to make effective. Even when watching a favorite video, young people will start getting up or fidgeting with things after 30 minutes. As classes get longer with block scheduling, the necessity for movement becomes even greater. Without the integration of movement into the curriculum, the middle school teacher will simply not be successful.

B. Integration

There are many ways to provide movement.

1. Retrieval

Having students get up to get materials can provide a good opportunity for movement. An orderly way to do this is to dismiss students by rows. This actually is more efficient than passing materials out. Some teachers work this into their daily schedule, having students keep notebooks or portfolios that they must retrieve each day in the room.

2. Cooperative learning

One of the best methods to get students up and around is through cooperative learning opportunities (page 57). Whether you call them "workshops," "committees," "teams," "staff," or just "groups," the process of cooperative learning stimulates the class. Students must physically get out of their desks and move the desks around to form groups and retrieve materials. Usually, there is a good amount of movement during this learning. It is important, however, that the movement be on-task and not off-task movement. As a teacher, you must monitor closely; if you are not alert, the play fight in the corner of the class may go on indefinitely.

Curriculum Development

(cont.)

B. Integration *(cont.)*

3. Providing tasks

For jumpy students who seem magnetically repelled from their seats, giving them tasks as student helpers can release their energies and keep them productive. Following is a good list of tasks:

- passing out papers/collecting homework
- running a cross-school errand
- cleaning transparencies

- erasing the board
- organizing bookshelves
- cleaning the room

4. Speaking

When conducting warm-ups, discussions, or other activities, have students walk up to the front of class to give the answer, comment, or speech.

5. Hands-on learning

Provide for hands-on learning as much as possible, where students can get up and learn by doing. Class museums, project displays, or work centers promote learning while moving.

6. Class outside

If you have good class control, try taking them outside for the lesson. This gets them up and walking and places them in a new environment. They can associate other places, like being outside, with learning. Learning takes place not only in the classroom but anywhere.

7. Emergency exercise drills

Sometimes, teachers feel it is necessary to have the whole class get up and do 20 jumping jacks or other physical exercises to get out the "jitters." Also, do not be shy about taking your class outside to play a team sport occasionally. This can do much for class morale.

8. Class activities

There are various class activities teachers use throughout the year wherein students are required to get up, change seats, move over, and walk around. The fact is that as a middle school teacher, you really do not have a choice in the matter. Without physical movement in your lessons, you will probably be prone to feelings of frustration, anger, resentment, and lack of control. Furthermore, you may find a lack of student interest in your class. This breeds a "me-against-them" mentality, and that is no fun.

Curriculum Development

(cont.)

II. Creating Instructional Units

All good teachers create their own curriculum. The days of the textbook teacher are coming to a close. A teacher must be not only an expert on the content but a master planner and organizer as well. In addition, as teaming (page 129) becomes prevalent in school structures, teachers are writing curriculum together, incorporating interdisciplinary concepts. We are in a new age of changing curriculum.

A. Planning an Instructional Unit

The most basic element of any curriculum is the instructional unit (IU) designed to last from 3–9 weeks. Plan on having about 5–8 IU's every year. Consider first your . . .

1. state's Essential Elements
2. district guidelines
3. team's agenda
4. specialities and interests
5. materials and resources

It is usually a good idea to make a calendar or a syllabus of the semester. Map out a rough idea of the year in units, but plan in detail for the semester. Effective teachers find 6–9 week instructional units are generally good time periods in which the cycle of learning can be completed.

Your IU will contain the set of concepts or learning objectives and the activities that are used to teach them. For example, here is a list of typical IU's and their subject areas:

1. **Math: "Integers," "Fractions," "Geometric Relationships"**
2. **American History: "The Colonial Period," "The Troubled 60s"**
3. **Science: "Solar System," "Circulatory System"**
4. **English: "Persuasive Essay," "Basics of Grammar," "Mythology"**
5. **Reading: "Story Elements," "Exploring the Biography"**
6. **Foreign Language: "Declensions," "Verb Tenses"**

Once you have these general concepts down, you should start gathering materials and resources. On your IU Sheet (page 248) write down the name of the unit and start jotting down ideas on the following areas:

- lesson plans
- cooperative learning exercises
- projects
- guest speakers
- field trips
- culminating activities

In essence, you subdivide your IU's into lessons. Your lessons should consist of a variety of means to achieve learning. If you want an overall picture, think of it as one big mixed pie. The unit is the pie itself, the whole thing. The lessons are the pieces of the pie, sliced into small parts. The methodology is the flavor of these slices. Cooperative learning might be pecan, lecture be chocolate, reading be lemon, and so on. As the chef of this pie, your job is to carefully plan and prepare it. If your pie is all one flavor, it will be bland and boring. But if it has variety and quality ingredients with hints of originality, your pie will go over well.

Curriculum Development

(cont.)

B. Lesson Planning

Dividing your instructional unit into lessons is the next step of organizing your curriculum. Planning a lesson is different for every teacher. Furthermore, teachers organize their lesson plans and curricula in different ways. Some teachers prefer keeping a lesson plan spiral book, while others keep notebooks, and still others keep lesson plans in file folders.

Basically, a lesson should always contain three elements: objective, procedure, and assignment. On your Lesson Plan sheet (page 249), you should record these three items.

1. Objective

The basic question you want to ask yourself is "What should each student know by the end of class?" Write this down and look at it after the lesson. Always ask yourself "Did this lesson meet the objective?" Objectives should be written not only for lessons but for units and projects as well.

Here are some common lesson objectives:

history lesson—*Students will **know** the events of the Russian Revolution.*

English lesson—*Students will **learn** how to write internal citations.*

science lesson—*Students will **understand** the qualities of igneous rocks.*

math lesson—*Students will **comprehend** what negative numbers are.*

Objectives from units and projects that stress higher level thinking might be the following:

history unit—*Students will **evaluate** the practice of the slave trade during the 1700's.*

science project—*Pupils will **analyze** bodily systems and create their own body system.*

math unit—*Students will **synthesize** previous knowledge to operate algebraic equations.*

English project—*Students will **explore** their personal values to create self-conceptions.*

Objectives that require emotional response are lessons that incorporate varied methodologies, such as thematic celebrations ("Medieval Festival")—*Students will **identify** with Medieval characters and their times.*

field trips (to "Pioneer Farm")—*Students will **feel empathy for** early Texas pioneers.*

cooperative learning (for conflict resolution unit)—*Students will **learn to subordinate** their interests for the good of the others.*

guest speakers (on WW II lesson)—*Learners will **see** the pains, joys, and experiences of a military man during war.*

Curriculum Development

(cont.)

Objectives can also be written for psycho-motor skills as well. Objectives which integrate physical movement might be these:

science lesson ("Frog Unit")—*Students will **dissect** a frog and physically identify parts of the frog's anatomy.*

math unit ("Geometry")—*Students will **manipulate** geometric figures to fit various forms.*

reading lesson ("Mystery Unit")—*Groups of students will **act out** parts of the mystery novel.*

foreign language project ("Mother Mexico")—*Each student will **design and make** a Mexican costume.*

Typically, objectives incorporate many designs, stressing cognitive, emotional, and physical needs, as well as high-level thinking.

English project ("Midsummer's Night Dream")—*Students will **learn** events and dialogue of a Shakespearian play, **act out** scenes, **construct** sets, and **identify** with their characters.*

science unit ("Ecosystems")—*Groups of students will **analyze** data, **prepare** speeches, and **construct** a research center on a given ecosystem of the world.*

After you determine what you want students to know when the lesson or unit is over, the very crucial next step is to define your procedure, also called methodology.

2. Procedure

The next step in planning a lesson is to figure out how the students will reach their objectives.

You must ask yourself "What methodology will I employ to teach this objective?" There are many methods. Most teachers have at least two types of teaching modes during a class period. Common classroom methods can be summed up in these basic categories:

- Lecture: Students take notes, listen.
- Cooperative learning: Students read information from books or handouts.
- Texts: Students do textbook activities.
- Worksheets: Students do exercises from activities on handouts.
- Discussion: Students ask questions, make comments (Psycho-motor).
- Presentations: Students speak and demonstrate (Psycho-motor).
- Writing: Students are given a writing assignment.
- Test/quiz: Students are evaluated.
- Technology oriented: Students operate or listen to media/computers (Psychomotor).

Curriculum Development

(cont.)

Dominant routines of traditional teaching have been *lecture + texts or reading + worksheets*

More progressive routines use various methodologies, and with the expansion of class period time (block scheduling), teachers can switch methodologies several times to teach a lesson. For instance, teachers can do . . .

- warm-ups +
- lecture + cooperative learning
- cooperative learning + presentations
- reading + lecture + cooperative learning
- writing + presentations + technology oriented
- technology + writing + cooperative learning
- texts + discussion + worksheets + speaking

Good middle school teachers use a psycho-motor activity in a lesson. The idea is to break things up every 20–30 minutes or so.

3. Assignment

Providing an assignment is most important for accountability. It should be able to tell you whether or not the student has mastered the lesson. Also, assignments are used to enrich and extend the lesson. Assignments are either in class or homework. The important criterion about assigning homework is to make it as meaningful and relevant as possible. In other words, home assignments should stress quality over quantity. One of the least successful home assignments is a text-reading task. If you need kids to read for understanding, have them read in class.

Other assignments include the following:

- textbook work
- worksheet
- writing assignment
- skill exercises
- oral presentation
- product
- performance

In-class assignments should introduce and reinforce content or concepts, while homework should reinforce or extend concepts.

Effective teachers always write assignments on the board or other device in the same place on a consistent basis.

Curriculum Development
(cont.)

C. The Learning Cycle

Successful units and quality lessons share a universal element—they follow a cyclical pattern. At first, the learning cycle starts with a curiosity or an emotional desire to learn. Then come the introduction of information and quest for knowledge. Next, the learner produces a product as a symbol of the quest for and attainment of knowledge. Lastly, the cycle of knowledge ends with the learner teaching and sharing the fruits of wisdom.

When students have a chance to experience the whole cycle, then the learning process will be completed and attained. Unfortunately, most of our students are stuck in section two—*information/ comprehension*. Sometimes they will venture out into section three—*products of learning*. What is ignored is section one—*curiosity/emotional desire*, and section four—*teaching/sharing*. We must give students the opportunity to experience the whole cycle of learning in both units and lessons.

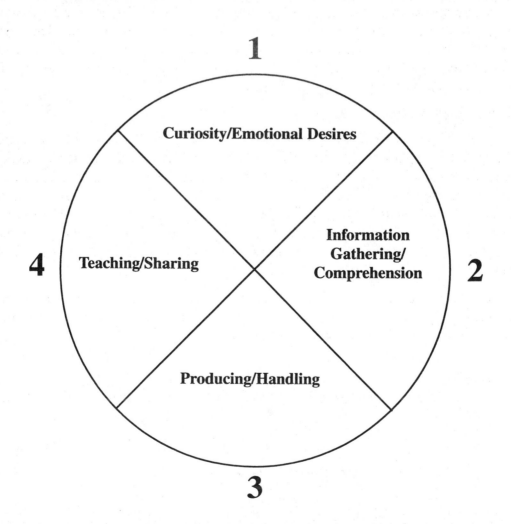

Curriculum Development

(cont.)

III. Cooperative Learning

A. Background

Much has been said about cooperative learning (CL) in the recent years. Some educational soothsayers have given CL the title of savior of education. They also are quick to point out that CL fits into the Total Quality Management (TQM) paradigm that is sweeping across businesses of America. In the TQM model, the power shifts to a horizontal mode which stresses teamwork, self-sacrifice, and loyalty for a greater purpose. These notions are contrary to traditional American entrepreneurship which stresses competition and rugged individualism. TQM was developed fully by Edward Deming to be used in post-World War II Japan. Apparently it worked, and many experts have suggested that the TQM model not only replace our business structures but our school systems as well. In essence, CL is aligned with a powerful movement within our country today.

What this means for the classroom teacher is that you may be expected to conduct CL as a basic part of your curriculum. CL is actually nothing new. Good teachers have been using CL since there were schools to use it in. Everyone sees the benefits of teamwork. The cliché "two heads are better than one" sums up this common-sense idea. The only thing that is changing is the form and frequency of CL. Experts stress that there are proper ways to use CL. There are basically two types of CL: informal and formal.

B. Informal Cooperative Learning

This type of CL uses teamwork on a moment's notice. The teacher simply assigns groups in pairs, triads, or larger groups to use teamwork to complete the assignment. This type of CL is used in classrooms all across the country. It is criticized by the educational elite as being unstructured and meaningless. However, if you as a teacher see opportunities to implement informal CL, stick with it. Giving students opportunities to help each other, discuss ideas, share responsibility, and complete assignments is very healthy. Also, it breaks up the monotony of "boring work" and provides an opportunity for movement. Informal CL has the added advantage of being easy for the teacher to plan.

The disadvantage of this type of CL is that there is no real accountability from the students. Students are likely to get off task or just copy from their partners. The teacher must monitor closely and suspend CL privileges if necessary.

Curriculum Development

(cont.)

C. Formal Cooperative Learning

Widely accepted in colleges and public schools throughout the nation is a more structured form of group work. It involves planning and preparation to avoid the pitfalls of informal CL. Books, seminars, courses, and workshops are devoted to formal CL, but it is not hard to understand. Distilled into its purest form, this method states that there can be no true CL without these two elements: individual accountability and positive interdependence.

Individual Accountability

This term requires that each student be held accountable for mastering content and doing a fair share of work. The CL lesson plan must provide a structure for this. Giving roles is the most widely used way to ensure accountability. The roles must fit together like a mosaic for the group to succeed and should be appropriate for the individual CL exercise. It is important to create roles which function throughout the activity. Common roles are these:

- leader: directs and manages the group, reports to teacher
- researcher: gathers information, teaches it to others
- speaker/presenter: prepares presentation, must know all facts
- writer: prepares written products
- artist: creates illustrations as necessary
- designer: makes format/designs visuals as necessary
- encourager: gives positive morale boost to teammates
- jack-of-all-trades: helps a little with everything

Positive Interdependence

Depending on teamwork to succeed is the basis for positive interdependence. When positive interdependence occurs, students are vocal about the assignment, share answers and information, encourage each other to succeed, and are generally motivated in a positive way.

Following are effective techniques to ensure accountability and positive interdependence:

- Require all group members to master the content, although one member from each group will represent that group in front of the class.
- Provide roles for each group member to fulfill completely in order to receive a grade.
- Have students teach the class what they learn or present to the class what they made.
- Have students take a post-test which all members must master before grades will be recorded.
- Record one group grade based on products, presentation, and cooperative skills.
- Require each student to fill out a self-evaluation of his/her contribution to the group.
- Require each student to prepare a peer-evaluation assessing the performance of the group members.
- Have students share materials and teach them to the other members for mastery.
- Using one or many of these techniques will give you a good start.

Curriculum Development

(cont.)

D. Heterogeneous Grouping

Another consideration of CL is how you group your students. This can make a big difference. Most of the time, students will want to sit with their friends. Rarely in the real world, however, do we get to pick our co-workers. Part of CL is learning how to deal with diversity and how to develop successful social skills. Hopefully, we can instill in our students the value of seeing others' sides of arguments and accepting diversity.

Therefore, the best method of grouping is putting different types of students together—heterogeneous grouping. Different races, ethnicities, class systems, genders, learning styles, and personalities will make interesting teams. They might not all get along at first, but they will learn. The more they get to practice, the better their social skills become.

Incidentally, the opposite of this is homogeneous grouping. A good application for homogeneous grouping is "home groups" which stay together all year. They meet once a week to share experiences. Home groups share each other's phone numbers in case they are absent or need immediate information. Such groups provide an anchor and a security blanket for class members. For a Home Groups form, see page 250.

E. Group Size

An important question of CL is "How many members are going to make a group?" The larger the group, the more complicated CL becomes.

Pairs: Pairing students is effective for a short term or daily assignment. Make sure, however, that sharing information does not turn out to be copying information. Group strong students with at-risk students to provide for student tutoring. Pairing is good for in-class assignments, especially textbook and worksheet tasks. Also, it can be used effectively for higher level jobs like interpretations and creative expressions.

Triads: By putting students in groups of three, teachers have the luxury of easily monitoring multi-student operations. Triads can work well with book work or higher level work.

Quads: A four-person group gets exciting. The teacher is now obligated to use formal CL to ensure proper technique. Assigning roles becomes imperative for group productivity.

Cincos: Probably the largest group you will use is a five-member team. The cinco can allow for complex operations and coordination within the group. Like the quads, the cincos are dangerously susceptible to a lack of individual accountability. Having systems in place to ensure accountability is crucial.

Other: Most teachers do not go beyond a cinco. However, having large groups of 6–10 students might be acceptable under certain circumstances. For instance, making group videos might require 6–8 group members, each sharing a different role. When making a class play, the whole class is basically one giant CL group.

Curriculum Development

(cont.)

F. Managing Cooperative Learning

CL enables the teacher to step back and monitor the students as they are learning. To see them talking over complex vocabulary, sharing ideas, teaching each other, and learning from each other, is truly a joy. Although there will be times when not everyone will share this enthusiasm, it will be much rarer than you might think. Specific negative behaviors encountered during CL are these:

- complaints about group members—"He's not doing anything!"
- complaints about instructions—"What are we supposed to do?"
- off-task behavior—wandering, daydreaming, ignoring discussion
- socializing—"Did you see that great movie last night?"

The teacher should handle these behaviors just like any other classroom offense.

If the CL exercise has been planned thoughtfully and directions are clear, most off-task behaviors vanish. If students complain about not knowing what to do (even though there are clear instructions), give them this chance to use their problem-solving skills.

The teacher should be omnipresent, monitoring groups. Try not to answer extraneous questions from group members. That is their job. During CL, the teacher is mainly a consultant and facilitator. The students are in the limelight.

G. Planning CL Exercises

The two most basic exercises are the CL lesson and the CL project. Use your CL Lesson Plan Sheet (page 249) to plan a CL lesson.

CL Lesson

A CL lesson usually takes a period (45 minutes) or longer. When conceiving a lesson, try to follow this general pattern:

1. *Objective:* Decide the objective of the lesson. This might be completing an answer sheet, taking a quiz for mastery, producing a group product, or teaching the class by presentation. Objectives usually share content information as well.

2. *Grouping:* Next, decide on group size, based on assignment and materials. (If a teacher has five class sets of group resources for 25 students, then obviously grouping will be in five-member groups, or cincos.) The second part of grouping is membership. At first, you can simply go down your class roster to get random groups. As you get to know the students, you can group them more appropriately. Heterogeneous grouping is more productive for the students' social skills.

3. *Materials:* Make a list of all the materials you will need to complete this project. Materials are the backbone of the CL exercise. The more advanced the materials, the better the CL experience will be. Materials can be as simple as a textbook and an instructional sheet, or they can be highly advanced, as in collateral readings, interesting objects and manipulatives, or other creative resources.

The more middle schoolers can put their hands on things, the more motivated and enthusiastic they become. CL exercises that are completely reading-based are generally not very successful.

Curriculum Development

(cont.)

4. *Making Instructions:* The final thing is to detail your instructions for the students. For efficiency, you might write these on a transparency. Instructions include group members, roles for the members, specific instructions for those roles, requirements to complete the product/assignments, presentation guidelines, and any other information necessary for students.

An effective form of a CL lesson that can be adapted to any classroom is described below.

Generic CL Lesson (using transparencies)

1. Decide on a content objective, like learning about famous women in the Old West.

2. Decide on group size, like a quad.

3. Assign groups members and roles. Suggested roles: leader, researcher, professor, scribe.

4. For your materials, provide the following: texts or handouts, transparencies for each group, and transparency pens.

5. Directions should be put on the overhead for the class to read. State that the **leader** must report to the teacher and manage the group's progress; also the leader is the only one able to speak to the teacher. The **researcher** has the job of finding the information and showing the professor. Determine the questions the group must answer. If you were doing a "famous women" lesson, you would pass out the reading/learning materials to the leader and have each group explain their women to the class. You would have the scribe use a list of biographical data like birth/death, childhood, jobs, accomplishments, and other interesting facts. The **professor** must explain it to the **scribe,** who must write it to show the class in presentations. Also state that you will pick one person to come up and explain to the class their findings.

6. When time is up (about 30–40 minutes), take up all pens from the leaders and choose the representatives from each team. Each representative must show a transparency of their teaching lesson. Stress audience behavior as reflective of the group grade.

CL Project

This form of CL is long-term based. The process can be very rewarding and a basis for CL to be used in the classroom frequently. Some examples of CL projects include these:

1. Make magazines/newspapers/brochures, etc.: The roles of editor, illustrator, writer, researcher, photographer, designer, computer formatter, etc., provide in-depth learning experiences while working with others. The CL exercises can be called "staff meetings."

2. Research-based products: Having students divide their roles to gather information on different subjects and then come together to synthesize information in order to form a product can be very rewarding.

    For example, let's check on Mr. Hamad's science class. He has written a CL project where different science teams must produce a visual display and oral presentation on "The Kingdoms of the Earth."

Curriculum Development

(cont.)

✉ Kingdom of the Air ✉

Mr. Hamad was nervous giving the students directions on their new cooperative learning project. He wondered if it would really work. "The teams are divided into cincos where each member is charged with obtaining information on his/her respective areas. The "Kingdom of the Air" team members will be subdivided into predators, water-based birds, tropical, common, and others . . . ." Thus did Mr. Hamad explain the directions and roles for this six-week project.

"But how are we supposed to get information on these things? The books in the library are all checked out," commented David.

"That's a good question, David," Mr. Hamad answered, "because there are many sources of information besides library books. From activities, lectures, readings, videos, guest speakers, and even a field trip to the wildlife refuge, you will gather research for your project. Sources will also be books, magazines, brochures, personal observations, and interviews with experts."

The same day, the Kingdom of the Air members Marcia and Ana got together after school and started on the project. They went to the park to observe different birds and their characteristics. Marcia took the journal to record their findings and sketches.

The other three members—Nolan, Dallas, and Viviana—went to the library to gather books. Viviana even found a record with bird songs.

After they gathered information, they all helped to create a research center with pictures, graphs, reports, and flying birds (papier mâché). Viviana, a clever enterpriser on the team, even made her own tape of bird songs for the research center. "This is going to be a great research center," Ana told Marcia while working on the project.

Mr. Hamad provided for a display of all the students' work in the common area of the school. At the thematic celebration, "Animal Land," the research centers were put up. Everybody remarked about the Kingdom of the Air center, but all the projects looked great, and people learned much from them. Many groups brought fish, pet dogs and cats, made animal costumes, and showed wildlife videos.

To the chagrin of the Kingdom of the Air group, the Kingdom of the Forest had created a "wildlife refuge" with plants, decorations, jungle sounds, and vines to swing on. But that did not bother Ana, who whispered to the others "Ours is still the best because we can fly!"

3. Film/Video: Making a film to achieve learning objectives can be one of the most exciting experiences for the young person. This requires many roles, such as writers, directors, actors, props designers, set designers, and editors. Using energy and enthusiasm to channel their creation can be an experience students will likely never forget.

4. Other: It is up to you as the teacher to create and explore how you can get CL groups to make long-term commitments. The following is a successful CL project.

Magazine Makers

Special Careers Unit—Journalism/Communications

Deadlines

- Outline Due: _____

- Rough Drafts Due: _____

- Hard Copies Due: _____

- Magazine Copy Due: _____

Purpose

In this project you will continue to refine your writing skills as well as to master the process writing technique. But more than this, you will have a chance to explore different roles as a magazine staff employee. You can even get fired if you do not pay attention to your deadlines! It is hoped that you will come to understand that a career in communications or journalism is an exciting prospect, but like all good jobs, it takes dedication and hard work to succeed. At the end of the project, your group will have a magazine copy of your very own.

Each group will name its magazine, design a cover for it, write articles, shoot pictures, draw illustrations, and edit it, as well. Have fun!

Getting Fired

If you do not make the deadline dates, your editor will fire you. At this point, you must see the teacher for extra assignments and other steps. Once you complete this work, you are available to be rehired (for lesser pay, of course).

Magazine Makers *(cont.)*

Step 1: Roles/Outlining/Brainstorming

As part of a small magazine staff (your group), you must pick roles which you are good at or just interested in. Every member must choose one of the following roles:

1. **Feature Writer**—Acts as a reporter, writes hard news as well as soft articles.

   Hard News: major world/government events, crime, police reports

   Soft News: lifestyle, sports, arts, movie reviews, personal interest, and fiction stories

   Interviews: Feature writers must interview for reports on their topics. Once you know whom you will interview, contact that person for an interview time during class or at another time.

2. **Columnist**—Writes a "column" in which the writer gives his/her own view on various subjects. The column can be humorous, and it usually has a certain popular style. Look in your newspaper for examples to read. (Many newspapers will carry a popular writer's picture above his or her regular column.)

In addition, every member of the staff must assume one of these following roles:

- **Editor**—Keeps track of deadlines, fires and hires, edits and corrects copy.
- **Illustrator**—Draws artwork for articles and magazine covers.
- **Photographer**—Takes pictures for articles.
- **Designer/Formatter**—Designs cover, formats the magazine into columns, fonts, etc.

Have a staff meeting to determine roles. If you cannot agree, the teacher will choose the roles for you.

My roles are . . .

_____

_____

The type of article I am writing is . . .

_____

_____

This article will basically be about . . .

_____

_____

My interview will be at . . . _____

with . . . _____

Magazine Makers *(cont.)*

Step 2: Writing/Revising Rough Drafts

After you know what kind of article you want to write and you have gathered information by reports or other means, you must write your rough draft.

A. **News reporting** is different from most other writing that you have been doing. In news reporting, you want to use "the pyramid" style of writing which gives specific facts first and provides secondary information later. Be succinct, to the point, and clear. Quoting a person involved in the story is essential to authenticate your article.

You must explain what your article is about and why it is important to your audience. Use formal writing style only (avoid using first or second person).

Other feature articles include movie/play/book reviews, sports features, personal Interest stories, and fictional stories. These articles use varying styles. Look in the newspapers or magazines for examples of these types of writing.

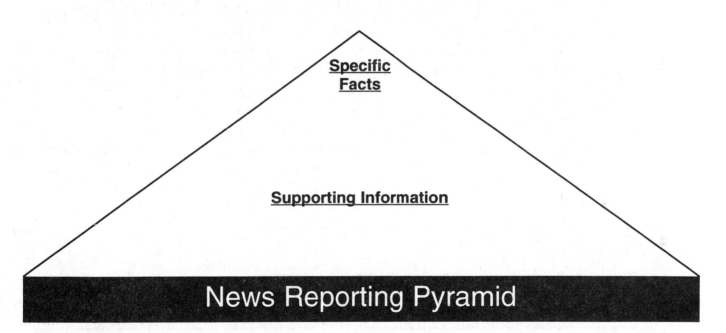

B. **Column writing** uses a more free-form style of writing than news reporting. Column writers are generally talented stylists who write pieces which people find interesting or amusing. Informal writing is permitted.

C. **Your article** must be two to three handwritten pages.

D. **By the deadline date**, give your rough drafts to the editor during a staff meeting.

E. **Once you receive your edited draft**, write up your corrected article and turn this in to the editor as well.

F. **Now start** on your secondary role. You will be drawing, shooting pictures, formatting, or editing.

Magazine Makers *(cont.)*

Step 3: Hard Copies

Typing: Now you must type your revised and corrected drafts. It is helpful to use a computer for this.

- Save your document as the headline title.
- Spell-check your document with a dictionary.

Formatting: Using your desktop publishing knowledge, and with the help of the formatter, arrange your article into columns, leaving spaces for pictures, designs, illustrations, etc.

Two-Page Spread

Once you are sure you are finished with your article, get the teacher's permission to print.

Now you are finished with your hard copy.

Step 4: Magazine Copy

At the final staff meeting, gather all the hard copies, pictures, illustrations, cover, table of contents, etc. You must cut and paste these all together.

Turn in your final copy by the deadline date. Be ready to present your contribution to your group's magazine.

Curriculum Development

(cont.)

H. Conclusion

It is time to check up on Mrs. Orangetree, the language arts teacher, who has been writing up lesson plans for her new folklore unit. To incorporate cooperative learning, she has prepared a CL lesson entitled "Find Any Gold in Them Thar Hills?" Let's peep into her classroom to see her progress . . .

✉ Mrs. Orangetree Strikes Gold! ✉

Mrs. Orangetree is giving instructions when a hand pops up urgently. "Yes, Jeremy, what is it?" Mrs. Orangetree asks.

"Are we really going to find gold today?" Jeremy asks.

"Absolutely," answers Mrs. Orangetree, "if your group completes the reading questions, makes the map, and finds the metaphorical 'treasure chest,' then you will be given the glittering gold."

"Wow! Is it really gold, Mrs. Orangetree?" questions Stacy.

"Well, have you ever heard of 'fool's gold'?" Mrs. Orangetree asks. "It's almost the same, and you get to have some if you can find it—but that's all in the directions. As I was saying, you'll divide up into cincos, or groups of five—"

"Mrs. Orangetree, cinco is the word for five in Spanish," interrupts Alice, who is quite proud of her contribution.

"I know," replies the teacher. "Isn't that a coincidence? Now, here are the groups." Mrs. Orangetree projects a transparency with the group members on it. Immediately there are reactions to the group selections.

"Ooooh, Mrs. Orangetree, do I have to be with Michael?" laments Suzanne.

"Listen," says Mrs. Orangetree, "You can forget about moaning to me for two reasons: number one, it's rude behavior and I don't stand for rudeness; and number two, your grade depends on your cooperative behavior, as we talked about before."

This sends a hush through the room. "Now, when you get into your groups, you will follow these directions:

1. Assign the following roles: a speaker/leader, two researchers, a map maker, and a jack-of-all-trades. However, you will all have to read the story "Folk Tales of the Gold Rush." If you can't decide on roles or if you're arguing, I will decide the roles for you.

2. The speaker will lead the group and present its findings to the class; the researchers will find information in the readings to answer the questions on your question sheets; the map maker will help the researchers and draw the map on the transparency; and the jack-of-all-trades must help everyone and encourage teammates.

Curriculum Development

(cont.)

 Mrs. Orangetree Strikes Gold! (cont.)

3. Once you've answered the question sheet and the map is drawn, tell me so I can write your group's name on the board.

4. After 30 minutes, all maps need to be made, and the speakers will present the group's findings to the class.

5. If the map is correct, according to the stories, then that group will receive the gold. Good luck, get into your groups and start working. You have 30 minutes to find that gold! Remember, part of your grade is cooperation!"

The students plunge into their assignments like gold-mad prospectors. Some groups argue about roles, but within five minutes, all roles are settled as they begin reading "Folk Tales of the Gold Rush." After about 15 minutes, students begin to start answering the questions as Mrs. Orangetree passes out transparency materials. "Organized chaos" breaks out as students try to answer questions, talk over problems, find solutions, map gold rush routes, and sing songs of the mountain men, the words and music for which were included in their packet.

"Mrs. Orangetree! I don't know what to do!" whines Miranda.

"OK," the teacher says. "What's your role?"

"Map maker," answers Miranda.

"OK, read the directions of the map maker." As she reads them, Mrs. Orangetree's instincts tells her Miranda isn't used to working with diverse students. "So what's your question?"

"I can't draw maps!" complains Miranda.

"You've got to do the best that you can. You see, Miranda," the teacher says in a lower tone, "life's not always going to be clear-cut, and sometimes you will just have to roll with the punches—so stop complaining, and use that brilliant mind of yours to help your group find the gold!"

Miranda laughs, then sighs and rejoins her group.

After 30 minutes, the teacher signals "OK, time's up. Speakers, get ready to present, and map makers, give me back all my markers."

As one group speaker gets up to present, Mrs. Orangetree reminds the students that audience behavior is part of their grade.

"OK," says Sharon with a giggle, "we thought the folk songs led the gold miners to Utah and then to Nevada, because it said in the song 'Going through the middle of the Rockies/ Us mountain men will find the luckiest . . . .' "

Curriculum Development

(cont.)

✉ **Mrs. Orangetree Strikes Gold!** (cont.) ✉

One by one, group speakers present their conclusions. It happens that four out of the five groups successfully analyze the story and are rewarded with small chunks of fool's gold. The other group receives bookmarks for trying.

After class, Mrs. Orangetree evaluates the lesson. She realizes that the objectives—understanding story elements of folklore and using problem-solving skills—were achieved. After making some notations on her lesson plan sheet, she decides to keep the lesson and place it in her curriculum notebook.

This CL exercise was a success because it channeled student energies productively. Students were "searching for the gold" but simultaneously learning story elements, western geography, folk songs, and other content objectives. Placed in heterogeneous groups, they had to form and practice social skills. They learned to synthesize their roles into one product. Mrs. Orangetree's providing fool's gold was both a reward and a stimulus to be followed up by the science teacher. Needless to say, it was a positive motivator for the students. Not much management was needed because preparation was thorough and directions were clear. As students become used to CL exercises and working with others, management becomes even easier.

IV. Projects

Projects are student tasks with tangible products. The stereotypical image of the project is the student carrying to school a bulky poster completed the night before. However, projects vary widely in form and substance, becoming very complex in some classes. Projects might be written products, research centers, models, or other visuals. There are a dozen varieties, but all share these basic elements: carefully detailed instructions, a forum to apply knowledge or creative expression, and a product applying that knowledge. Kids tend to remember doing projects if they are interesting, thereby internalizing what they learn.

The steps to a successful project can be identified in five basic parts: *conception, resource accumulation, writing/typing, management,* and *presentation.*

A. Conception

Some projects are already written, ready for you to teach. However, you may want to be creative and come up with an original idea, incorporating your learning objectives.

For example, if you are going to study Greek myths, obvious project ideas are to have students write original myths, to act out myths in a sketch, to make myth research products, or to combine them all and give options. When thinking of an overall project objective, try to reach all levels—cognitive, emotional, and psycho-motor. For example,

*Students will **identify** and **analyze** Greek gods, heroes, and monsters, **infer** values of their culture from readings, and **create** their own expressions of myths through writing.*

Also, projects with an element of fun increase motivation. Design ways kids can do unusual activities in class, at home, and in the community. Projects can keep a class motivated throughout a unit, especially CL projects.

Curriculum Development

(cont.)

B. Resource Accumulation

It is important that you use a variety of resources. Besides providing copies of the instructional packet, typical materials to help students on projects are these: books of all kinds (usually topical), reference sheets, manipulatives, video/audio materials, transparencies, art and craft supplies, technology-related materials, costumes, and bulletin board materials.

C. Writing/Typing

After you have your concept and basic objective, it is time to put it all down on paper. This can be time consuming, but it will be worth it and you can save it for future reference. Some teachers have developed quite a formidable portfolio and can pull out a project for any occasion.

The essential elements of writing your project follow:

1. Name/Due Dates

The name of the project is the title. Provide a space for the student to write his or her name. Next, it is a good idea to provide the due date spaces at the top for quick reference. It is important to have many due dates to check development and progress. Students will sometimes wait until the last moment to do projects if not monitored. Leave the spaces blank for the students to fill out. This does two things. First, it impresses the dates on the students because they have to write them. Second, it leaves the project open for use at other times of the year.

2. Purpose

Provide the background and purpose for doing this project. Give the students a clear goal and tell them what skills they will be expected to use. This will keep the students focused.

3. Steps

Give a clear set of steps that each student must follow. Start with "Step 1" and continue until the whole project is completed. List the resources and materials that the students are going to need and tell them exactly what to do. The last step should be a wrap-up telling the students exactly what they need to turn in.

It is a good idea to have steps last a week or so. In other words, a six-step project lasts six weeks. Check students' progress each week. Discuss progress with the whole class. Have students bring in their projects to work on in class.

4. Extra-Credit

Provide extra assignments in case students are interested.

An example of a successful project, Medieval Diary, follows.

Medieval Diary

Purpose

The purpose of the medieval diary project is three-fold. First, this is a chance to show and improve your descriptive writing skills. Second, you will keep developing your research skills to follow your interests. Finally, you will dig deep into medieval history and geography!

Materials

- spiral binder or journal book
- poster board/drawing paper/colors
- reference books

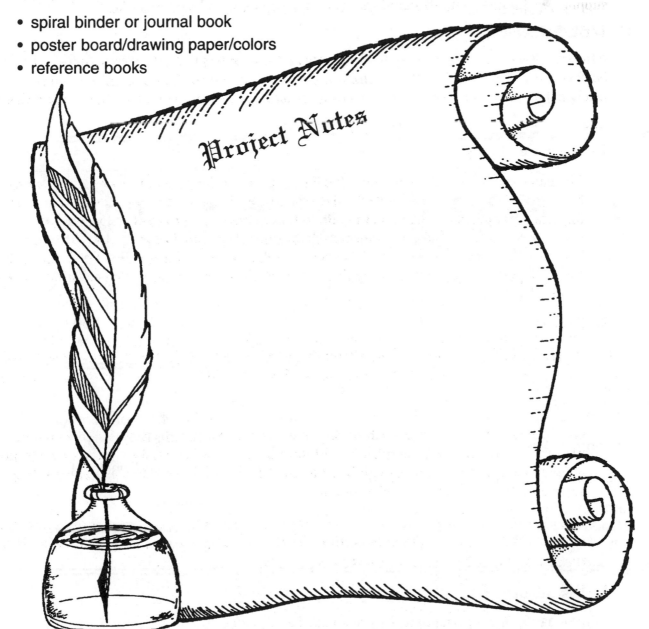

Project Notes

Timetable

- Outline Due:_____
- First Five Pages Due: _____
- First Ten Pages Due: _____

- Maps/Pictures/Diagrams Due: _____
- Final Project Due: _____

Medieval Diary *(cont.)*

Step 1: Roles/Places/Outline

For the medieval diary, you will have to choose a role to play. Here are some recommended roles:

A. Knight/Lord	G. Nun	M. Doctor
B. Lady in Waiting	H. Sorcerer/Alchemist	N. Miller
C. Sailor/Pirate	I. Moor	O. Cook
D. Servant/Maid	J. Yeoman	P. Carpenter/Mason
E. Priest	K. Bishop	Q. Court Jester
F. Monk/Friar	L. Ballad Singer/Poet	

My Role: _____

In addition to playing the role, you must also travel to different places in medieval society. In your diary you will write about all the experiences you undergo in your life and travels. Name the place where you reside and the different areas through which you travel. You will chart this travel on a map (see page 74). Here is a list of major regions during the medieval period:

Kingdom of Italy	Kingdom of Norway	Serbia
Kingdom of France	Kingdom of Denmark	Caliphate of Cordoba (Moors)
Kingdom of England	Kingdom of Burgundy	
Kingdom of Scotland	Kingdom of Castile	Russian Principalities
Kingdom of Wales	Byzantine Empire	Ireland
Kingdom of Sweden	Holy Roman Empire	Papal States

Place of Residence: _____

Other Places My Character Will Travel:

_____   _____

_____   _____

_____   _____

Medieval Diary *(cont.)*

Step 2: Writing and Researching

In your journal, you will write about your experiences, travels, the people whom you meet, the things that you see, etc. Write in first person (I, me) and use vivid description and detail. If, for example, you assume the role of a servant living in a French castle and your name is Monique, the following diary entry might work well.

The Diary of Monique Montrealle, September 4, 1244

Dear Diary,

Today we were attacked by those vicious English rats! They besieged our castle with flaming arrows and catapults. One side of the north wall was completely demolished. The Lord and Lady were hiding in their citadel—what low-down cowards! I will go and fight these English pests if I have to.

The terrible noises can still be heard from the wounded soldiers. Their groans and screams torment the night. Sadly, there is little you can do for a man whose legs are torn off . . .

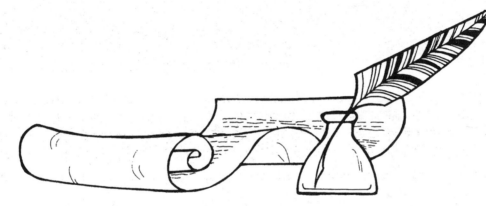

In addition, research the people, behavior, and events of your time period, country, and nearby areas. Here is a list of related topics:

- Charlemagne
- Crusades
- Knights/Knighthood
- Moors
- Boyars
- Islam
- Celts
- Roman Catholic Church
- Constantinople
- Byzantine Art

- Charles V
- Vikings
- Cathedrals
- Castles
- Henry VII
- Monks
- Gothic Art
- Marco Polo
- Scottish Wars
- Robin Hood

- Dark Ages
- Feudal Manors
- King Arthur
- Pope Gregory
- Richard the Lion-Hearted
- Monasteries
- Danube River
- Pilgrimages

Medieval Diary *(cont.)*

Step 3: Drawing Maps, Diagrams, and Pictures

On half a poster board, draw a map of where you live and your travels. Depending on all the places you go, your map might include most of the known world (if you were Marco Polo) or just a map of a local parish or region. You should use authentic geography of the medieval age, but you may also use your creativity to create towns, roads, etc. Make sure to color your map!

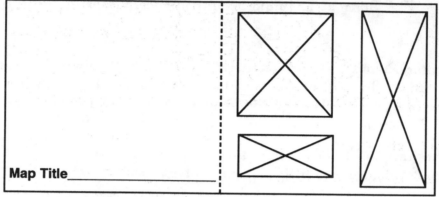

On the second half of your poster board, paste other pictures, photos, drawings, diagrams, architectural plans, or anything else that is relevant to your experiences.

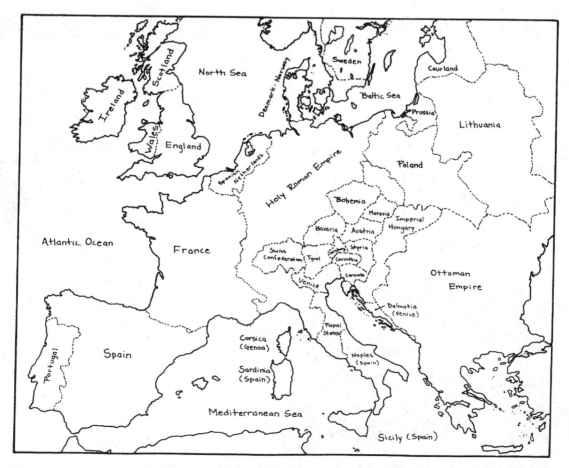

Medieval Diary *(cont.)*

Step 4: Putting It All Together

Now, once you have completed your visuals and your diary, turn them in together. Be sure your name is on them both!

Step 5: (Optional Extra Credit)

You can design and create a medieval learning center for extra credit. You might consider including models of castles, drawings of knights' armor and weapons, typical women's dress, enlarged maps, illuminated manuscripts, shield designs or coats of arms, art, and collections of stories or reference books about the time. You may also do any of the extra credit projects that are approved by your teacher. Have fun!

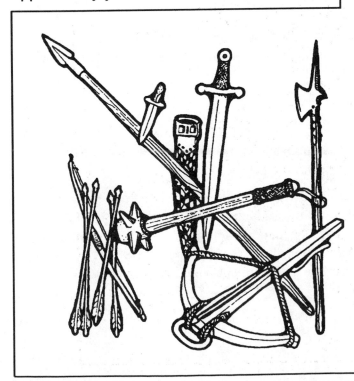

Curriculum Development

(cont.)

D. Management

After you have written the project and gathered your materials, get the class started.

1. Explaining Directions

Read the instructional packet to the class. Explain guidelines thoroughly and quiz the class on what you just talked about. Answer any questions. Have students write names and due dates on their projects. Explain that they will be checked at least once a week for a grade.

2. Checking Progress

You might conduct projects solely in the classroom or have students do them mostly at home. Whatever the case, you must check their progress at least once a week. For at-home projects, send information home with a parent signature requested. Keep a sharp eye on the at-risk students. It is often a good idea to have them bring the project to school to work on.

In class discuss how the project is going and show examples of student progress. Examples from years past will show students what final projects look like and serve as models.

3. Dealing with "Slackers"

Some students may make little or no progress. Try to find what the problem is. They may lack money to buy materials or be genuinely confused about directions. Other factors include emotional distress, lost materials, lack of interest, or laziness. Give the student the benefit of the doubt and help all you can. If this does not succeed, you must treat it as a discipline problem. Refusing to do work is a referrable offense.

4. Collecting Projects

When all projects are turned in, store them in a safe place while presentations are given. After presentation or display, return the projects to the students. If they are proud of their work, they will want to keep them.

E. Presentation

Presentation is essential to the learning cycle. Have the students individually get up and spend about three to five minutes explaining each project. You can use this opportunity to assess speaking skills. For a Presentation Evaluation form, see page 252.

Students often get nervous when facing the class. This is a healthy way to help them face their responsibilities. Also, presentations serve as a test of productivity. Students who do not try hard will face the wrath of the class. On the other hand, some learn so much they cannot keep quiet about their discoveries. Their comprehension is also tested by their peers' questions. Generally, presentations are successful exercises because students like learning about one another.

Curriculum Development

(cont.)

E. Presentations *(cont.)*

After presentations, display the projects to promote an atmosphere of learning and pride of accomplishment. Some display methods are the following:

1. Classroom Display

Put projects on the walls and doors of your room. For a dramatic display, hang the projects from the ceiling, turning the classroom into a "learning festival."

2. Hallway Display

Attach projects to the hallways outside your classroom or other appropriate places. Be careful not to infringe on other teachers' space.

3. Schoolwide Display

Turn the front of your school into a "learning maze" where projects stand up by themselves. In essence, this is a project museum where parents or other visitors can see what students are producing.

Always get the permission of your principal for such displays. The other person to consult is the head custodian. Explain your plans and ask for advice or any special suggestions.

V. Guest Speakers

A significant way to spice up learning is to build a good list of qualified guest speakers. Real people with real stories will leave an indelible imprint on the minds of your students. Before speakers come into your classroom, be sure to get administrator approval.

Use the Guest Speakers Matrix (page 253) to record names and numbers. This will coordinate all your contacts and be a handy reference sheet for addresses when you need to send thank-you letters.

It's good to have at least one guest speaker for every unit. People from all walks of life are usually very accommodating, happy to come speak to a classroom, especially if you plan well in advance. Some institutions, like the police force and community groups, have members who visit schools. It is your job to pick up the phone and make the calls.

Some ideas for guest speakers are these:

- authors
- lawyers
- politicians
- medical professionals
- business people
- armed forces personnel

- police officers
- clergymen
- journalists
- scientists
- high school students/college students
- other teachers/administrators

Curriculum Development

(cont.)

VI. Field Trips

An even more dramatic impact on students than guest speakers is a class field trip. Unfortunately, field trips connote a host of negative ideas for some teachers—obnoxious children screaming on the bus, running after students, worrying about liability, mounds of paperwork, and permission forms—so they are naturally hesitant to take one. But the rewards of field trips outweigh the minor inconveniences. Of the activities that students do, the field trip is probably their most anticipated and remembered event.

A. Ten Steps to a Successful Field Trip

There are good ways and bad ways to take a field trip. To ensure a successful event, fill out your Field Trip Form (page 254). Here are some ground rules:

1. **Clear your idea with administration.**

    The first thing to do is present your field trip ideas to the administration, preferably the principal. There are district guidelines which you may not know. In addition, your administration must know where all students are during school hours. They want a detailed agenda with learning objectives. If the principal clears your idea, then start planning.

2. **Confirm destination.**

    Confirm your destination with a phone call. The place you wish to visit might be closed on the days that you are interested. Confirm exact dates and times. Tell them how many students you will be bringing. Familiarize yourself with their house rules and write these down for the students. Express your appreciation to all who help you because you might want to come back.

3. **Confirm transportation.**

    You will have to call the transportation division of your district to arrange for a bus. Sometimes these busses are only available at certain times. There is usually a fee involved as well. Get exact numbers so you know what to charge students. Usually exchange of money is made through the office. Confirm times and places. Depending on your district rules, you might want to charter a private bus. This can be a creative solution for longer field trips.

4. **Make eating arrangements.**

    How will the students eat lunch? The easiest solution is to have students bring their own lunches. **Make sure names are on the lunches.** You might decide to eat out, especially for long trips. This method is sometimes easier on you, and the kids love eating in restaurants. Just make sure all the kids have enough money and bring some extra cash just in case. Notify the restaurant in advance, if possible, of the number and time.

Curriculum Development

(cont.)

VI. Field Trips *(cont.)*

5. Write parent letter/permission form.

Write a letter to the parents which explains your field trip plans, gives exact times and locations, indicates requirements for attending, provides for parent volunteer information, specifies any money needed, and provides for a permission slip which needs to be signed.

On the permission form, provide blanks for parent numbers in case of accidents. You should keep all your completed permission forms in an envelope and take them with you on your trip. In case there is an accident or emergency, you will have the parents' work numbers at your fingertips. Pass this letter out well in advance of your trip (three weeks is recommended).

6. Inform students and go over rules.

Thoroughly go over the field trip routine with the students. Detail any special requirements to be eligible, like passing scores, behavior, etc. Answer any questions or concerns the students might have. It is extremely important that you go over the specific rules of the location and rules governing bus rides. Make clear that breaking these rules is unacceptable. Here are some common field trip rules:

- Never leave the sight of an adult.
- Observe the buddy system at all times.
- Behave appropriately at all times.
- Use quiet voices on the bus.

7. Make arrangements for nonparticipants.

Some parents might not want their children to go for various reasons. For a Field Trip Parent Letter Form, see page 256.

For those students who cannot go, make arrangements with other teachers to have them in their classrooms. Provide a stimulating, but time consuming, activity for them to complete. If you have more than five nonparticipants, make arrangements to send them to more than one room. Prepare a list of "who and where" for the teachers and the office. For a Nonparticipant Form, see page 257.

8. Take up permission forms and prepare list of participants.

Collect all permission forms promptly on a daily basis. When you have all the permission slips, write out exactly who will be going on your trip.

9. Provide a list of participants to the office and teachers.

Give this list also to all the teachers who will not have that student in their classes for those appropriate periods.

10. Specify a designated meeting place and time to depart.

Tell your students where and when to meet you. On the day of the trip, have students prepare themselves and sit quietly while you go over your Field Trip Checklist (page 255). Make any last-minute arrangements. Take careful attendance and head count. Organize any volunteers. Before you get on the bus, go over the rules one more time and double check your list. Have fun!

Curriculum Development

(cont.)

B. Liability Factors: Negligence and Accidents

While conducting a field trip, the responsibility of caring for the children belongs to the teachers. If you are the only teacher, then you are solely liable. If anything were to happen to the children, it would be technically your fault. You must take this responsibility seriously because teachers can be sued for negligence or not exercising due care. There is a difference, however, between gross negligence and common accidents. Here are some examples of both:

Gross negligence: Your class gets to the museum. As the students get off the bus and mill into the museum, you make sure all the lunches are in the boxes on the bus. Suddenly, you hear a screeching car slam into a student. Billy has been hit and his neck is broken. He will be paralyzed for life. The parents of Billy can legitimately sue you for not exercising due care. They would probably win.

The most dangerous part of field trips is getting off the bus and to the location. You should have been supervising the unloading process and acting as a street guard. Then you could have directed Billy, who is prone to wandering, across the street safely.

Accident: At the park, your class is enjoying the playground. You are sitting on the bench supervising and talking to some students. Suddenly, Rebecca falls off the swings and cuts her lips wide open. When you get there, she is a bloody mess, with tears, saliva, and blood mixed together and running down her chin. After her parents get her to the emergency room, she will have irreparable scars on her face. Can Rebecca's parents sue you for negligence?

The answer is they can try, but they will not have much of a case. You were doing all you could do at that time by supervising. In addition, there was no way you could have prevented Rebecca's fall.

Gross negligence: On a trip to an archeological dig, your class is listening to a speaker. When you realize that you forgot your sunglasses, you inform the speaker you will be right back and run to the bus to retrieve them. When you return, Wayne has fallen into a mine shaft and lies unconscious. He will be in a coma for five years. Wayne's parents can easily sue you for negligence, even though you left him in the care of another adult.

You are the caretaker of your students, no matter what other adults are around. Leaving your class (even for a minute or two) in unfamiliar, dangerous terrain constitutes gross negligence—especially when done for a pair of sunglasses.

Accident: Your class is preparing to depart from the ballet. You are in the middle of the stairway supervising students. Dana slips and rolls down the steps, too late for you to catch her. She seems unconscious. Later, it is found that she broke her hip and will be bedridden indefinitely. Can Dana's parents sue you for negligence?

In this case, you were not negligent. On the contrary, you placed yourself in the middle of the stairway in order to prevent any falls. Dana's fall was probably caused by a shoelace or clumsy step, and you are not liable for accidents of this nature.

Curriculum Development

(cont.)

These cases are overly dramatic, although not out of the realm of possibility. As a teacher, the last thing you want to do is inadvertently ruin a child's life. Therefore, it is always extremely important that you follow safe procedures. It is not possible to be too careful on a field trip.

C. Ways to Make Trips Safe

1. **Supervision:** Sign up as many parent volunteers as possible to help supervise. As always, keep a close eye on all the students and vocalize the rules and procedures often. Taking head counts is essential in crowded areas.

2. **Planning:** Plan your trip to the minute. Let the students know exactly what they are going to do and when. Assign timekeepers who will help keep the class on schedule.

3. **Rules:** Go over the rules of behavior and procedure at the location thoroughly with your students. Provide immediate consequences in case they break those rules. One consequence kids usually take seriously is never being able to go on a field trip again. Explain to them the reasoning behind the rules.

4. **Dangerous Areas:** Field trips to places where liability runs high, like swimming areas (drowning), caves (falling), forests (getting lost), and the beach (drowning), should be cautioned against. Remember, middle schoolers, above all other students, tend to run and jump on things a tremendous amount.

D. Conclusion

Field trips are enjoyed by students all over the country, and the educational experience will be something they are not likely to forget. They can be fun for the teacher as well. With proper planning, most field trips go as planned. Take this job seriously, and you should never have any real problems.

When you get back to school, you might have some extra time. Prepare a post-trip packet filled with activities about the trip. Have the students discuss their experiences and share what they learned. Your students will appreciate you for taking them, even if they do not say so.

Remember to send thank-you letters to parent volunteers, signed by the students. The addresses you can get from your Personal ID Sheets.

FIELD TRIP Follow-UP

1- Discussion   2- Reports

3- Drawings   4. models

5- Skits   6- Research

Curriculum Development

(cont.)

VII. Thematic Celebrations

An exciting way to close the learning cycle is to create a thematic celebration or culminating activity. The core aim of thematic celebrations is that the students express what they have learned in a lively and colorful manner. In essence, they are celebrating their success. Unlike the typical presentation, thematic celebrations encompass a whole class effort. Some examples of these activities are the following: class museums, festivals, ceremonies, assemblies, field trips, and school-wide presentations.

Class Museums

Set up projects or products of student work in the classroom. Design a day when students walk around these displays and do an activity based on the projects, such as having them vote for the best displays and award prizes. A structured activity based on other students' work can be very educational.

Festivals

Plan a festival where food and drink are provided. The festival should adhere to the theme of the unit. Wearing costumes and eating content-appropriate foods will be an activity that students will enjoy. After all, information is only meaningful when it is remembered and applied. Having a festival is a meaningful learning experience because kids will associate the knowledge from class with the fun of the festival and always remember it.

On a practical level, conduct festivals in the cafeteria or outside. Also, do the following:

- Clear the idea with the administration and fill out any necessary forms.
- Provide for as many parent volunteers as possible to help with food and drinks.
- Make sure there are adequate trash cans for waste.
- Secure any necessary materials, like public address equipment or tables.
- Arrange food and utensils—cups, plates, napkins, etc.

Suggestions follow for a medieval festival which might culminate the Medieval Diary unit.

Medieval Festivals

When studying the Middle Ages, have students create a medieval fair. Kids love to dress up like knights, jesters, kings, queens, magicians, minstrels, monks, dragons, and other characters. Some ideas to spice up a Medieval Festival are these:

1. Elect a king, queen, duke, and duchess of the festival.
2. Provide for a red carpet (red butcher paper) and build medieval sets.
3. Allow extra privileges for those who dress up.
4. Eat medieval-style food—turkey, chicken, breads, pies, etc.
5. Always have students be responsible for cleaning up.
6. Provide for jugglers, magicians, and jesters to perform.
7. Bring in science experiments (alchemists).
8. Have game tables up for chess, checkers, and backgammon.
9. Provide ballad singing and dancing. Some ideas for ballad dancing technique are on page 83.

Curriculum Development

(cont.)

Circle Dancing

Have students gather in a circle and hold hands. Tell them to go to the right for two steps, kick and then go to the left two steps and kick. Once they have done this two times (4 beats x 2 = 8 beats), have them run in a circle to the right for 8 beats.

Diagrams of Feet

 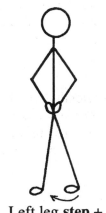  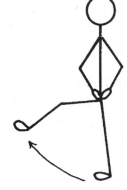

Left leg **step** +   Right leg **step** +   Left leg **step** +   Right leg **kick** =   4 beats

Right leg **step** +   Left leg **step** +   Right leg **step** +   Left leg **kick** =   4 beats

Repeat, different direction = 4 beats.

Run right in a circle for 8 beats = 8 beats.

Go back to the beginning.

                             #548 How to Manage Your Middle School Classroom

Curriculum Development
(cont.)

Line Dancing

Have students get in rows of four or five. Based on the four-beat rhythm, have them do the same steps as in the circle dancing, except now they step in a line and not a circle. Since they are not holding hands, they are free to move their arms while they line dance. Arm moves that change every eight beats follow:

The Greek

Extend arms fully, bring in, and then extend back again. Touch nose or head to vary moves.

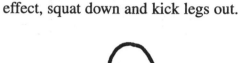

diagram of arm movement

The Russian

Fold arms in and flap: to get the true effect, squat down and kick legs out.

diagram of arm movement

Dances are sure to be a big hit, especially with sixth graders. Seventh and eighth graders tend to be more self-conscious, so they might need a little more sophistication. Utilizing classroom singing and dancing talents can be a big hit.

Ceremonies and Assemblies: Having award ceremonies to honor those who deserve recognition is essential. Having your own "award-of-the-week" or "award-of-the-month" can let those who are really trying know that their efforts are appreciated and admired. At the end of a unit, those who showed outstanding effort should be recognized. Teams of teachers can have their own assemblies to honor those in their teams. It is a good idea to conduct an assembly in a meeting place like the theater or cafeteria. For a Student Award Form, see page 258.

Field Trips:

You can choose to cap off a unit by going to a unit-appropriate location—for instance, visiting historical sights that were associated with your unit. Seeing plays, performances, museums, recreations, or other content-related locations not only provides for application and extension of knowledge, but it gives a real-world framework to classroom concepts.

School-Wide Presentations:

You can plan for school-wide **assemblies, shows, exhibits, interactive learning centers,** and more. Your students can be the performers, facilitators, or tour guides. Plays can be put on in the theater or cafeteria at a low price. Drama is not the only class that can put on plays. English teachers do it frequently. History, science, and math students also could easily express their knowledge through dramatic interpretations in front of an audience.

Curriculum Development

(cont.)

VIII. Organizing Your Curriculum

After you finish planning thematic celebrations, field trips, guest speakers, projects, instructional units, and lesson plans, you will need to have a system for storing and categorizing your work. For most of us, this means keeping a file cabinet and a few notebooks.

Summoning all the ideas and strategies from the previous chapters, organize them into a convenient, effective system:

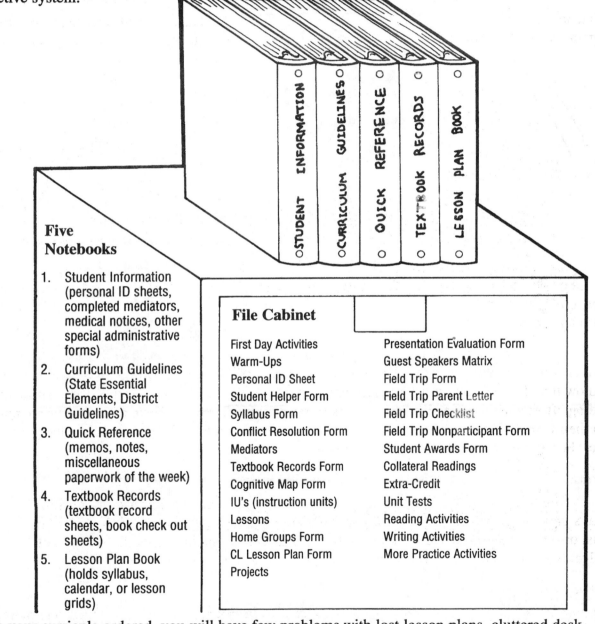

Five Notebooks

1. Student Information (personal ID sheets, completed mediators, medical notices, other special administrative forms)

2. Curriculum Guidelines (State Essential Elements, District Guidelines)

3. Quick Reference (memos, notes, miscellaneous paperwork of the week)

4. Textbook Records (textbook record sheets, book check out sheets)

5. Lesson Plan Book (holds syllabus, calendar, or lesson grids)

File Cabinet

First Day Activities	Presentation Evaluation Form
Warm-Ups	Guest Speakers Matrix
Personal ID Sheet	Field Trip Form
Student Helper Form	Field Trip Parent Letter
Syllabus Form	Field Trip Checklist
Conflict Resolution Form	Field Trip Nonparticipant Form
Mediators	Student Awards Form
Textbook Records Form	Collateral Readings
Cognitive Map Form	Extra-Credit
IU's (instruction units)	Unit Tests
Lessons	Reading Activities
Home Groups Form	Writing Activities
CL Lesson Plan Form	More Practice Activities
Projects	

Notebook spines: STUDENT INFORMATION | CURRICULUM GUIDELINES | QUICK REFERENCE | TEXTBOOK RECORDS | LESSON PLAN BOOK

With your curricula ordered, you will have few problems with lost lesson plans, cluttered desk, misplaced activities, and other symptoms of ineffective teaching. Your curriculum file and notebooks are the core of your teaching success, for they hold the floor plans that will shape ideas and change lives for the better.

Effective Classroom Administration

In building an effective classroom, a teacher must perform the important task of administrator and manager. You have already raised four strong supports: understanding the micro and macro worlds of middle school (Chapter 1), creating order in the classroom (Chapter 2), laying the foundation for teaching the basics (Chapter 3), and writing quality curricula (Chapter 4). Keeping up with details and handling administrative matters is the fifth support for your learning structure.

Outline of Chapter 5

I. Attendance
 A. Marking Your Attendance Card
 B. Dealing with Tardies

II. Grading
 A. Gradebooks
 B. Grading Scale
 C. Grading Efficiently
 D. Handling Homework

III. Authentic Assessment
 A. Observations
 B. Portfolios
 C. Self-Evaluations

IV. Keeping Up with Students
 A. Locker/Notebook Checks
 B. Hall/Restroom Privileges
 C. Administering Medical Care to Students

V. Preparing for Substitutes
 A. Making a Substitute Folder
 B. Substitute Lesson Plans

VI. Administering Standardized Tests

VII. Systemizing Red Tape

Reproducibles for Chapter 5 (See pages 259–265.)

1. *Class Grid (all purpose)*
2. *Teacher-Parent Warning Forms*
3. *Homework Weekly Planner*
4. *Self-Evaluation Form*
5. *Hall Passes*
6. *Health Notice to Parents*
7. *Substitute's Record Form*

Effective Classroom Administration *(cont.)*

I. Attendance

Attendance accounting is crucial to the teacher and school. Most schools are funded on the basis of average daily attendance (ADA), where one or two percentage points can mean hundreds of thousands of dollars. Also, attendance records show where the student has missed important days, field trips, needs to do make-up work, etc.

A. Marking Your Attendance Card

Every period, take a few minutes to fill out your attendance card. Wait about five minutes after the bell to account for tardy students. It is very important that you mark both your attendance card and your gradebook to have accurate records for the office and for yourself.

Absent: Marking the appropriate box is the usual method of noting absence. The first period of the day you should wait at least 10 minutes to put out your card to catch late comers. Late busses, traffic, and weather are other variables that complicate first period attendance. Mark your grade book as well. Always keep duplicate attendance records in your gradebook. Attendance and grades often have high positive correlation.

Tardy: This is usually marked either with a "T" or a diagonal line where a previous absence mark was made.

In-School Suspension: If students receive in-school suspension, they are not counted absent. This is usually indicated with an "S." You must provide a make-up assignment for that student.

Home Suspension: Students suspended from the campus are absent and marked appropriately. Some teachers write them letters giving assignments, assurances of encouragement, and words of wisdom.

Field Trip: Field trips are excused absences. Undoubtedly, you will receive advance notice of field trips. Mark this on your cards and gradebook immediately.

Excused/Unexcused Designation: Most attendance systems indicate the difference between an excused absence and unexcused. This is often done by circling the excused dates. Many schools set a limited number of unexcused absences for eligibility to pass the class.

B. Dealing with Tardies

Tardiness, excused or unexcused, is distracting. Students with legitimate reasons for being late must have a pass with the proper information and signature. Unexcused tardies should always result in a discipline consequence, like a mediator (see Chapter 2). Sometimes, students actually do have reasonable delays, like a jammed locker or a hallway incident. However, frequent tardiness is a major problem which should be handled firmly. Mediators, after school detentions, and parent conferences will usually end this misbehavior.

Effective Classroom Administration *(cont.)*

II. Grading

Since students are judged in your class based on your grading system, it is imperative that you keep an efficient, organized, and fair grading system.

A. Gradebooks

Every teacher keeps a gradebook. The gradebook usually doubles as a class roster and attendance record as well. Fill out your gradebook fully for your instructional period, with dates, assignments, and grades. Schools provide each teacher with a gradebook, but you might need class rosters for special grades or lists. An all purpose class grid is available for you on page 259.

Periodically, make copies of your gradebook in case you lose it or it gets irreparably damaged. A recent development has been the computer gradebook. There are programs which simulate gradebooks (spreadsheets) and do all the calculating for you according to programmed scales. The only real differences between a computer gradebook and a handwritten gradebook is that the computer does all the calculating. An ideal situation would be having a computer in your room for class records. Another effective feature of a computer gradebook is that you can get printouts of grades for each student. Many teachers in the future will have a "gradedisc" rather than a gradebook.

B. Grading Scale

After you know what you will teach and the assignments you will give, you must determine how everything will be weighted. For instance, a grade on a final project normally should count more than a spelling assignment. No teachers have exactly the same grading structures, but some common types of grading scales follow.

The Traditional

- daily assignments 50%
- tests 50%

In this scale, the emphasis is on traditional teaching methods (teach and test). It is assumed that students will learn from lectures, textbooks, and worksheets and then be tested on them to assess comprehension.

Effective Classroom Administration *(cont.)*

The Progressive

- class activities 10%
- cooperation 10%
- homework 10%
- quizzes 20%
- projects 50%

With this scale, students are evaluated in a range of areas, including the behavioral (cooperation). This scale emphasizes the project more than anything else in the class.

The College

- exams 90%
- discretionary 10%

This scale would not work well in middle school. It places an emphasis on final exams, which would not assess middle school children fairly. The "discretionary" is a professor's way of saying "I can give or take away up to ten points if I feel like it."

The Authentic

- portfolios 33%
- self-improvement 33%
- cooperation 34%

The portfolio here becomes a record of the student's progress and accomplishments. Self-evaluation should stimulate improvement. Cooperative and intra-personal skills are seen as the third component to a well-rounded youth.

These are only a few of the variations which teachers use across the country. Part of teacher autonomy is deciding how you will grade and what emphasis you will put on your course. It is important to be fair, and always remember one thing about assigning students a grade. In middle school, *you are grading learning*. Grading on effort helps students and individualizes their education. Being flexible on grading and taking into account individual concerns is not unheard of in the realm of good teaching.

Effective Classroom Administration *(cont.)*

C. Grading Efficiently

On any given day, a teacher's desk can look like an office explosion—worksheets, homework, memos, flyers, markers, etc. There may be no magic remedy for this, but effective teachers clear a special shelf or box for homework.

A good teacher assigns many great activities but might get bogged down grading daily papers. *How can you accurately grade and record papers without examining each one intensely?* Here are three methods:

Student-Graded

Have students grade their own papers. To preclude the temptation to cheat, switch papers among different students to ensure variety and fairness. Students can switch papers with the person in front or behind, the person to the left or right, or however you choose.

Next have all the students write "Graded by . . ." and then their names. Go over all answers, responding to any questions. Finally, have students compute the grades according to your direction (a mini-math lesson, with each one double checking the other).

This method produces grades accurately and immediately. Moreover, students get immediate feedback on what they did right or wrong. There are drawbacks, however. You can use this type of grading only with assignments like spelling tests, vocabulary quizzes, text work, worksheets, and other low-level assignments with clear-cut answers. Short story writing cannot be treated quite like this.

Student Aides

Have student helpers with a zest for accuracy grade papers where applicable. Provide sample perfect papers or grading rubrics to follow. Student aides enjoy helping the teacher, gaining responsibility, and will almost always do their best. Follow these guidelines when using student graders: Never take student aides out of normal class activities to grade; never let student aides grade major tests, private journals, or assignments open to interpretation; supervise grading to answer questions or make corrections.

Using student aides can be a break for you and a learning experience for the student; but remember, it is technically your job to assign grades, not theirs. So use this method with caution.

Spot Checking

When in a crunch, you might have time only to spot check papers to make sure of the major requirements of an assignment. Spot check marks can be the following:

(check plus) = Outstanding! (100)

(check) = Complete (95)

(check minus) = Tried, but not complete (75)

(N/C) = No credit, must do again

This method lets you grade a paper rapidly. The drawbacks are that you do not get to check real progress or what the student is saying. In addition, you do not have time to make comments.

Effective Classroom Administration *(cont.)*

Stamp Pads/Stickers

An efficient way to make comments is to buy some stamps and pads or stickers. Stamps are actually more efficient because they last years, and you can order them with encouraging messages like *Excellent Work!, Good Job!, Magnificent!, Well Done!, Fabulous Work!,* and *I'm proud of you!*

Stickers are more varied and colorful. They are usually inexpensive. In general, middle schoolers seem to have a fascination with stickers, so they can be used as rewards and incentives as well as comments.

Grading Presentations Efficiently

If students give presentations, it is essential that they receive feedback to improve. Using your Presentation Evaluation form (page 252), you can easily check off student progress and give them instant feedback on the following:

Eye Contact: Did they make good eye contact with everybody in the room?

Voice Level: Was their voice loud, clear, and commanding?

Gestures: Did they gesture effectively?

Movement: Did they move around the room effectively?

You will be surprised how much speaking skills improve with proper feedback.

Teacher Feedback

Part of a teacher's job is to assess student output thoroughly, seeing progressions or digressions, remarking on excellence, and thanking for hard work. Teacher feedback is very important to the learning process. Giving valuable time and thoughtful reflection to student work is essential. Sometimes, in our hectic world of middle school affairs, we may overlook that one student who really needed a boost. Even vocally remarking to individual students that you liked their work will bond you to those persons. This will ensure a source of energy that feeds on itself.

D. Handling Homework

Homework Routines

All effective teachers have a specific method to deal with homework. One effective way is to have student helpers take it up, noting any who did not have it. It is imperative that you have a system in place for those who did not do their homework. Simply saying, "I guess you get a zero then" does not help anybody. In addition, students will offer all kinds of excuses:

"I left it at home."

"It's in my other binder at home."

"I didn't finish."

"I forgot."

"I didn't understand."

Sometimes, these can actually be legitimate, but most of the time they are not.

Effective Classroom Administration *(cont.)*

D. Handling Homework *(cont.)*

In dealing with those who do not have their homework, the most important concept to get across to students is not that they will be punished but that they will do it. Some effective consequences for this annoying syndrome are the following:

1. Write names on the board of those who did not turn in homework.
2. Remove offending students to an isolated booth to finish the assignment.
3. Assign lunch detention (15 minutes) to finish homework.
4. Assign after school detention (1 hour) to finish homework.
5. Write a note home to parents on your Teacher-Parent Warning forms (page 260).
6. Call parents and inform them of their child's progress.

Above all, never let a student slide by without turning in homework. These methods will eliminate most homework problems, but not all. If a student is having a continuous problem, try intervening. Some interventions which could help are these:

Homework Weekly Planner: This is a calendar of the week in which students write down each night's homework for all subjects. It is a quick reference sheet for the student to look at before he or she goes home and before school to make sure they have everything. For a copy of Homework Weekly Planner, see page 261.

Homework Binder: This is a notebook which just carries homework. It is especially good for students with poor organizational skills and those prone to lose and misplace assignments.

Assigning Homework: Homework should never introduce lessons or concepts that the students are not familiar with, unless it is for a specific purpose. It is your job to introduce and activate prior knowledge and motivation. There are basically four types of homework: *process, product, reminders,* and *special.*

Process: Home assignments of this nature require students to continue working on a process, like a project or other long term assignment. These types of assignments would appear on the board like the following:

- *Complete third page of journal.*
- *Finish step two of invention project.*
- *Create last part of solar system model.*

Process homework is useful because it prods students to keep on task. It is especially good for the teacher because there is no immediate grading needed. The drawback to assigning process homework is that it is impossible to account for who has done it and who has not.

Effective Classroom Administration *(cont.)*

D. Handling Homework *(cont.)*

Product: Product-oriented homework is the traditional type of home assignment. The student completes a task and has a product ready the next day.

On the chalkboard, it looks like this:

- *Complete page 156, Questions 1–11.*
- *Read pages 3–27 TXT, answer Q 1–5, page 27.*
- *Write a one-page story about losing your best friend.*
- *Complete Geography of England word search, do crossword on back.*

Product homework provides instant accountability and can be graded immediately for feedback.

Reminder: Middle school students tend to forget things. Homework that simply reminds them of upcoming events or activities helps them cope with the world of middle school. Typical reminder homework follows: Bring novels to class tomorrow, Have map pencils for tomorrow, Don't forget permission slips, Bring money for fair tomorrow.

Special: Special assignments are unusual and go beyond the scope of classroom activities, involving parents, friends, and the community. Some examples are these:

- Do something with your parents this weekend.
- Write a letter to a relative.
- Explore a new park.
- Try a new sport.

At first, these types of tasks are greeted with surprise and laughter because students are not used to them. However, you may be surprised at the number who follow up and do the assignments. You may have many good discussions in class about these assignments.

One way to ensure accountability is to have students write in class about what they did.

Frequency of Homework: When will you assign homework? Some teachers give homework every day and some not at all, preferring that students do all their work in class. Most probably give homework at least two or three times a week. It is important to be consistent. Let's go back to Mrs. Clay's English class and find out how she assigns homework.

Mrs. Clay's Homework Policy

day	assignment
Monday	spelling exercises (product)
Tuesday	story (product), project (process)
Wednesday	project (process)
Thursday	Study for spelling test (process).
Friday	Special (Forgive somebody, or make a new friend).

In this example, Mrs. Clay seems to have most of the heavy work at the beginning of the week. She assigns process homework for most of the middle of the week. On the weekends, she wants students to have a special task, which usually involves mental health activities.

A happy medium of assigning homework is important to the success of teachers and students.

Effective Classroom
Administration *(cont.)*

III. Authentic Assessment

Recently, a more legitimate and productive way to assess students is being called for. Traditional means of assigning intelligence levels are under attack. Some argue that grades are useless. Far from genuine feedback, they are merely arbitrary numbers which represent how well a student conforms to a certain set of expectations and particular assignments. Is it really productive to have students complete worksheets that they will just forget anyway? To prepare them for life after school, shouldn't we concentrate on how the world will assess these students?

These are some of the questions being debated today. Many propose a level-of-mastery system with a simple pass/fail designation. A student cannot continue unless he/she has passed. Conversely, if students are motivated enough, they can move up in grades faster. In essence, classes would be based on mastery of a set of criteria and not based on age level as is done today.

Traditional assessment tools are unlikely to change drastically anytime soon, but teachers recognize that assessment should be as authentic as possible. Some ways teachers achieve this besides traditional pencil-and-paper assignments are the following:

A. Observations

By keeping observation journals and notes, teachers can assess student performance. Observations are efficient assessment tools.

Cooperative Learning: Observations are the main means of assessing student performance in cooperative learning. An observation notebook is good for recording important notes. It serves the dual function of alerting students that you are assessing them as they work, keeping them motivated. Usually notes are quick and diagrammatic. Observation notes might look like the following:

- Johnny—won't compromise
- Heath—isolated, no social skills
- Sarah+Sheldon—good teamwork

Presentations: Use your Presentation Evaluation form (page 252) to assess speaking techniques. Students need feedback on speaking skills if we are to nurture and improve their rhetorical abilities. Think of the everyday occurrences when speaking ability changes situations—a phone conversation with a potential client, a disagreement about procedure, a meeting about a salary raise. All these situations demand a command of the English language.

Participation: Many teachers include participation in their grading systems. The idea is to motivate students to add to class discussions to help other students and the teacher. Developing motivation is one of the best life skills that we as teachers can instill in students.

Citizenship: This system of evaluation assesses students' ability to act morally upright, lead others in a positive manner, and sacrifice for the greater good. You will find natural leaders in your classroom. Use them for good in your classroom and have them model leadership skills.

Effective Classroom Administration *(cont.)*

B. Portfolios

A ubiquitous buzz word going across the discussion tables of our nation's schools is the term *portfolios*. The idea behind a portfolio is that each student should keep a record of his or her best work to show two things: progress and products.

Progress: A portfolio system is supposed to measure how the student has progressed since the beginning of a course. Comparing samples of the same type of work in different time periods, teachers can see what learning has taken place. For example, an English teacher asks all students to write a description of a certain scenario. She repeats this assignment three months later. Using both samples, she is able to evaluate student progress in descriptive writing. The expectation is that the second sample will be much better, using all the techniques and knowledge developed in class. When both students and teachers actually see improvement, that should spur motivation. This is genuine portfolio evaluation.

Product: Besides measuring progress, the portfolio also showcases student products. The portfolio system implies that students should work on meaningful, long-term projects. The thought is that in the real world, people mainly focus on projects requiring a complex synthesis of information.

- Construction workers build houses.
- Doctors operate on patients.
- Business people negotiate contracts.
- Politicians create laws.
- Archeologists initiate digs.
- Portfolios are designed to hold large projects for others to see.

How to Start a Portfolio System: If you want to start a portfolio system, follow these guidelines:

1. The actual portfolios to put student work in can be as simple as a manila folder or expandable envelope. Have one for every student.

2. Have students mark their names neatly on the portfolios and provide a place for storage. Organizer boxes usually do well.

3. Design a table of contents outlining what will be included. Let's say Mr. Hamad starts a portfolio system in his class.

✉ Mr. Hamad's Portfolio Table of Contents ✉

I. Science Writing, sample 1	VI. Research Paper
II. Lab Sample, biology	VII. Science Writing, sample 2
III. Lab Sample, chemistry	VIII. Self-Evaluation
IV. Home Observation, biology	IX. Open
V. Home Observation, chemistry	X. Open

Mr. Hamad has created a flexible portfolio system accounting for progress as well as product, ensuring that quality projects will overshadow traditional daily assignments.

Effective Classroom Administration *(cont.)*

C. Self-Evaluations

Historically, student input about their own progress has not been valued. Many teachers and administrators are reevaluating this assumption. Indeed, asking students how they think they are doing is seen as a key for assessing student learning. Middle schoolers, in particular, are usually extremely honest about themselves. In addition, providing opportunities for self-evaluations gives students a sense of ownership in your class. Students tend to respect teachers who ask for students' opinions.

For a Self-Evaluation form, see page 262.

IV. Keeping Up with Students

A. Locker/Notebook Checks

Check on student organization as much as possible. Middle schoolers have major problems keeping up with social concerns, let alone school work. Occasionally, however, you will find students with strong organization. You can let these people serve as models for everyone else. Be very meticulous about student organization. Ignore this point, and students will think you really do not care what they do. That will produce bad habits. You simply have to make time during your busy schedule to check on your students.

If your distrtict requires or allows a locker check, there is an efficient way to do this. Supply each student with a locker standards checklist like the following:

Locker Standards Checklist

❑ No extraneous papers in lockers   ❑ All books covered

❑ All library books OK   ❑ No unnecessary items in locker

❑ Locker neat and tidy

With a simple checklist like this sent home as advance notice and a competent student helper, a teacher can check lockers quickly and thoroughly.

You will remember from Chapter 2 how important it is for students to keep an organized system for each class. You can help this process by providing checks either randomly or routinely. Student helpers can help here also.

Notebook Standards Checklist

❑ All sections designated properly with divider   ❑ All papers filed appropriately

❑ No damaged papers   ❑ No misplaced papers

❑ All other requirements met

Effective Classroom Administration *(cont.)*

B. Hall/Restroom Privileges

There will come times when students need to leave your classroom. Legitimate causes for these interruptions include summons to principal's or counselor's offices, medical appointments, or family emergencies. For these cases, passes are usually already provided, and you just have to sign and time them. Do not forget to note the absence.

However, there will also come times when students need to leave class momentarily without an official excuse. These occasions are known as privileges to distinguish them from rights. The most common form of this privilege is going to the restroom. Other causes are getting drinks, going to the nurse, and running errands. The teacher needs to use discretion when giving students these privileges. Allow for one student at a time. To save paper, some teachers use one pass for the whole year. Find a permanent object of some kind (driftwood, plastic toy, shoe, etc.) and label it with your name and room number. Have a designated location where students who are eligible for privileges can get the pass and proceed on their errand. For generic Hall Pass Forms, see page 263.

C. Administering Medical Care to Students

You know by now that a teacher is really many persons: leader, professor, biologist, physical therapist, philosopher, accountant, manager, parent, disciplinarian, conflict mediator, psychologist, writer, organizer, fund-raiser, technician—just to name a few. If you are a teacher, then you are also a nurse.

The most fundamental aspect of student well-being is health. You will probably encounter a range of physical ailments you should be aware of. There will be two kinds of conditions—documented and common. A documented medical condition is important to understand. Common ailments are less serious but still important to treat.

Documented Health Conditions: (Check with your school health officials for more information.)

Asthma: If these students start wheezing or have other complications associated with breathing, they probably need their inhalers, devices which provide immediate relief.

Migraines: These students might need to lie down, go to the nurse, or go home because of serious head pain. Migraines complicate blood flow to the head, making learning a low priority. Be sensitive to these students and let them relax.

Allergic Reactions: This term covers much ground. Be careful with foods, dyes (crafts), drinks, and activities where bees, hornets, or wasps are present. Some students have such bad reactions they can go into seizures.

Seizures: Seizures can be quiet, or they may involve muscle spasms. Make the student as comfortable as possible while the seizure works itself out. Usually, the nurse has special instructions for prolonged seizures.

Effectve Classroom Administration *(cont.)*

Common Maladies

Colds: Many students will have at least one or two colds during the year. It is important to treat these appropriately.

Stomach Aches: These conditions can be serious and are usually documented with an explanation of what to do in case of emergency.

Keep all these medical documents in your student notebook right behind Personal ID Sheets for quick reference. Also have these basic items in your classroom at all times:

1. First Aid Kit: Students will receive minor cuts, rashes, scrapes, and other ailments which young people are susceptible to over the course of the year.

2. Tissues: Provide an ample supply for colds. If your school does not supply tissues, an efficient way to do this is to write to the parents explaining your concern about student health, requesting that they contribute. Do not administer any medications. Check with your school administrators on this policy.

V. Preparing for Substitutes

Preparing for substitutes is a major reflection on your professionalism and organization. When you are not there, the show must go on. Many teachers complain about substitutes. "He didn't teach anything!" "My classroom's a mess!" "She didn't even look at my lesson plans," and "The sub was awful!" Unfortunately, many teachers have never substituted and have little idea of what a difficult job it is. Even perfect lesson plans cannot save substitutes lacking training or familiarity with school policies. This is because middle school students are likely to observe the following behaviors when a substitute appears:

- excitedly run down the halls screaming, "We've got a sub today!"
- think of the day as a holiday where no real work can be done
- be uncharacteristically rude or testy with the substitute
- try to sit in other seats
- be purposely tardy to class
- do anything to sabotage the lesson
- be extremely resentful at any disciplinary measures
- think of the substitute as a person to toy with and never see again

Being a sub is much like keeping the lids on a kitchen full of boiling pots while trying out a new recipe. Just to finish is a major accomplishment. So it is only humane that you recognize the problems of a substitute and adjust accordingly.

One effective measure is to have formal substitute rules. These are usually the same class rules with a bonus if everybody follows them—outside privileges, parties, reprieves, enrichment activities, etc. Leave a Substitute Record form (page 265) to be filled out. Also, you can do two things which will ensure a proper transfer of power in the classroom: make a Substitute Folder and create substitute lesson plans.

Effective Classroom Administration *(cont.)*

A. Making a Substitute Folder

A three-ring spiral notebook makes a good folder. In the folder you should include the following items:

1. Attendance Records	6. List of Helpful Teachers
2. Seating Charts	7. Names of Administrators
3. List of Class Rules	8. Mediators
4. List of Helpful Students	9. Discipline Referral Forms
5. List of Problem Students	10. Lesson Plans (prepared or emergency)

B. Substitute Lesson Plans

1. **Prepared:** This form of planning occurs when you know you are going to be absent. Funerals, special leaves, professional opportunities, and other obligations allow you to write a well-considered substitute plan. You may continue with regular plans but provide buffers for the substitute. You can spell out everything about your class and give detailed lesson plans. Substitutes appreciate this. If you have trained your students well, you can provide for quality learning opportunities where the substitute can actually teach.

2. **Emergency:** These plans are a permanent set that you should leave in your substitute folder, intended for immediate use. Sometimes, you cannot foresee disabling incidents in your life. The next day a substitute gets a call early in the morning but often will show up late because of legitimate reasons (for example, not having the classroom key). A set of emergency materials can keep the first class operating while the substitute or administrator can prepare for other activities. In these plans, you should have the following:

   a. Worksheets that are visually appealing but cognitively challenging—crosswords, word searches, and any other word or math puzzles can be found in workbooks and resource guides. You may make your own so they are content specific to exact class needs.

   b. A challenging set of warm-ups for the substitute to present. A substitute can supervise and read the answers.

   c. A transparency or other type of message for the class. An effective simple message might read like the following:

You will have a substitute today because I had an unexpected emergency. If you finish your assignment early, ask the teacher if you can use the reading center to read. All hall and restroom privileges are prohibited. The teacher will write down names of students who do not cooperate. The class will lose its privileges if any disrespect is shown to the teacher.

   d. A lesson which will last all period. Provide a quality assignment that is easy for the substitute to administer.

   e. Materials, instruction sheets, transparencies, etc.

Effective Classroom
Administration *(cont.)*

VI. Administering Standardized Tests

At some time during the year, you will have to give basic standardized tests to your students. Each state handles its own tests differently. Whatever version of the tests you have, the procedure is fairly uniform. To properly administer standardized tests, follow this sequence:

1. Get testing information from your counselor or testing coordinator. Make sure you keep abreast of any innovations in testing procedures. For security purposes, you will not receive the testing materials until the first day of testing.

    You probably have been talking about the upcoming test with your students and reviewing the format. Make sure you tell the students when testing will begin. Their homework during testing days should be only the following:

    • to gets lots of sleep
    • to eat a good breakfast
    • to bring two pencils with erasers
    • to bring reading materials in case of finishing early

2. On the day of the testing, explain the rules thoroughly by reading directly from the teacher's manual. Your job is almost robotic. To validate standardized procedures, there should be no variation from the exact printed directions.

    If the students have to bubble in personal information, make sure they do it right by checking their answer sheets. Read the directions to them and the sample questions. Have them start. Then give time information on the board if administering a timed test.

3. Walk up and down the aisles every now and then to check that students are marking their answer sheets correctly. You may not answer any questions related to the test while the students are testing. You are allowed to respond to non-test questions.

4. When students finish a section, make sure they close their testing booklets and wait until the next section is started. They may look at the section they have just completed, but they may not look at any other section. A good idea is to have students read or work on extra credit after they are finished with the test.

5. At the end of the testing day, take up all materials in order. You will probably test part of the day for three to five days. At the end of the testing week, gather all materials in the order that the counselor or testing coordinator requests, which is usually testing booklets, completed answer sheets in alphabetical order, blank answer sheets, student testing attendance record, testing oath signature, and extraneous testing materials.

Effective Classroom Administration *(cont.)*

VII. Systemizing Red Tape

Especially if you work at a large urban middle school, you will receive a shower of memos, reminders, staff reports, meeting minutes, special activities, faculty meeting announcements, etc. It is easy to misplace all this "red tape" because it comes on small strips of paper and is generally hard to keep track of. The following is a suggested system for organizing the paper river:

1. **Quick Reference Notebook:** Obtain a small binder to hold all your memos of the day/week. These papers will probably arrive in your mailbox. Visit your box at least twice a day and put your correspondence in your notebook to review later.

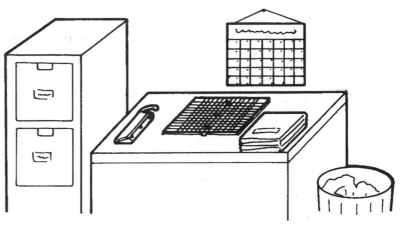

2. **Review Paperwork:** When you get a spare moment, review all your communication. While you are doing this, have the following items ready: calendar, file cabinet, notebooks, three-hole punch, trash can, and gradebook/attendance records.

Notebooks

If you remember, you have five notebooks: curriculum guidelines, student information, textbook records, quick reference, and a lesson plan notebook. This chapter introduced you to one more—the substitute notebook. So you have six notebooks altogether. There is a strong chance that some paperwork needs to be stored in one of these. For instance, there may be a medical alert sheet describing a student's allergic reactions to bees. This should be punched (with three holes, that is) and stored after the student's Personal ID Sheet in your student notebook. A memo about textbooks, of course, would go in your textbook records notebook.

But what about information like library overdues or special activity memos? This is where your quick reference notebook comes in handy. Keep these memos here, announce them to the class, or put them on the board, and then discard them after they expire.

Attendance Roster

You have transferred all the paperwork efficiently on your calendar, in the appropriate file, or in a notebook. Now, why would you need your attendance records? The answer is field trips and student disciplinary removals.

Frequently, you will receive memos about students going on certain field trips. You will also receive lists of students who are on in-school or at-home suspensions. Record this immediately in your gradebook/attendance. This is important because they should not be counted absent. If you mark your attendance record immediately, you will not have to worry about making attendance errors.

In conclusion, systemizing the red tape can be made effective and efficient. In addition, you can rest assured that all the important information is recorded or stored appropriately.

Technology in the Classroom

The new source of power is not money in the hands of a few but information in the hands of the many.

—John Naisbitt

Technology is rapidly changing our lives. Technology actually does not change anything in the classroom except the medium of learning. Every teacher should be an expert in some technology. Our culture is dependent on it.

Outline of Chapter 6

I. Background

    A. The Information Age

    B. Why Teachers Resist Technology

II. Audio-Video Technology

    A. Traditional Technologies

    B. Laser Disc Players

III. Computers

    A. Background

    B. Geography

    C. Modes of Integration

    D. Word Processing

    E. Spreadsheets

    F. Data Bases

    G. Graphics

    H. Desktop Publishing

    I. Hypercard/Hypertext Programs

    J. CD-ROM

    K. Computers at Home

IV. The Computer Lab

    A. Networks

    B. Computer Lab Rules

V. On-line Systems

    A. How Modems Operate

    B. Applications

VI. Desktop Publishing

    A. Background

    B. Design/Formatting

    C. How to Make a Professional Newsletter

VII. Knowing the Copyright Laws

    A. Buying the Rights

    B. Fair Use Exemption

    C. Face-to-Face

    D. Software Copyright Laws

Technology in the Classroom *(cont.)*

I. Background

A. The Information Age

Technological advancements are sweeping into our lives. Microwaves in the kitchen, electronic garage door openers, laser-guided home security systems, and home computers are widespread. The changes in only half a century are truly remarkable. After all, many of our grandparents grew up without electricity!

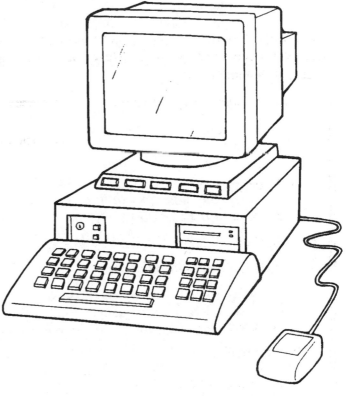

Author and researcher John Naisbitt has spent a good part of his life following economic trends in society. His exciting thesis of a new age in history is based on humankind's past progress from a hunter/gatherer society to an agricultural society to an industrial society.

The Rumblings of a New Society—The Information Age: Are we still in an industrial age? The answer is *no*. In 1979, the number one occupation in America became clerk, succeeding laborer. The clerk job is based on technology. We are on the threshold of a new age, whether we are aware of it or not. Our economy, national defense, government, business, and other vital areas depend on tools born from the information revolution—in essence, almost a "silent revolution." This subtlety of change is a characteristic of all ages.

Naisbitt's prophetic volume *Megatrends: Ten Directions Transforming Our Lives* describes the beginning of our new age. We still have one foot in the industrial era and one foot in the information age. This may be evident in your school. Think about it.

- Do you have a typewriter class and a computer literacy class simultaneously in your school's curriculum?
- Have you ever seen a student in the library looking in a hardbound encyclopedia while another is searching a CD-ROM encyclopedia?
- Have any of your students turned in their papers typed on computers, while others turned in handwritten copies?
- Have you ever seen two people making notes, one on paper and one on a laptop computer?
- Do any of your students know more about computers than you do?

Technology in the Classroom *(cont.)*

If you answered yes to any of these questions, then you are witnessing the rumblings of the information age. The new technologies making the greatest impact on our society are computers, satellites, micro-circuitry, robotics, laser technology, and advanced electronics. The new millionaires are not making cars or steel; they are inventing microchips and software programs. The new fuel for our society is no longer capital but information itself. As Naisbitt explains,

But in our society...the strategic resource is information. Not the only resource, but the most important. With information as the strategic resource, access to the economic system is much easier.

...That is the most important reason for the current entrepreneurial explosion in the United States, the huge growth in new small businesses. In 1950 we were creating new businesses at the rate of 93,000 per year. Today (1983), we are creating new companies in this country at the rate of more than 600,000 a year. (Megatrends, page 7)

Myths of the Information Age:

In essence, new technologies have revolutionized our society. Our grocery prices are read by lasers, we telebank our finances, our taxes can be done by computer, we "e-mail" correspondence, and this is only the beginning. We live in a digitalized world that is advancing and changing as you read this sentence, leading to the myth that we are losing our "humanness" and becoming cyberunits in a cyberuniverse.

But far from losing our humanity and becoming computer-like creatures with no feelings, the information-age person loves nature. The more we look at computer screens and deal with electronic devices, the more we want to get back to nature and our natural lives. Nature hikes, camping, religious movements, family values, social concerns, interest in the supernatural, and basic escapism are just a few examples of the patterns which are coloring the information age.

Another myth of the information age is that computers and the "information highway" will eventually keep everyone at home in "electronic cottages." This will not happen, for humans are social animals; we crave company and deplore isolation and loneliness. People will still want to go to work and interact with the energies of others. Socializing is a basic part of the human experience. This is also why home videos have never replaced movie theaters. We want to get out and enjoy experiences with other people. Seeing plays, live music, festivals, and other entertainments is as popular as it always was. This basic need to get in touch with our humanity will grow proportionately as we become more advanced.

In conclusion, world systems are changing to reflect an information-based economy. This has serious consequences for how we train students for the future. Employers need workers familiar with high technologies and technological principles. Because of the communication-based systems, basic academic skills like reading and writing are more important than ever.

Technology in the Classroom *(cont.)*

B. Why Teachers Resist Technology

The main reason teachers resist learning and teaching new technologies like computers is because they feel threatened by their awesome power. Many teachers feel that computers will replace their jobs.

Most people are fearful of change. If everything seems to be going fine, it is only natural to feel uncomfortable about changing. The adage "If it ain't broke, don't fix it," reflects a common attitude. By ignoring technology, however, teachers are turning their backs on society, producing a work force incapable of meeting the demands and challenges of a new era. If our job is to give students the tools for the future, we have to expose them to as many technologies as possible.

On another level, resisting basic tools like computers is being hypocritical. If we require that students adapt and change to our instructions on a daily basis in order to learn, then we as teachers need to learn and change as well. In other words, we should practice what we preach.

The fact is that anyone can master the latest technology, and you do not necessarily need a book or training course. Just get your hands on the equipment and experiment. This chapter will help orient you to all the different technologies influencing education today. Most of these innovations are already in your school, and it is wise to take advantage of all your resources.

II. Audio-Video Technology

A. Traditional Technologies

Giving students opportunities to experience sights and sounds is part of every exciting curriculum. Some students learn better by seeing and hearing than by reading. The traditional technologies which you are already probably familiar with are overheads, audio tapes, film/video, and slides. Integrating these into your lessons can be worthwhile. They can break up monotonous readings and lectures. For more ideas on audio/video, see Chapter 3, section 3.

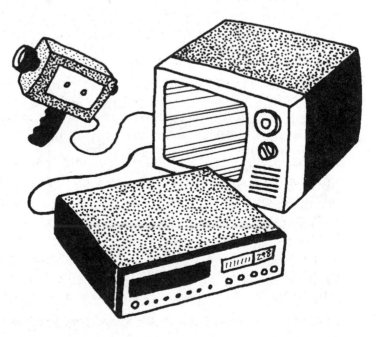

Technology in the Classroom *(cont.)*

B. Laser Disc Players

Probably less familiar to you is the laser disc player. Relatively new to the classroom, it is an exciting new technology which is only in its infancy. A laser disc player at first seems just like a VCR and TV. Indeed, it serves the same function: video and audio display. However, what laser disc technology can do goes far beyond traditional VCR systems. The difference is that between the automobile and the horse and buggy.

The main contrast of a laser disc player compared to that of a regular video system is basically how it works. The laser disc operates by storing vast amounts of information which is read by a laser eye. Through the wizardry of those who brought you the wonders of microcircuitry and microchips, this information can be instantly accessed. Have you ever played a CD? Then you know that you can skip around to different songs at your whim. The same is true for the laser disc which operates on the same principles as the CD player.

A programmed laser disc stores vast amounts of information in the form of pictures, photos, film footage, sounds, and written information. A list of all these items forms a master menu for the disc. The best thing about laser discs is that you can sequence the exact images or sounds that will correspond to your learning activity. If you ever have programmed a set of songs on a CD player, then you know you simply select the item number and push "program."

Laser discs have the added benefit of crystal clear images produced by the pinpoint precision of lasers, vastly superior to video analog signals. Furthermore, you can shuttle backward or forward on a laser disc with incredible clarity; one frame at a time or a variety of speeds is at your fingertips.

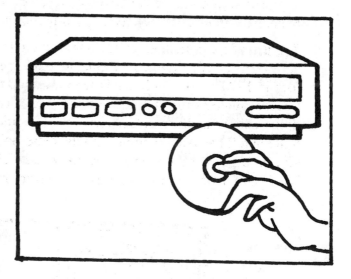

The possibilities of laser disc use in the classroom at present seem endless. At this time, teachers mainly use laser discs like slide projectors or videos. The laser discs that are made for teaching, however, are growing in quantity and quality. Reviewing your library's stock of discs can mean many future "laser lessons." Also, if you are really motivated, then you can apply for some grants for specific discs that could help your school. Being laser friendly means not only having a fascinating hobby, but it also means providing students with excellent learning opportunities.

Technology in the Classroom *(cont.)*

III. Computers

Let's now embark on a journey through the wonderful world of computers. Once teachers get to know the "lay of the land" and feel comfortable with computers, then the computer can become the teacher's best friend and helper.

A. Background

Computers have been in use in this country since the early part of this century. The word "computer" comes from the same word as "compute" (Latin: com = together, thoroughly + putare = consider, calculate). The first company to make large-scale computer equipment started small but thought big. The International Business Machines (IBM) company was a wildly successful venture. World War II greatly accelerated the need for improvements in communication, calculations, and high technologies. However, it was the Cold War which financed large amounts of computer research and manufacturing. The realization that the United States was falling behind in math and science was a cause of great concern for intellectuals as well as politicians. With the launch of *Sputnik* in 1957, it was widely thought that the U.S.S.R. would gain the upper hand in world power through their technological knowledge. In 1965, the United States government apportioned billions of dollars to the application of computer technology in the classrooms by passing the landmark Elementary & Secondary Education Act (ESEA), which focused on math and science instruction.

The use of the computer in the classroom gained serious momentum after ESEA. However, computers at this time were too large and expensive for efficient use in schools. The brilliant idea in 1975 of two individuals who invented the integrated circuit led to the first microcomputer or personal computer (PC). Their company is now the world-famous billion dollar enterprise of Intel Corporation. The microcomputer is what you are probably familiar with, and it has been coming into the classroom by the millions. Almost one hundred percent of all schools now have at least one computer. The two modes that people are familiar with are the IBM and the Macintosh systems. However, these are becoming more alike all the time.

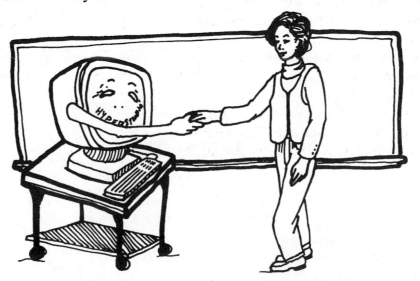

Technology in the Classroom *(cont.)*

B. Geography

The typical computer system used in schools is contains the following components:

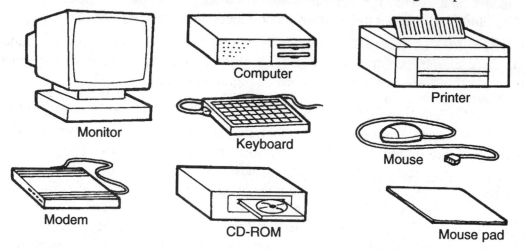

Monitor Computer Printer Keyboard Mouse Modem CD-ROM Mouse pad

1. **Monitor:** The monitor is like a TV screen. You can adjust the imaging of your monitor by turning the adjustment knobs. All monitors have an on/off switch.

2. **Keyboard:** The keyboard is nothing new if you have ever used a typewriter. However, you do have different function keys not on typewriters. Also, keyboards are usually provided with a "punch pad" for typing numbers efficiently.

3. **Computer:** The actual computer itself is the central command of the whole system. It is equipped with microchips that store billions of bits of information. The computer will be the "electronic shed" into which all the other components will connect. It contains an on/off switch.

4. **Mouse:** The mouse is simply a quick and easy tool for getting around the screen and activating functions. If you click the mouse by pressing down on its top part, it activates a function the cursor is indicating on the screen.

    If you click onto a menu heading at the top of the screen, the menu unfolds. If you are an IBM veteran, the menus correspond to the function keys.

    The other technique of using a mouse is to click and drag. This will highlight areas of text or implement menu commands. The mouse is something that only experience can teach, but its simplicity is its genius.

5. **Mouse Pad:** This pad aids the mouse in movement and protects the mouse from dirt and debris.

6. **Printer:** The printer makes your hard copies. A laser printer is the best quality. Next, letter quality printers are almost as good. Lastly, the old dot matrix printers might still be lurking around.

7. **CD-ROM Player:** This box plays CD-ROMs. In order to load a CD, you must have a carrier to put the CD in. Then you load the carrier with the CD into the CD-ROM player.

8. **Modem:** This device transduces electronic phone signals into computer talk. In other words, it creates on-line services.

Technology in the Classroom *(cont.)*

C. Modes of Integration

There are basically two ways you can use the computer in the classroom: as a tutor or as a tool.

Tutor: In the tutorial mode, the computer acts as a teacher and guide.

As more software becomes available, tutoring uses for the computer expand. Today, most educators think of the computer mainly as a tutorial instrument, the most important effect of which is a one-on-one relationship. Most programs tutor in this fashion:

- introducing information: give a reading, list vocabulary of content, chart formulae
- providing practice: ask questions, list options, go over right and wrong answers
- assimilating information: compile previous entries, show relationships
- testing comprehension: give formal evaluations
- showing mastery: chart progress
- creating product: print out results of work

The tutorial success of computers has more to do with the quality of the software than anything else. With new mega-memory systems like CD-ROM's, first-class tutorials are just around the corner. The main advantage of tutorial software is that it provides a context for one-on-one learning consistent with the mastery learning concept.

Educational Games: Types of tutorials with huge impact on students are educational games. While they play these games, students are learning about content. Even more exciting, though, they are using problem-solving skills. Software like *The Oregon Trail* (history), and *Where in the World Is Carmen San Diego?* (geography) are superb learning tools. Try out as many programs as you can to determine usability.

Tool: The computer in the classroom can also be used as a tool. Like a hammer, it helps build a structure or complete a project. This mode provides much flexibility for the teacher and student. In fact, tool-oriented software lets the imagination run wild.

Examples of tool software are these:

- Word Processing: typing up papers and other written products
- Spreadsheets: organizing and computing data
- Data Bases: organizing, sorting, and retrieving data
- Graphics: creating visuals
- Desktop Publishing: synthesizing text and graphics; good for newsletters, brochures, flyers, invitations, newspapers, magazines, etc.
- Hypercard/Hypertext: lets the student build a program

Technology in the Classroom *(cont.)*

D. Word Processing

Computers have virtually eliminated typewriters. The ease and flexibility of writing and printing with a computer can only be topped by the fact that it all can be stored in memory.

Rewriting draft after draft or having to type over a whole page because of a missed comma is a thing of the past. Now, deleting, adding, modifying, rearranging, and reformatting are all as simple as a touch of a button. Some basics of word processing are finding the program itself, typing the documents, formatting, editing, and saving.

1. Finding the Word Processing (WP) Program

After you have turned on your computer, find the word processing icon or label. If you are using Macintosh, some common WP software titles are MacWrite, MS Word, and Claris Works. If you are using an IBM, you will probably use WordPerfect. If you click twice on these programs, you should be in a WP document.

Another way to do this is to open an already existing WP document. Once you have opened one, click on the file menu and drag to "new." Let go and the computer will give you a clean new document ready for you to type on.

2. Typing

Wherever the cursor is blinking is where your words will appear. Just as with a typewriter, you can type words, return, space over, tab, and set margins. In contrast to a typewriter, however, you can change your text in terms of style or placement at any given time. When you are typing, the computer will automatically return for you. By clicking and dragging with your mouse, you can highlight certain areas. When areas are highlighted, it means they are ready to be changed. Common changes you will probably want to make are in font, size, and style.

Fonts: These are on a menu that is located at the top of your screen. Fonts are the style of character. Examples of different types of fonts are the following:

Chicago	**Helvetica**	9 point
		12 point
Courier	**Times**	18 point

There are actually hundreds of fonts you can load into your computer. Find the font which is appropriate for your communication. After highlighting the areas you wish to change, simply click on the font menu, drag down to your font choice, let go, and the highlighted area immediately changes. Click anywhere on the screen to remove the highlight.

24 point

48 point

Size: The size of your characters might be important. Sizes are measured in points. Regular size is 12 point. But you might want to go higher for headings or lower for special purposes.

Technology in the Classroom *(cont.)*

D. Word Processing *(cont.)*

Size can also be programmed to meet your individual needs. You can program a size that is so big that one letter takes up a whole page or so small that it can barely be discerned.

Style: You probably have noticed the different styles of lettering used to add organization to this book. Remember the old days when if you wanted to boldface a word, you typed it in twice? With WP, just highlight and choose the appropriate style. Following are type styles:

By carefully selecting font, size, and style, one is able to control the organization, clarity, and visual appeal of WP documents.

3. Formatting

Formatting refers to the arrangement of your paper. Mainly, its application is in *setting margins, aligning print, spacing lines,* and *providing columns.*

Setting Margins: To set margins, go to the format menu. You should see "document." If you open "document," your margin measurements will be in boxes labeled "margins." Click in those boxes to change as necessary.

If you want to reset your margins, you can do this at any time, and your entire paper will automatically reset itself.

If you need to set a part of the paper with different margins, you can use the triangle icons that appear on the ruler at the top of your screen. Highlight the area which you want to change. Click on the left triangle and drag it where your new left margin will be. Let go and watch the highlighted area immediately fall in line. Do the same with the right margin if desired.

Alignment Controls: Alignment refers to the orientation of your lines of print. There are basically four types of aligning your print: right, centered, left (traditional), and justified, or even. Do you see the ruler at the top of the screen? On the bottom of the ruler there should be a number of boxes. You are interested in the four boxes which contain three lines, all differently configured. If you look carefully, you will see that the lines represent the four types of alignments. You can set your text to conform to these styles by clicking on them before you type or by highlighting the area of text you want to justify and then clicking the appropriate box. If you are on an IBM, you might have to push the appropriate function keys.

Technology in the Classroom *(cont.)*

Alignment Controls: (cont.)

 This indicates the traditional type of alignment: all print is aligned to the left of the paper, and the right side is uneven.

 This indicates the center mode: all print is centered in the middle of the page.

 This indicates the right mode: all print is aligned to the right side, and the left is uneven.

This is the even mode: used when you want both sides to be completely even. In newspapers, magazines, and books, this technique gives a sense of balance.

Spacing Lines: Again, this is on your ruler or function keys. By clicking on the appropriate box, you can go from single spacing to double spacing and beyond.

Providing Columns: Usually, you will want to write in a one-column format. However, if you wish to use two or three columns, this can be done with a click of the mouse. You might find the column changer on your ruler. Click the box which has two columns represented and watch your entire paper line up into two columns. If you click it again, your paper will be formatted into three columns. To go down to one column, click the box with a single column represented.

The column function is also on the format menu. Drag to the column function and a window with column calculations will let you set widths and other measurements.

4. **Editing:** The most common editing functions are deleting, adding, cut-and-pasting, and checking your text for errors.

    Deleting: To delete portions of the text, you have options. After highlighting the part you want to delete, simply push the "delete" button on your keyboard. Also, you can click to the beginning of the lines you want to erase and then keep pushing "delete" until satisfied.

    Adding: To insert text, click the cursor to the appropriate place on the page or anywhere in the entire document and type away.

    Cut and Paste: You can use this function to rearrange text or to copy a portion of text and use it repeatedly. First, click on your edit menu. You will see "cut," "copy," and "paste." If you want to cut a sentence or paragraph, highlight the whole thing and then click on the edit menu and drag to the "cut" function. The highlighted portion will disappear but do not worry; it is waiting for you to paste it somewhere. Click your cursor where you want to paste it. Go back to the **edit** menu and drag down to "paste." Let go and you will see your cut portion appear.

    If you want to copy a portion of the text, follow the same procedure as cutting except go to "copy" instead. In this case, your highlighted portion will not disappear because a copy of it was created and is ready for you to paste it somewhere.

Technology in the Classroom *(cont.)*

Checking Your Text for Errors: On your edit menu, you may see functions that are labeled "spelling" and "grammar." You can check those areas appropriately. These functions do not correct the text for you. You have to decide the best choice among options. The grammar-checks provide grammar lessons according to the type of error. These functions often come bundled in the word processing software.

Saving: Once you have typed, formatted, and edited your document, you need to save it. This is done by clicking on the file menu and dragging to "save." Give your document a name by typing the title in the box which is labeled "untitled." Click "save" and your document name will appear on the top of your screen. Your computer will save it on your disc or on the hard drive. To make a copy of your documents, you can use the "save as" function. Follow the same procedure as save, except provide a new name. When you click "save," a copy of your original document will be saved under its new name. If you try to quit a program without saving, a box appears, asking you if you want to save the document or not.

Caution: *If you click "no" to saving, your document will be erased.*

What if you have an important disc that you want to copy onto a backup? Or what if you need to make multiple copies of discs for legitimate purposes? It is very simple. Load your original disc into your computer. Do you see its icon? Now click and drag the icon and superimpose it on your hard-drive icon. Release and the entire disc will be copied onto the hard drive. It will appear on your hard drive as a folder with the disc title. At this point, you can load another disc and copy the original off the hard drive onto the new, empty disc.

Printing: To print your document, click on the file menu and drag to "print." Let go and you should see a window which provides all kinds of printing functions. To print your entire paper, just click on "print" and wait for the printer to print.

If you need to print just a selected number of pages, the options to do this are in the same window. Click on the box after the word "from" and type what page you want to start with. Then click on the next box after the word "to" and type what page you want to end with. Next, click on "print" and you will print only those pages.

Quitting: When you finish or need to leave your document, make sure you save and then quit. The quit function is on the bottom on the file menu. When you quit, you should see the main hard-drive window where you started. If you are using a disc, you should see the icon of your disc. Click on your disc and drag it to the trash can. Let go and your disc will come out. Don't worry, you are not erasing your disk—just setting it free. Your **special** menu might also have an "eject disc" function that you can use.

To ensure a clean retirement, click on the special menu and drag down to "shut down." Then turn both your computer and monitor off.

Technology in the Classroom *(cont.)*

E. Spreadsheets

Spreadsheets are simply tables and charts of information that can be manipulated many ways. They look like this:

	A	B	C	D	E	F
1						
2						

Spreadsheets are made up of columns and rows. Columns go top to bottom. Rows go left to right. Where a row meets a column is a "cell."

When information needs to be charted and then calculated, the spreadsheet is your tool. For example, Mr. Hamad's science class is charting weather patterns every day by using newspapers and direct observations and measurements. They are recording this information on spreadsheet software. Their first column lists cities: Topeka, Chicago, Baltimore, New Haven, Phoenix, San Antonio, Tallahassee, and San Francisco. The next four columns are days of the week. The cells will store the rainfall amount for each day. After four days, the records looked like this:

Topeka	1.3	.5	.2	0
Chicago	1.5	1.7	1.8	2.3
Baltimore	.5	.4	.5	.2
New Haven	1.2	1.3	1.4	1.4
Phoenix	0	0	0	0
San Antonio	1.7	.3	0	0
Tallahassee	0	.2	.2	0
San Francisco	1.3	1.6	2.6	.5

By entering formulae into the cells, averages of rainfall counts can be calculated. The cities can be sorted, and multiple combinations can be calculated.

A more advanced spreadsheet that is programmed by professionals is the computer gradebook. These programs let teachers enter student names and assignment grades. The computer instantly calculates the students' grades according to the weight you assign to each assignment. This eliminates the calculating for the teacher. For instance, say you have 120 students. Your grading scale was daily work = 50%, homework = 10%, projects = 40%. For each new task you enter, you give its weight or scale. When you enter the student's grade, a new calculation appears, reflecting your specifications. Another nice feature of the gradebook programs is the sorting and printing. You can print a copy of grades for the whole class or just for an individual.

Technology in the Classroom *(cont.)*

F. Data Bases

Data bases are information storing devices—"electronic file cabinets." They store records for later retrieval. Students can develop organizational skills by creating their own data bases. The business applications of data bases are obvious. Banks, agencies, offices, restaurants, and businesses of all kinds have customer data bases to serve their clientele better. For educational resources, you cannot beat the data bases which are collected at our nation's universities and libraries. These colossal information storage and retrieval systems can be accessed at the touch of a computer keyboard now, thanks to on-line systems.

G. Graphics

Graphics software is getting very advanced. Three-D imaging is enjoying a prominence among science, business, and the entertainment industries. On a smaller scale, graphics programs are entering the school through Macintosh bundles like Claris Works or MacDraw. Graphics software comes in two main varieties: drawing and painting.

Drawing: In the drawing mode, you can create designs, pictures, graphs, signs, flyers, brochures, and other products. Everything will work the same as in word processing except for a few things.

The Toolbox: A toolbox is a window which displays command functions for drawing on your document. It usually appears on the left side of your screen. You can hide the toolbox by clicking the **view** menu and dragging to "hide tools," or you can click on the show/hide toolbox control at the bottom left of the screen. The toolbox usually has the following tools:

> **Pointer** (arrow): Selects objects and frames. The pointer can "block" an object by putting small square blocks at the four corners of the object. When an object is blocked, it can be manipulated by moving it anywhere on the screen, filling it with a color, pattern, or gradient, or deleting it entirely.

> **Text Tool** (the letter A): To create a text frame (words and sentences), select the text tool, click and drag for amount of text space and release. Start typing as necessary. Within your text frame, all the rules from word processing apply. After you are finished typing and stylizing your text, click anywhere on the screen. You will notice that your text frame is blocked. While it is blocked, you can move it around the page by clicking and dragging.

> **Line Tool** (a diagonal line): To draw a line, select the line tool. Click where you want the line to start and drag for the length and direction of the line. Press shift as you drag the crosshair to draw horizontally, vertically, or at a 45-degree angle.

> **Rectangle Tool** (a box): To draw a rectangle, select the rectangle tool and drag the crosshair. Press shift as you drag the crosshair to draw a perfect square.

> **Oval Tool** (an oval): To draw an oval, select the oval tool and drag the crosshair. Press shift as you drag to draw a perfect oval.

Technology in the Classroom *(cont.)*

Arc Tool (an arc): To draw an arc, select the arc tool and drag the crosshair diagonally.

Polygon Tool (irregular polygon): To draw an irregular polygon, select the polygon tool, click to set the starting point, drag the crosshair, and click at each angle of the polygon. Double-click to end the polygon.

Freehand Tool: To draw a curving or irregular line, select the freehand tool and drag the crosshair.

Fill Indicator (paint bucket): Shows the current fill attributes. To change the fill color, pattern, or gradient, select the appropriate command functions that are usually below the fill indicator.

Fill Color (rainbow/multi-colors): Displays a palette of colors you can use to fill objects. To set the fill color, click here and select a color. If an object is blocked, and you change the color, the object will be filled with that color. You can only get a color print if you have a color printer cartridge.

Fill Pattern (thatched design): Displays a palette of designs you can use to fill objects.

Fill Gradient (color fade): Displays a palette of air brush quality gradients you can use to fill objects.

Pen Indicator (a pen drawing a line): Shows the current pen attributes. To change the pen color, pattern, or width, or add arrowheads to lines, select options from the commands that are usually below the pen indicator. These commands are like the fill commands: pen color, pen pattern, pen width, and arrows.

Zoom Control Commands: Most drawing programs allow you to zoom in on your document or zoom out. Claris Works has small zoom controls at the bottom left of the screen. Other programs might have zoom controls under a **view** menu. Clicking these will let you look and work on your document at different zoom lengths. This is important when you design documents like flyers, where you want to see the entire document as you design it. It will also be necessary to look at a small portion of the document to provide extreme accuracy.

Arrange Menu: Use the functions under the **arrange** menu to move objects or text frames into vertical, flipped, or other irregular formats.

From a look at all tools, you can see how adaptable the drawing software is.

At the very least, you spice up a document with interesting visuals. Combining all the tools is an art in itself. On the next page is an example of a document made by a drawing program.

Technology in the Classroom *(cont.)*

Drawing Tools

Technology in the Classroom *(cont.)*

Painting Programs

Paint programs are software which takes the drawing concept one step further. The same type of format is used: a toolbox and zoom controls. The main difference is that there are more tools you can use. Apart from all the other drawing tools, there are also these:

New Tools

Paint Brush: To paint brush strokes in the current fill color and pattern, select the paint brush and drag to paint. Under the options menu, you can change the size and texture of the brush.

Pencil: To paint fine lines in the current pen color, select the pencil and drag to paint lines. Hold the shift button down to paint perpendicular lines.

Paint Bucket: To fill an area with the current fill color, select the paint bucket and click the area you want to fill.

Eraser: To erase unwanted parts of a painting, select the eraser and drag over the unwanted areas. Double click on the eraser to erase the entire painting.

Spray Can: To spray fine dots in the current fill color, select the spray can and drag over areas of spray flow.

Options Menu

A new menu will appear for the painting mode. The options menu lets you have further control of the tools. Brush shapes, spray-paint sizes, and other manipulating devices can control your painting even further.

The following will show you how the different tools look on a painting document. Remember, there are a million combinations to consider. Colors work beautifully on a painting document. Do not be afraid to experiment.

Both drawing and painting programs can enhance students' computer literacy and creativity. After they master these formats, the next step is three-D imaging. These are important skills for students to learn, since experts in the field of computer graphics production get paid well for their knowledge. In addition, advertising agencies and almost all businesses have graphics experts on their staffs, for promotional design material.

Technology in the Classroom *(cont.)*

H. Desktop Publishing

Desktop publishing is simply a synthesis of graphics and word processing for a specific communication purpose. Although professional publishing houses have specialty software that is industry standard, like Quark Press, many desktop publishing software programs and applications are filtering down to the microcomputer.

With this type of software, it is possible for the student to experience the entire writing process—conceiving, writing, typing, editing, making graphics, designing, formatting, and printing. For an example of a cooperative learning project using desktop publishing software, see Magazine Makers, pages 63–66.

Desktop publishing will be addressed in detail later in the chapter, section VI, page 123.

I. Hypercard/Hypertext Programs

The Hypercard programs can be found on both Macintosh and IBM (Hypertext). In this software, you or a student can build a program consisting of cards, stacks, and graphics. The program can become interactive, giving choices and showing options.

In an exciting development, the Hypercard producers have come up with HyperStudio, a program which can add video footage, photos, music, sound effects, and other media to your stacks. It is recommended that you take a workshop on the intricacies of Hypercard programs.

J. CD-ROM

A CD-ROM is not software. "Compact Disc-Read Only Memory" refers to the actual marvel of the compact computer disc. The device that plays the CD-ROM is loosely titled the CD-ROM player. It is called hardware because it is a vehicle to play the software, or discs, in this case.

A CD-ROM has only one basic difference with a regular computer disc—more memory! For this reason, it can display animation, video footage, complex sound effects, three-D imaging, and other features which need mega-memory to operate.

How to Load a CD-ROM

When you buy a CD-ROM, you will need a carrier case to load it into the CD-ROM player. Plastic carrier cases hold the CD-ROM in place for the player to read it properly.

1. Open the carrier case by pressing in on the indicated corner latches. The clear plastic window should open.
2. Place the CD-ROM in the case and close the window.
3. Load the case into the player. It should catch the case and draw it in.
4. On your computer screen, you should see the CD-ROM icon of what you just loaded. Double click on this icon and the program will begin.

Technology in the Classroom *(cont.)*

Applications for CD-ROM

CD-ROMs are proliferating by the minute, and many are ideal for the classroom.

Multimedia Encyclopedia: A great tool for classroom use is the CD-ROM encyclopedia. There is so much memory on a CD-ROM that the entire 20-volume set of *Grolier's Electronic Encyclopedia*, with nine million words and an extensive index does not even fill up one disc. In addition, these programs allow one to print out any portion of the text desired. Along with the text, the multimedia CD-ROM encyclopedia can store 15 hours of audio and 15,000 color images.

Learning Subjects: Other educational discs can be lumped into this category. Profiles on animals, historical periods, scientific phenomena, educational locations/landmarks are just a few of the subjects on CD-ROM's. These learning tools use incredible graphics, video footage, musical scores, actual photos, and animation to become state-of-the-art computer software.

The variety of CD-ROM's is increasing geometrically, and many computers already have CD-ROM drives built in.

K. Computers at Home

If students already have computers at home, it is strongly recommended that you build on this natural resource. Encourage students to use their computers for school work whenever they can. It makes it a lot easier for teachers to read student work, and it increases their computer competencies.

A question of grading fairness arises regarding the home use of computers. Should a teacher give more points for work that is typed? Teachers sometimes look on work that is typed as being superior. However, it is recommended that the teacher not give any extra points for typed assignments. After all, most students do not have the luxury of computers at home, and it is not fair to them that someone else should get a better grade just because he or she has a computer at home.

IV. The Computer Lab

Many schools are finding that a centralized location works best for computer classes. A recent trend has been in content-specific computer lab rooms, like the "Writing Lab," the "Science Lab," or the "Math Lab." The software is geared around those individual disciplines. For instance, the "Writing Lab" contains word processing, desktop publishing, and Hypercard. The "Math Lab" loads software like spreadsheets and math games. The "Science Lab" acquires excellent CD-ROM's on nature and animals, has spreadsheets, word processing, and science tutorials.

These labs are usually the product of someone's good sense. The two main things you want to know about computer labs are networks and computer lab rules.

Technology in the Classroom *(cont.)*

A. Networks

Several computers connected together qualify as a network. There are three basic parts to a network—the computers, an interface board, and the cables which connect everything. An advantage of networking is to save text that a normal microcomputer cannot. The network acts as a "file server," a master hard drive. These large storage capacities allow advanced programming.

Passwords: Most computer labs have a system to stop anybody using the computer without permission. Also, the system limits the user to a select personal file. Once you have entered your correct password, the "master hard drive" will reveal your personal file with saved documents on it. Also, you might see a menu with software icons appearing on the screen. This can be referred to as the "at ease" screen.

At Ease Screen: Sometimes, networks are programmed with preset software, the only options you can use in that system. For instance, you might see an icon for a CD-ROM encyclopedia. It will always be there, whether the CD-ROM is loaded or not. If you try to load another CD-ROM that is not part of the at ease menu, you will find it will not accept it. Basically, the at ease menu is the master menu which connects directly with the file server.

Saving Documents: When you save documents, they will appear in your file. Do not worry about filling your file with icons. There is probably enough storage in your file server to save everything you do on the computer for the rest of your life.

B. Computer Lab Rules

You must give students direct rules to follow. Generally, young people like going to the lab and are responsible in their actions. However, rowdy behavior can damage equipment. CD-ROMs are attractive. They should be locked up when not in use. Check your students' stations before they leave. Also, assign student helpers as lab techs to help others with computer problems and keep an eye on the equipment.

A suggested list of rules for students follows:

Computer Lab Rules

1. Come in and sit down at the station where you are assigned.
2. Do not turn on your computers until the signal.
3. Turn on your computers and go through the access sequence.
4. Start work on your project; raise your hand if you need help.
5. The computer assistants who can assist you are . . . .
6. When finished, make sure you save and quit properly. Work will be checked before you quit.
7. At the signal, get up and stand in line at the door and get ready to go back to class.

Technology in the Classroom *(cont.)*

V. On-line Systems

An exciting application for computers in school is to connect to world-wide information systems through the telephone. This is called "going on-line." A world of information is transmitted daily through electronic signals by business, governments, schools, and individuals. Getting on-line can access you to a million resources, and all you need is a modem.

A. How Modems Operate

Modem stands for modulator-demodulator. To "modulate" means to turn the computer signals into analog signals which can race across the country at incredible speed. To demodulate is turning those analog signals back into computer signals. To make an on-line system work, all you need is two computers, two modems, and a transmission line.

computer   modem   transmission line   modem   computer

The direct connect modem currently in use is a small box and a wire which plugs directly into a standard phone jack on the wall. The other side of the wire attaches to a port in the computer. Once you have hooked up your modem, you need to know whether your computer has the terminal software built in to facilitate on-line activity. If not, you have to install this terminal software.

To get the on-line services, you will need to pay hook-up fees and receive an account number with a password. Making these arrangements by telephone is the standard procedure. The two biggest on-line agencies in this country are CompuServe and America Online. They will make arrangements to send you the software. Billing for these services is usually a small monthly fee and charge-by-the-hour fees. Most on-line systems are under 20 dollars a month for home use.

Some schools are already hooked up with on-line services.

B. Applications

The numbers of services available on-line are growing daily. Buying flowers, booking a plane ticket, and downloading information for a student report are some current possibilities. E-mail has already caused mention of the modem eliminating the need for parts of the postal system. Paying bills through modems is another popular idea.

On-line systems can provide basically three services for the classroom: reference services, program swapping, and communication exchange. The titanic data bases that store and retrieve this information are changing names and faces rapidly as business mergers take place and investment in these technologies expands.

Technology in the Classroom *(cont.)*

Here is a list of some of the common on-line systems available on a national basis:

Internet: You have probably heard of the Internet network. On this system students can access almost anything under the sun. Access to newspapers all over the country, special services, small interest groups/topics, encyclopedia, and even a student/educational forum are options for referencing different topics. Research can be very efficient on the Internet. In effect, a giant electronic bulletin board is now accessible for various data requirements or interests.

National Geographic Kid's Network: A wonderful contribution to electronic academics is the creation of the Kid's Network. This system distributes software and curriculum materials via computers. It also provides ongoing ecological studies and other scientific activities. Schools, classes, and students are encouraged to participate in these nationwide projects.

World Wide Web: The WWW is just that; it has connected networks around the globe and given access to users. International libraries, news reports, special information, and communication services are the tip of the iceberg.

Dialogue: The Dialogue service has been used by libraries for over ten years. This network collects reports, statistics, and doctoral dissertations from 140 different corporations, universities, and government agencies. In-depth information can be accessed and printed for research purposes.

Other useful on-line systems are Genie, Dow Jones News and Quotes Reporter, and the McGraw-Hill Information Exchange. An interesting metaphor for using these systems is "surfing the net." This poetic comparison is appropriate, for when you see the ocean of information available in the world, it is challenging to stay afloat.

VI. Desktop Publishing

A. Background

True publishing started in the 1500s. This development quickened the dissemination of information throughout society. It is not an exaggeration to say that the printing press revolutionized the world. An interesting parallel to the printing press is the microcomputer: both have created new standards of information processing. The intricacies of a printing press once restricted the printing process to a handful of technicians. As printing procedures advanced, it became simpler for operators. Today, the secrets of the printer are no longer available just to the apprentice. They can be learned easily with the application of word processing and graphics software.

To continue through the next sections, you must be familiar with the word processing and graphics vocabulary that were mentioned earlier in this chapter.

Technology in the Classroom *(cont.)*

B. Design/Formatting

Of the basic graphics tools, there are three main areas which you need to know: text boxes, picture boxes, and design graphics.

Text Boxes: In text boxes, all the rules of word processing apply. To create a text box, select the text icon (the letter A) from the toolbox. Click and drag to set box dimensions. When you see the cursor blinking in the box, you can type normally.

To create a heading for the text (a headline), enlarge the font accordingly. After you start typing, you will notice that the text box enlarges downward to fit more text in. However, the left and right sides of the text box always remain in place.

You might want to add to the headline with a by-line naming the author. You might also want to provide columns of print, especially for magazines and journals. Select the "increase columns" control to create more than one column of print.

Picture Boxes: To place picture boxes on a page, select the rectangle tool. Click and drag for the shape of your box. In your picture box, you can fill computer art or clip art immediately, or you may leave it blank to fill with computer art or photos later.

1. Find where your clip art page is in your software. When you see the clip art, scroll through it and select an object you want to transpose onto your newsletter. Block it with the pointer.

2. Using your cut-and-paste skills, either copy or cut the object by selecting the edit menu and clicking on the appropriate command. Now the object is in the invisible holding area.

3. Go back in your document to the area where you want to paste the clip art. You must make a picture box, thus creating a field to place the clip art in.

Computer art can be created by using the tools in the graphics tool box. Zoom in for a detailed look at your artwork. Hand-drawn art can be done after the prints are finished. Photographs can be used to fill the picture boxes as well.

Photographs rarely reproduce well on a copier. A device which translates any picture or photo with superb accuracy onto the computer screen is called a "scanner." These tools are a designer's joy. When the image is saved on the computer, it can be manipulated by filling a picture box. High-tech computer graphics programs can also transform a picture in many ways. This process, known as "morphing," is used in films to create the illusion of people turning into bizarre shapes and substances.

Design Tools

Visually appealing publications often use borders, frames, and other designs around a page. This can be done with the tools in the graphics toolbox, like straight lines, box frames, etc. Such design features create a professional look, pleasing to the viewer.

Technology in the Classroom *(cont.)*

C. How to Make a Professional Newsletter

When you gain practice in designing and formatting, then you can make a great newsletter! The configuration of all your design techniques is called the *layout*. If you are really professional, you will draw out a "dummy" sheet, depicting your layout scheme. In the old days, the newsletter was made by drawing a dummy, typing articles on a typewriter, cutting those articles to conform with measurements, and pasting the articles and other visuals onto the master copy. In the information age, the computer can do most of that for you.

1. On your computer, create the text and picture boxes on a given page and type in articles as needed. Using the computer, fill in boxes with print or pictures. Put the name of the publication in big letters (36–48 point) at the top of the page. Have the most important or gripping articles on this page. If you can manage a photo on the front page, it would help.

2. Put in your design graphics to enhance visual appeal. Take a look at some popular magazines to see how the professionals lay out their graphics. Providing long straight lines as borders is basic. Framing a text box is simple. Select the rectangle tool and click and drag around the print. If your print is covered up, go to the fill pattern command and select the transparent icon; it should look like two intertwining boxes. Your box now will be transparent, so it does not cover up any print. An option is to provide a line down the middle of the columns of print.

3. When you are satisfied with the layout, have written all your articles, and have finished using all your graphic design features, print out final copies.

4. Next, get all pictures, photos, or illustrations together. Cut them to match their picture boxes. You will need a ruler, scissors, pencil, and glue. Cut and glue your photos or other pictures to the hard copies. These will be your master copies. Put them in a file or other protected place.

5. Make copies of the newsletter on the copier and distribute. If you give them to the kids directly, have an incentive or assignment which makes sure it gets into the hands of their parents. A parent signature is good evidence. If giving copies to other faculty, assign student helpers to distribute during appropriate times (not during regular class hours). Give one to the principal and/or to district personnel (they appreciate getting exciting information about what is happening in classrooms).

The following is a simple two-page newsletter, "Dream Express," produced for a sixth grade team during their first week of school.

Dream Express

If you can dream it, then you can do it!   *August, 1996—Issue 1*

WELCOME TO THE 6TH GRADE!

You've really made it! You are out of elementary school and into the complex world of middle school. But you are not alone! You are now on a team with other students and teachers who will provide support for you all year long.

We teachers of the Dream Team want you to be as successful as possible in this new world. So buckle up, here we go!

THE DREAM TEAM

What is the Dream Team? That is the team of students and teachers you will be working with all year. You are a valuable member on this team, and you will get to know your classmates and teachers very well.

Who are the teachers on the Dream Team? The teachers you will see all year long are the following:

Ms. Jackson — *Colt Connection*

Ms. Groves — *Language Arts*

Ms. Schulte — *Math*

Mr. Padillo — *Science*

Ms. Williams — *Language Arts*

Mr. Hagerty — *Social Studies*

ASSIGNMENT BOOKS!

The Covington Assignment Books are here! All students are required to have one, so if you have not picked one up yet, ask a teacher where to get them. They cost $3.00 and are filled with important information you will need all year. Each teacher will go over the information in the assignment books thoroughly.

COLT CONNECTION

Because we are so concerned about the success of our 6th graders, we have a special class just for you! In your Colt Connection class, you will learn different strategies to succeed in school, how to cope with problems, and other great stuff! We think learning should be fun, and we try to make it that way.

BLOCK SCHEDULING

Block scheduling is important to understand. Basically, you will get twice the normal time in every class period. This means that you will spend one and one-half hours in each class. Fortunately, you will not be in school twice as long. Instead, you will have "A" days and "B" days. On "A" days you will go to one set of classes, and on "B" days you will go to another set of classes. Confused? Look at this example:

"A" Day	"B" Day
1. Math	1. Science
2. English	2. Reading
Lunch!	Lunch!
3. Elective	3. Colt Connection
4. PE	4. Social Studies

So, you still take all the same classes, but they will meet on different days. We use block scheduling because we know that spending more time with the student makes a better learner. If you are still confused, don't worry, you will get the hang of it!

Dream Express *(cont.)*

TEAM RULES

In order that you have success, we have agreed upon the following rules for the Dream Team:

C — Come prepared for class.

O — Obey the student handbook.

L — Listen and follow directions.

T — Treat others with respect.

We have also agreed to reward students with good behavior in the following ways:

1. positive reinforcement
2. frequent feedback on student progress
3. tangible rewards at teacher discretion
4. recognition of outstanding students
5. group celebrations

LATE WORK

Turning work in late is considered a major offense in the Dream Team. However, you do have a chance to make it up—with substantial penalties. Remember, "better late than never."

For daily assignments, work will be penalized 25 points a day. Work that is over three days late will not be accepted.

For major projects, work will be penalized 10 points a day.

Keeping up with all your assignments will be a breeze with your assignment book, and Colt Connection will also aid you in other time-management skills. Sometimes you will be asked to have your parents sign the assignment book to make sure they know of your progress.

CONSEQUENCES

When students do not follow rules, they interfere with everybody else who is trying to learn. We realize that some students will not follow the rules, and they will have to accept the consequences of their behavior. When there is a problem, one or more of the following will occur:

1. warning and/or talk with student
2. phone call to the home
3. classroom discipline (mediators)
4. detention during lunch or after school
5. team conference with student
6. referral to counselor or principal

WHY AM I SPECIAL AT COVINGTON?

Because we teachers love all our students! We want you to be happy, successful, and feel good about yourselves. Also, we will be glad to discuss any concerns you might have. Why? Because we are here for you! That's our job. We want to make Covington the best school in the nation, and we want to give you skills that will last a lifetime.

STUDY TIPS

1. Use a "home office" (desk or work space).
2. Set a "work time" every day.
3. Stock up with school supplies.
4. Have a dictionary and thesaurus handy.
5. Keep up with your assignment book!

Technology in the Classroom *(cont.)*

VII. Knowing the Copyright Laws

It is extremely important to be aware of laws regulating the video and computer industries regarding use rights. Failure to recognize these laws can result in lawsuits and suspension of privileges for an entire school.

A. Buying the Rights

When you purchase a video, you buy the right to exhibit it under reasonable circumstances. Showing it to your class, school, or the entire district for educational purposes is allowable. Purchasing a video, however, does not grant you rights to air it over public airwaves. Your library and district media center probably have purchased many videos that are legal to exhibit to your students.

If you have recorded or received a video but not purchased it, the law states that you may not exhibit it to a crowd other than your family. That means if you tape something from TV and show it to your class, you are breaking the law. There are two exemptions from this law; the *fair use exemption* and the *face-to-face exemption*.

B. Fair Use Exemption

This exemption allows for portions of a video to be used legally as part of a greater product— for instance, making a montage of different TV shows for a presentation. As long as the portions of the work are not the most important part of the work, then using these clips is covered under the fair use doctrine. For instance, if you just used the million-dollar graphics sequences of a popular movie, like the sequences on *Forrest Gump* where Forrest meets the presidents, then that would be considered unfair and an infringement on copyright law.

C. Face-to-Face Exemption

Under the face-to-face exemption, you may use the whole video for class instruction, with some rules. First, you must be instructing the students literally face-to-face. A librarian or other aide cannot play the video without you. Secondly, you must erase the video in a reasonable amount of time (usually within three months). So, you can use the whole video, but you must erase it later. In essence, **the only lawful procedure for building a permanent set of class videos is by buying them.**

D. Software Copyright Laws

The ease of copying programs from disc to disc has caused a strict set of copyright laws teachers need to know. The basic law is that copies of programs are forbidden, except for one back-up copy. Other copies are considered pirated software, and the person responsible can be prosecuted. To protect yourself and your school, always buy the software which you or the students use.

Teaming

Reproducibles for Chapter 7 (See pages 266–273.)

1. *Team Procedures Checklist*

2. *Team Calendar Form*

3. *Detention Hall Pass Forms*

4. *Team Instructional Unit Form*

5. *Team Meeting Record*

6. *Team-Student Conference Form*

7. *Team Assembly Form*

8. *Team Assembly Notice*

I. Background

Teaming is a word used to describe the process of teachers working together. Informal teaming has been around since the first school. Good teachers have always tried to carry over knowledge and procedures from their colleagues to their own classes. Since the 1950s, approaches to team teaching have been implemented in our nation's schools. Today, however, teaming has become more formal. Furthermore, the implementation of formal teams on campuses all over the country can be seen as the advance guard of oncoming educational reforms.

The emphasis on cooperative learning has attracted new methods and opportunities to our schools. Building students' social skills and developing their team ethic are necessitated by the fact our world demands that we work together and build for the common good. Students are not the only ones who need this practice. Teachers also need to create formal systems where their shared work makes a difference. Together, teachers can make more impact than alone.

One purpose of teams is to ensure consistency across all classes. Also, the team acts as a security blanket for students and an efficient administrational vehicle for the teachers. It would be difficult to argue against the benefits derived from a team-centered faculty as opposed to a non-team faculty. Furthermore, the need for teams becomes greater as our schools get bigger.

Teaming *(cont.)*

II. Forming a Team

Let's take a look at Pine Oaks Middle School before and after the implementation of formal teams. Remember Eloise Agrippa, the math teacher? She is getting ready to prepare for a new year. Pine Oaks will have about 1,200 students this year. This means there will be about 400 sixth graders. Mrs. Agrippa knows that she will probably receive about 150 students to be spread out in six classes. How will she know which students will be scheduled to her class?

Before teaming, she would receive her 150 students randomly, like all the rest of the teachers. Her friends down the hall—Mr. Hamad, the science teacher, and Ms. Clay, the English teacher—might have a coincidental student that she has as well. Here is how a pre-teaming 6th grade scheduling of students would be diagramed:

Student Body—6th Grade

Classroom Assignments (a typical period): Students are spread evenly into different classes, assigned different teachers and schedules until class sizes are evened out (about 22 students per classroom).

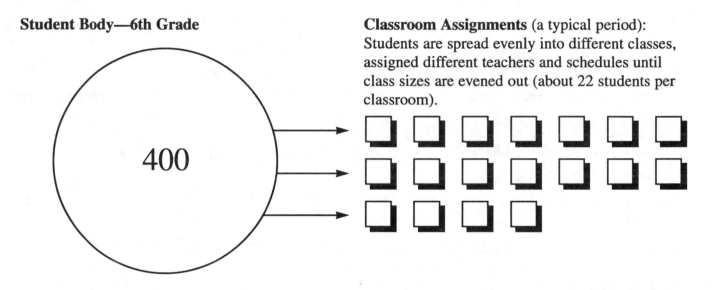

In other words, few if any students would have exactly the same schedule. In fact, it would be a stroke of luck if a student had two or three classes that were shared with a friend. Mrs. Agrippa as a math teacher would find it hard to develop a thematic unit with science when her students have three different science teachers teaching three different curricula. On the same note, Ms. Clay complains that she has to work with three different history teachers to try to make relevant spelling lists. Unfortunately, she is frustrated because one history class is studying China, one is studying Africa, and one is studying the Age of Exploration.

In addition, class rules change from class to class, confusing students and causing misunderstanding. When Mrs. Agrippa complains to the principal, he tells her that if everybody just stuck to the textbook, then everything would be fine. Finally, she gives up, and all the teachers decide to cloister themselves in their own classrooms.

This common occurrence, sometimes labeled the "monastery effect," is probably what most of us grew up with and a lot of us continue to teach with. In this scenario, teachers close their doors on any outside influence and focus on one thing—teaching their subjects their way, with no outside interruptions.

Teaming *(cont.)*

The next year, Mrs. Agrippa is ready to retire, but she has hope because a new principal has been assigned to her school. This principal talks of reform as an ongoing process, and the first thing to change will be the implementation of teams. Here is how the new schedule will be processed:

Student Body—6th Grade   **Classroom Assignments:**

Students and teachers are pooled into teams.

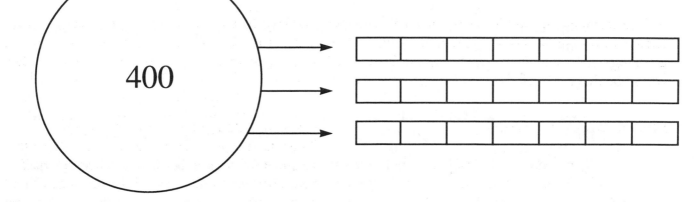

The idea here is to pool the 6th grade into three groups, where each group will share a set of six teachers. Mrs. Agrippa has been informed that her team will consist of herself (math), Mr. Hamad (science), Ms. Clay (language arts), Mr. Rockler (history), Ms. Hernandez (language studies), and Ms. Orangetree (language arts).

Together they share a group of about 150 students. At long last, Eloise is excited about the possibilities of working on a team, and she can't wait to get started.

In this example of Pine Oaks Middle School, the need for students to share commonality and identify in such a big school is paramount to their success. Otherwise, students will get lost and probably forgotten. The metaphor "falling through the cracks" is all too applicable in these circumstances.

Teams provide a security blanket to wrap around their students for the love and support which is completely necessary in middle school. Students go from class to class, knowing exactly what to expect and, hopefully, seeing the connections between disciplines. Some teams provide more connections than others. But all teams can learn to achieve a level of education in which students find more meaning and are better behaved than in any one-teacher-oriented system. Team maturity can be seen as existing in four levels of curriculum lining. Each level has its own characteristics and rewards.

III. Curriculum Lining

The most important function of a team is to line the curriculum. You can think of this phenomenon metaphorically as a railroad system. Your team is traveling on the train to reach their learning objectives. The railroad tracks are the different strands of curricula taught in each class. Usually, the train must stop and the students must get off and walk over to another train. This stop-and-start motion causes obvious interruptions and confusion within the team. But what if that train could continuously ride across tracks that were in line? The train could probably go much farther than it ever had before.

Building a smooth, durable railroad system does not happen overnight. It takes hard work and skillful engineering. In building your railroad, there are basically four stages or levels.

Teaming  *(cont.)*

A. Level 1: Procedural

When a team first comes together, many tasks confront it. Your principal will probably give each team a checklist of items that need attention before any students come into your classroom. If no checklist is provided, or if it is inadequate, refer to the Team Procedures Checklist on page 266. The basics of these items are usually the following:

❑ **Team Roles**

Roles for members on a team cannot be taken lightly. Roles vary from school to school but commonly include these:

Leader—A team needs a person to provide a strong sense of duty. The leader should be voted on or simply volunteered. The leader should make sure the job gets done and that power is delegated responsibly. Leaders are usually the liaisons to the principal as well. It might be a good idea to switch leaders every now and then or to have co-leaders.

Secretary/Scribe—The scribe records the team minutes and other important policy-making documents. Secretaries should always forward courtesy copies of team documents to the principal's office. Some principals will want to mull over every word, while some may not even want to see team minutes. A good idea is to mark team communication "FYI" if it is routine information that just needs to be filed. Marking "Response Requested" is a way for the principal to know that a major issue needs his or her attention.

Communications/Journalist—The communications person makes the team newsletter. Refer to Chapter Six in order to make a professional newsletter. Team newsletters are important for the parents to look over, as well as for the students themselves. A great idea is to create a student newsletter staff. Have them write articles and use computers to make the newsletter process more efficient.

Events Coordinator—This role involves setting up all the extra classroom activities. This includes assemblies, field trips, guest speakers, or schoolwide events. Obtaining proper equipment, handling student organization/passes, and coordinating with outside personnel are common activities associated with this role.

Curriculum Coordinator(s)—If a team has exceptional writers of curriculum who have experience or motivation to write instruction for a whole team, it is advantageous to give these people opportunities to create team instruction. Writing, receiving feedback, typing, and copying are the major tasks of this team player.

Ideas Person—The ideas person has a hard job. This person is the problem solver. His\her commission is to solve a problem immediately by listing options and ideas. Also, this person must regularly provide ideas on instruction and policy. Above all, the ideas that the ideas person comes up with must work!

Teaming *(cont.)*

❑ **Team Roles** *(cont.)*

Parent Coordinator—A crucial role to play is that of parent coordinator. The major tasks for this player are to ensure that parents are happy and well-supplied with communication. Also, working with the PTA is another job that the role entails.

Community Coordinator—If at all possible, teams should have someone getting the community involved somehow in the team or school. Writing grants, receiving sponsors, getting community speakers like police officers—all these are vital tasks for the successful team. See Chapters 11, 12, and 13 for more information.

Treasurer—The team will find itself collecting money at some point. An efficient system for handling student monies is important so there is no lost or mishandled money. The treasurer not only collects and stores the money, but he also fills out deposit slips (just like a bank deposit) and gives those to the office staff.

Technology Coordinator—A great idea is to have a team member be responsible for all technology-related situations. Someone who provides scheduling for VCR's and other media, trouble shoots, and helps with computer instruction is a great resource for a team.

Discipline Coordinator—Somebody has to keep up with the discipline situations in the team. Creating contracts, managing detention halls, and administering other systems that keep an orderly team are essential tasks of this role.

There are many other roles that can be created and incorporated into your team. Roles are flexible, but members need to stick to their roles or the team will not run efficiently.

Continuing the Pine Oaks story, their team roles have been decided. Mrs. Agrippa will be the team leader. Mr. Hamad will be ideas person and technology coordinator. Mrs. Clay wants to be secretary and treasurer. Mr. Rockler likes event coordinator. Mrs. Orangetree wants to do the team newsletter. Mrs. Hernandez decides to be the parent coordinator. They all decide to be curriculum and discipline coordinators, sharing the roles equally.

❑ **Team Name/Identity**

In addition to roles, vote on a name for your team. Team names can be effective for creating team spirit. The more pageantry, color, and symbolism involved in a team, the more the students will identify with it.

Mrs. Agrippa's team decides on the name *Star Team,* with colors of blue and yellow. Their symbol will be the star. The teachers can use this theme to decorate bulletin boards, halls, doors, and walls.

❑ **Academic Standards**

The students should know how they will be graded in each class. No two teachers grade the same and should not have to. However, items such as penalties on late work, amount of homework, makeup work, extra-credit work, and grading standards should be relatively uniform.

Teaming *(cont.)*

❑ **Creating a Mission Statement**

Each team should always make a statement of goals and beliefs. Hang this in every classroom so you and the students get to see it often. Mission statements are sometimes seen as corny and superficial, but if you do not have a greater purpose in mind, you will not be satisfied as a team. Following is an example:

Star Team Mission Statement

Clay, Hamad, Agrippa, Rockler, Hernandez, and Orangetree

The Star Team pledges to . . .

1. promote the academic and emotional growth of Star Team students.
2. provide quality, challenging education.
3. handle discipline problems firmly and consistently.
4. strengthen learning by curriculum lining and interdisciplinary units.
5 honor excellence with frequent assemblies and activities.
6. recognize success with thematic celebrations.
7. involve parents in the learning process.
8. reach out to the community as much as possible.
9. provide all Star students with support and encouragement.

Everyone is a star on the Star Team.

Teaming *(cont.)*

❑ **Behavioral Standards**

Use the Team Procedure Checklist form (page 266) to make sure your team is consistent in basic behavioral rules and consequences. Consistency in this area is essential for a smooth transition from class to class. While filling out the Team Checklist, answer the following questions.

Homework Policy: When can students expect to have homework on your team? Every day? On weekends? What will be the penalty for late work? How will late work be handled to ensure mastery learning? Will students always be expected to make up missing work? How will projects or other long-term assignments be penalized if they are late?

Tardies: How will tardies be handled in team classrooms? What consequences will be administered for an unexcused tardy?

Food/Drink: Will food or drink be allowed in team classrooms? What about special events? What will be the consequences for chewing gum, eating candy, etc.?

Discipline Consequences:

- Warnings? What kinds of warnings will team teachers give to misbehaving students? How many warnings should you give? How can you stop misbehavior without interrupting class?

- Mediators? Will your team administer mediators or discipline essays? If so, what kind? Will you have mediators for rudeness, silliness, tardiness, excessive talking, or other misbehavior?

- Loss of Privileges? Will your team suspend privileges for misbehaving students? If so, what kinds of privileges will be lost—outside activities, class celebrations, field trips, assemblies, in-class enrichment activities?

- Detentions? Will your team assign lunch or after school detentions for misconduct? Will team teachers rotate turns each day or week to preside over d-halls? What will students do in d-hall? Should they be made to sit quietly as punishment or to work on class assignments? For D-Hall pass forms, see page 268.

- Time-Out? Will team classrooms have a time-out station? What will be the rules of going to time-out? What will students be expected to do while in time-out?

- School-Home Contracts? Will students be required to have contracts, promising certain behaviors? What if students break the contract? Will the contract be handed over to the student each day or each week?

- Parent Involvement? When should parents be notified of their child's behavior? Will parent conferences be necessary? Should the whole team meet with the parents or just the teachers who are having problems with that child?

- Referrals? When will it become necessary to refer a student? What are the specific behaviors that will end up in a team referral?

Teaming *(cont.)*

❑ **Team Calendar**

The last step to attain a Level 1 designation is to make a team calendar with all teachers' schedules included. Use the Team Calendar form (page 267) or make your own. When all team members have their curriculum planned, integrate it into one master team calendar. (If a fellow teacher has trouble making plans, direct him/her to Chapters 1–6 of this book.) A team calendar provides a map of what all teachers are doing; it should provide the following information:

Important Testing Dates: List dates and times that teachers will administer important evaluations. Other team teachers should assign homework appropriately the night before those dates. Also, teachers might avoid testing on the same day. Other team teachers should announce these dates frequently and help students to study for them. Team members should help each other as much as possible.

Important Due Dates: Specify dates when projects or long-term assignments are due. Many teachers complain that students do not turn work in on time and do not care about deadlines. Much of this would improve if all team members reminded students of important due dates in other classes.

Team Events/Activities: List major events, like assemblies, that the team has planned. Other activities involving one class or the whole team need to be indicated. Then, if Mrs. Agrippa cannot find Mrs. Orangetree, she can look on the team calendar. Mrs. Orangetree might be in the cafeteria giving a class assembly.

Curriculum Strands: Record the main curriculum strands that each teacher will be working with. This helps all teachers realize what students are studying in other classes. In essence, the right hand will know what the left hand is doing. For example, Mrs. Clay is diagramming sentences. When looking at the team calendar, she notices that Mr. Rockler is teaching native American cultures. She decides to have students form the sentences from their Indian studies, thus focusing on sentence structure while simultaneously reinforcing another subject.

When listing curriculum strands, be general and brief. Give a basic idea of the areas in which each class will be involved.

School Events/Holidays: List all important school events, like pep rallies, assemblies, track and field day, play performances, etc.

Conclusion to Level 1 Alignment: It takes energy, planning, and consistency to achieve the Level 1 designation. The benefits from lining the curriculum in these basic ways become obvious and immediate. Students are better behaved because they know what to expect. They have more academic success because classes support each other. In addition, the team itself will run more efficiently.

Teaming *(cont.)*

B. Level 2: Activity

The major difference between a Level 1 and a Level 2 team is that in addition to uniform procedures a Level 2 team conducts team activities. This calls for much planning. Team activities are usually outside the classroom. Team assemblies, field trips, celebrations, games, etc., are included at least once every six weeks.

After teachers get over the initial rough spots of creating an ordered team, their meetings can be used for more important planning. Instead of talking about how bad student behavior is and what should be done about it, the Level 2 team concentrates on team activities because the discipline systems are already in place. Activities are extremely important to building a team identity and instituting team morale. They include assemblies, field trips, outside activities, reward parties, guest speakers, and other activities in which the whole team can participate.

To organize a team activity like an assembly, read further in this chapter. Field trips and guest speaker presentations are outlined in Chapter 4. A Level 2 team can create enthusiasm for school by having students participate in team-wide situations, thus expanding their sense of belonging.

C. Level 3: Multidisciplinary

A team that has fulfilled the first two prerequisites of procedural systems and activity coordination is doing a great job. In fact, they are way ahead of most teams. The next order of business is going to the heart of the curriculum itself: classroom instruction. This initially involves working together to create projects and instruction which cross many disciplines or subjects. Any instruction which directly involves more than one subject can be labeled *multidisciplinary*. A solid example of a multidisciplinary project is the Medieval Diary packet on page 71. This project can be transferred from English (writing journals) to history (researching historical concepts) very easily. Although other subjects like foreign language, science, or art may become involved, the core of the instruction will come from two teachers.

Use your Team Instructional Unit planner (page 269) to help organize your preparation. The process of creating multidisciplinary instruction is the same as creating your own instruction, except it is twice as fast and twice as effective through synergy. If there are three teachers preparing, then the process is three times as fast and three times as relevant. The formula continues for four, five, or six teachers. This process can be summarized into seven steps:

1. Set a meeting time and place.

Teachers should set a date where all can sit down and plan. A conference period or two usually works, although lunch dates are also effective. Give yourselves as much time as possible. Create a relaxing atmosphere where everybody can concentrate. It is not unheard of for teachers to plan together at their homes. Visiting fellow teachers at home is relaxing and builds a special bond.

Teaming *(cont.)*

2. Decide on theme/objectives.

First decide on the overall theme that will color the whole unit. "The Ancient Greeks" is a good example of a theme to which many subjects can relate. History classes can study the military, political, governmental, artistic, and philosophical aspects of this broad subject. In English classes, students can practice reading skills, learn about the Greek alphabet and language, read myths, and write about their learning. Math sections can delve into the geometry of the Greeks. Science classes can examine the astronomy, biology, and chemistry of the time.

Other themes might come from science. For instance, a "Jungle Unit" or "Birds" is conceivable. Math may be a more difficult subject to integrate; however, themes like "problem solving" or "business careers" can work well. From English class, themes like "Famous Authors," "The Novel," or "Persuasion" are a few of the topics around which instruction can be centered.

3. Determine activities and lessons.

After setting the general theme, each teacher must implement activities to reinforce the content. A popular method is making a project applicable to all classes involved. A project is efficient because it gives a basis for all other assignments. Also, students are usually expected to take their project home and work on it in a continuing manner. The project becomes the focus for the multidisciplinary unit. For project writing, see Chapter 4.

Projects are not the only basis for a multidisciplinary unit. Many teachers like the idea of having specific lessons. For Lesson Plan sheets, see page 249. For instance, let's say that Mrs. Clay and Mr. Hamad want to team up for a "Bird Unit." They decide that instead of a project, they will co-teach different lessons during a four-week period. Mrs. Clay plans to teach these individual lessons:

- famous myths involving birds—Greek, Native American, and Egyptian (1 week)
- writing and editing a creative story from the point of view of a bird (2 weeks)
- mini-research paper—"My Favorite Bird"

Mr. Hamad will prepare the following lessons:

- the anatomy and biology of a bird (2 weeks)
- "create-a-bird" arts and crafts activity (3 days)
- mini-research paper—"My Favorite Bird"

Mrs. Clay also uses the bird theme to color her grammar exercises, integrating relevant information into the exercises. Following is an activity for her grammar lesson on pronouns for that week:

Identify the pronouns in the following sentences.
1. My bird is a canary.
2. I call him "Joe."
3. He is nice to my friends, but Joe is mean to my sister, Tabitha.
3. She hates him and tries to trick him sometimes.
4. Joe knows that she tricks him, but I protect him from her.

Teaming *(cont.)*

Even the simplest exercise can be made more relevant by coloring it with the theme of the unit. Mrs. Clay may not have the ability to bring bird-associated ideas into other lessons all the time, and neither will Mr. Hamad. Diversity is part of life. A good rule is that you spend a majority of time in ideas and concepts of your unit. Be realistic about your capabilities.

Notice also that both teachers will be teaching a mini-research paper. Mrs. Clay will handle the writing and editing part, while Mr. Hamad agrees to provide the research materials and study skills. They both agree that a thematic celebration should occur at the end of the unit where students can present and display their research and their birds.

Planning a whole project is beneficial because it is a single, effective instrument to tie together unit themes and activities. Also, planning for individual lessons can be just as effective.

4. Gather materials.

After you have planned your unit, project, and activities on paper, the next step is to accumulate as many materials as you can. Continuing the Bird Unit, Mrs. Clay must gather the following:

- The bird myths she plans to teach: She may run off a class set (30) and laminate them for preservation, or she may just make transparencies for the students to read from the screen in class.
- An instructional packet on writing a short story and point of view: This could easily be a set of transparencies. It is a good idea to encourage students to illustrate their stories, so Mrs. Clay might want to gather some art supplies that week.
- An instructional packet on mini-research paper guidelines: Mrs. Clay already has many research-skill worksheets and transparencies that she can use for note-taking, bibliographies, citations, and purpose/audience considerations. A page or two of time lines, length, and basic requirements will be needed to give to students. For the research paper, Mrs. Clay could also bring in enrichment resources on birds. An audio tape of bird songs, a video of "Birds of America," and other books related to birds would be appropriate.

Mr. Hamad also has many supplies to gather. All in all, both teachers can write the unit and gather all their supplies in the course of a few days. In essence, quality preparation translates into the ability to concentrate on teaching.

5. Type and distribute.

You have written the unit, planned the lessons, and gathered materials. Now you must type any necessary instructions or communication. Use your word processing skills from Chapter 6 to create visually appealing documents. Run these off on the copier for all your students. Next, enthusiastically announce to your students (if you are not excited about it, they won't be either) that they will be studying the same overall theme in several classes. Distribute all your information and go over the unit with your students thoroughly.

Teaming *(cont.)*

6. Manage.

During the unit, you will teach and manage. Be prepared to bend a little for the adjustment that is part of life. For instance, Mrs. Clay might have to take two days on thesis statements instead of one. Or maybe Mr. Hamad has to change the due date of the research paper because it falls on a day of a major test. Be flexible and adapt to change.

7. Assess learning.

Assessment is needed for all classes. Each teacher could test what he/she taught, or one teacher could give an overall test. Other useful assessments are the following:

- Have students write self-evaluations of their experience. Was it educational? Did they learn more from having it in two classes? What was their favorite aspect? Have attitudes changed from before the unit? How can they apply the newly acquired knowledge?
- Keep observation journals of the students. Who was really working hard? Who seemed to be off task? What social skills were being used? Were students learning during activities or just playing around? Were student attitudes towards learning better during multidiscipline instruction?
- Provide portfolios of the students' best work, using items from all classes. Short stories, mini-research papers, or a model the student is proud of can show much about learning.

D. Level 4: Interdisciplinary

The highest level of teaming results in true interdisciplinary instruction. In middle school and high school, teachers usually focus on a single discipline. This makes it harder to plan and requires total commitment from all teachers on the team. Because of the planning, coordination, materials, and outside influences that six or more teachers experience, true interdisciplinary instruction is rare but is steadily increasing.

Unlocking the power of interdisciplinary instruction is simple. First, interdisciplinary learning does not mean . . .

- scrapping all your former instructional methods.
- having to accept other instruction given by someone else.
- conforming to new regulations and rules about education.
- adding yet more things to an already overburdened work day.
- teaching the same thing in different classes.

What interdisciplinary instruction does mean is . . .

- working together, sharing ideas, and coordinating schedules.
- using old and new instructional materials.
- teaching the basic academic objectives of the state.
- sharing a theme that ties all classes together.
- not being isolated in one's own discipline.
- using creative and high-level thinking skills.
- motivating students to learn more.

Teaming *(cont.)*

The fundamental metaphor for understanding interdisciplinary instruction is a theatrical presentation. Interdisciplinary instruction provides the set or backdrop of a team's unit. Classrooms are like the scenes within the acts. Like Shakespeare, teachers are both the playwrights and the actors. The students are both the actors on the stage and the audience watching intently. Within this set or theme, the student watches and performs in various scenes (classes). An interdisciplinary unit consumes an "act," and the whole year can be considered the "play." The advantage of this scenario is that the students can concentrate in one area and not be moved from theater to theater. In turn, this provides relevance and meaning. Just think how disjointed watching random scenes from various plays would be! (See the Team Instructional Unit planner on page 269.)

Here are some ways to implement interdisciplinary instruction:

1. Umbrella Theme

To plan interdisciplinary instruction, use the same process as the multidisciplinary unit, with the following exceptions. In this mode, every teacher has a role in the overall theme. Like a puzzle, the unit must be comprised of pieces that fit together perfectly. Themes are broad enough to encompass all subjects. For instance, the theme of "birds" might be hard to integrate into Mrs. Agrippa's math classes. Therefore, themes of true interdisciplinary units generally follow these examples:

- change
- conflicts/resolutions
- values
- "our town"
- the ancients
- connections
- careers

- problem solving
- emotions
- communities
- courage
- revolutions
- improvements/advancements
- patterns

- cycles of life
- reasoning
- business
- effectiveness
- cultural diversity
- creativity
- cultures

2. Equal Roles

After themes have been decided, the role of each teacher must be defined. For instance, let's say the Star Team wants to do a unit on values. Each teacher must use this concept to color his/her instruction, listing broad learning objectives that use the umbrella theme. The Star Team decides to try an interdisciplinary unit using values as their theme. Here is a list of how the teachers break down their roles.

Star Team Interdisciplinary Unit on Values

Math—values of numbers, positive and negative values

Language Arts—exploring personal values through language

Science—value of the rain forest and endangered animals

History—cultural values of Native Americans versus settlers

Foreign Language—the value of bilingualism

Teaming *(cont.)*

3. Planning Activities

Writing cooperative curriculum is a challenge for many teachers used to traditional teaching methods. After your roles are defined, each teacher should break down the unit into lessons, activities, projects, and exercises. Making a syllabus or calendar of how the unit will shape up is necessary for a broad perspective. For example, the foreign language teacher, Mrs. Hernandez, breaks down her ideas on lessons that will be taught in sequence.

Lessons

1. Introduction—the value of bilingualism
   Cultural diversity cooperative learning exercise

2. Situations involving bilingualism (the value of Spanish in the real world)
   Student skits

3. Verb Tenses (The value of correct grammar)
   Text, student skits

4. Irregular verbs in Spanish (the value of correct grammar)
   Text, oral reports

5. Situations involving bilingualism (the value of Spanish in the real world)
   Text, student teaching

6. Mexican Fair (appreciation of other cultural values)
   Thematic celebration

In this example, Mrs. Hernandez plans for the overall concepts of values to color her lessons. She stresses the value of knowing Spanish, as well as the cultural values of Spain and Mexico. However, the specifics of teaching her subject change little. She still teaches basic grammar and will use textbooks frequently.

4. Coordinating Schedules/Gathering Supplies

The other teachers will plan around the general theme as well. When everyone is finished, all the schedules should be put on the team calendar. After this is done, any conflicts can be smoothed out. For example, Mrs. Hernandez probably does not want the Mexican Fair to be on the same day as Mr. Hamad's thematic celebration "Rain Forest-Rama." Copies of the team calendar let each teacher know what the others are doing at any given time.

You will probably make many copies, formulate instructional sheets, label text areas to be used, and develop transparencies. For instance, Mr. Hamad plans his supply list:

- butcher paper, all colors (for decoration and papier mâché animals)
- encyclopedia/books on the rain forest
- "Rain Forest" CD-ROM
- science text (class sets)
- various worksheets
- transparencies for rain forest lectures
- slides of rain forest (from personal vacation)
- cooperative learning instruction sheets

Teaming *(cont.)*

5. Managing the Unit

Once the team has created the theme, decided on equal roles, planned lessons and activities, coordinated schedules, and gathered supplies, it is ready to start the unit with the students. At first, the students will be surprised that all their teachers seem to be doing the same thing. Then, they will find that the information they learned in one class enriches the next class. This raises their level of thinking exponentially, and you will be amazed at how motivated students become when they see connections.

Flexibility is important to remember. Sometimes planned lessons will flop, and spontaneous lessons will be successful.

6. Assessment

Develop methods to assess student performance and learning, as in the multidisciplinary mode. Be sure to develop a method to assess the success of the unit itself. Did it work? Were students learning more than a regular unit? Was it easy or hard on the teachers? How can it become more beneficial?

All this preparation might seem burdensome, but it is the core of the interdisciplinary process. More preparation means more success. Preparation is like a treasure map. The more detailed and accurate the map is, the better the chance that you will find a chest full of gold. Poor maps result in no treasure.

IV. Dynamics of a Team

In general, teachers are a mature breed. Since they are not divine, however, problems can arise on teams. Knowing ways to resolve difficult situations makes for a more effective team.

A. Problems Within Teams

One aspect of teaming which creates potential problems is the constant interaction with other team members. You see them at meetings, in the halls, at lunch, and after school. In addition to standard social etiquette, you must work with these people to solve complicated problems on a daily basis. The sheer amount of time spent with your teammates might cause your team to suffer normal interpersonal problems.

Personality Conflicts

The people on your team might come from diverse backgrounds. Furthermore, teachers rarely get to pick and choose teammates. Often teams are assigned on the basis of heterogeneity. Some teachers are not used to working with other types of people. The range of personalities you may encounter could cause conflicts. Little details may begin to irritate you. A colleague might tap a pencil repetitively, have a tendency to stray from the subject, be very loud, or be extremely negative.

A proven technique to combat these minor but dependable irritations is "bracketing." This method trains your mind to completely ignore those outside stimuli which break down your concentration. Bracketing is also successful in the classroom where minor annoyances from students create stress for teachers every day.

Teaming *(cont.)*

Power Struggles

Some people insist on having it "their way." This impulse is strong in middle school teachers who have to command large groups of students on a daily basis. Having strong leadership skills in teaching carries over to team dynamics. Members on a team might be at odds on different issues. One member might try to take over, and this can lead to feelings of anger and resentment.

For example, let's say you have an idea for an interdisciplinary unit about "nature." You explain your ideas and the activities to your team. One teacher opposes the unit, citing the small learning value and the labor-intensive characteristics of the idea. In essence, she shoots it down. She concludes with the remark "Besides, they already did that in elementary school."

The other team members retreat and do not come to your support. You feel like standing up for yourself, but you are so angry and embarrassed nothing can come out. The team moves on to other topics, and your great idea is dropped. The scenario is common within teams. Sometimes the power struggles can be subtle, and sometimes they are blatant.

Ganging Up

Think back to middle school: Did you ever feel alone, defenseless, or awkward when a group of kids rejected you? Sometimes in a team, teachers can "gang up" on others in the team. If this sounds cruel, it is, unfortunately, a reality. Teachers start ganging up when they feel threatened or mistreated by another teacher. They might go to lunch together and purposely not invite the neglected teacher. They might be friendly and warm to other teachers but not to the mistreated teacher. This spiteful behavior erodes professional relations and poisons team success.

Gossip

As human beings, we exhibit the need to talk about each other. Whole industries in entertainment cater to this trait by fabricating gossip. Sometimes, teachers like to turn their lives into soap operas by gossiping about other teachers. Usually, gossip is harmful in nature, and rumors can ruin careers and lives.

B. Ways to Be a More Effective Team Member

There are many ways to deal with interpersonal conflicts. The more you use these techniques, the more positive energy and mutual respect will spread throughout your team and school.

Communicate Immediately

At all times, be quick to communicate your feelings. A firm tone helps others to listen. Writing memos is important also. Get into the habit of open reaction so others can know how you feel.

Listen to Understand

Many times when we talk to people, we do not listen. We hear, but we do not listen. Instead, we rehearse our answers to their discourse, thinking about what we want to say. This is only natural, but this type of "listening" is counterproductive.

Teaming *(cont.)*

If you want effective communication, you must first listen to the tone and message of the sender. Ponder what is being said and see if you can read between the lines to determine attitudes, motives, and emotions. This listening skill is an art which can be refined through practice.

After you have internalized this message, make your own thoughts completely understood. There may be some middle ground for consensus. Listen in on a discussion between two very different types of teachers—Harry Hamad and Linda Clay.

✉ When Harry Met Linda ✉

HARRY (walking into the room): Linda, I need to talk to you. Students tell me that you stopped doing the writing portion of our Birds Unit. If you don't do this, no one else will.

LINDA: Oh, I could do it—it's just . . . well, I just don't see the learning value in it.

(At this point, Harry's blood starts boiling. He wants to lash out at this teacher for insulting him like that. But he decides to use his listening-to-understand skills. He asks himself, "Okay, what is she trying to say?")

HARRY (sits down): Linda, you seem like you have a lot to do. Do you feel that the writing project is too much right now?

LINDA: Well, it does take a considerable amount of time to grade those papers.

HARRY: It is asking a lot, but I think it's working. What if we worked out a compromise? Let's look at where we can reach an agreement.

LINDA: That sounds good, Harry. I didn't mean to put down your unit; maybe it just needs some modifications.

Honest attempts to communicate require effort and patience, but they will pay off in manifold ways. Genuine understanding and mutual respect will go far toward successful team achievement, resulting in student progress and joy in school.

Stand Tall

The heart of success in a person is an unflinching integrity. Never let others run over you without standing up for your principles. You know you have to be flexible in this business, but you have a core of principles, like self-respect, fairness, and honor, that should never be compromised. The educational field is no place for meekness. Moreover, your colleagues will respect you more if you "stand tall" when it comes to personal principles.

Compromise

Be at peace with the fact that you can never have your way all the time. Your ideas might be changed or not used at all. But remember, if progress is to be made, ideas must be shaped so a consensus is reached. Offering compromises is an art in itself. Compromising is being realistic, practical, and efficient. No laws in this country would ever get passed without compromise. This is just and right because the process of compromise reflects the ideas of a diversity of people. People can disagree and still get along and work together.

Teaming *(cont.)*

V. Conducting Team Meetings

The most time-consuming activity for teams is conducting meetings.

A. Regular Meetings

A teacher's schedule should allow periods meant for planning, preparing, and conferencing, including a regular conference time for team meetings. Using the Team Meeting Record (see page 270), the team secretary records the major resolutions of the meeting.

Team Agenda

Team agendas usually cover the following areas:

- Administrative Matters: Issues like discipline procedures, scheduling, office memos, special school activities, and other details will continuously arise during the year. Ideally, discipline will not occupy much team time, but it frequently does.
- Policy: One team responsibility is to formulate and execute policy. Academic and behavioral policies may need frequent attention.
- Planning Curricula: The vital task of a team is to plan instruction. At the very least, all teachers should know what the others are teaching. At higher levels, teams plan multidisciplinary and interdisciplinary instruction.

Bad Habits

- Tardiness: Lateness is unprofessional and shows lack of discipline.
- Absence: Unnecessary absence from team meetings magnifies the problems of tardiness tenfold. Always attend team meetings.
- Gossiping: Team meetings should contain productive discussion. Gossip is a gigantic waste of everybody's time.

B. Team-Student Conference

It will be necessary to sit down with certain students to assess problems and solutions. Use your Team-Student Conference form (page 271) to record these conferences. Teams call in students at times for behavior problems; at other times, teachers will discuss academics. In these conferences the student is confronted with all teachers, reinforcing that all classes use uniform standards. The student cannot play one teacher against another.

The procedure for an effective team-student conference follows:

1. Schedule a meeting time.
2. Explain the situation/problem. List the documented situations and observations from the concerned teachers. Be specific.
3. Ask for feedback. What does the student have to say? Are there deeper problems? How can the teachers help?
4. List solutions for success. Brainstorm ideas to help the student. Emphasize that if these solutions do not work, other measures will be forthcoming.

 *(cont.)*

5. Make a contract if necessary. Contracts should list desired behaviors and have places for each teacher to check if that behavior was performed. For instance, common types of contracts include categories for each teacher to check at the end of the period.

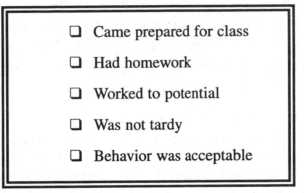

❑ Came prepared for class

❑ Had homework

❑ Worked to potential

❑ Was not tardy

❑ Behavior was acceptable

VI. Conducting Team Assemblies

Team assemblies can build team spirit and break up the monotony of classroom instruction. Use your Team Assembly form (page 272) for preparing. Also, see Chapter 4 under "Thematic Celebrations" for more ideas and details. When arranging a team assembly, consider the following:

A. Determine Details

Why?

What purposes will your team come together for? Usually, giving awards and honors is appropriate. Other reasons for assemblies are thematic celebrations, performances, plays, shows, or guest speaker presentations.

When?

Plan your assembly well in advance—at least two weeks.

Where?

You will need a large area for an assembly. Cafeterias, theaters, gyms, football fields, courtyards, and other large areas can hold hundreds of kids. If you are going to prepare food and drinks, you need a place that is spill friendly, like outside. The cafeteria is the safest inside spot. Never have drinks or food in the theater or gym—the coach or drama teacher will strangle you!

Who?

As a team you must decide who is eligible to attend the assembly. Some students may have lost privileges, and you might have to assign a classroom where nonparticipants can make up work. This means that at least one teacher must stay behind.

How?

What materials or equipment will you need? Decorations, tables, food, drinks, plates, cups, ice, PA system, and trash cans are usual considerations. If you are presenting awards, then the awards themselves must be designed and completed. For an attractive all-purpose award form see page 258.

Teaming *(cont.)*

B. Informing Parents

Parents usually want to watch their students receive awards, and students are proud to have their parents watch. Bringing parents in for assemblies is a a useful and easy way to promote community awareness. Use your ready-to-copy Team Assembly Notice (page 273) to inform parents of this occasion. Also, don't forget the powerful resource of parent volunteers. Recruit as many parents as you can to help with the details.

A visitors' sign-in sheet can be placed near the entrance. After the assembly, teachers can use this register to contact parents again, thanking them for attendance, support, and participation in school events. Personal attention to such details leads to strong parent-teacher bonds.

VII. Team Field Trips

A challenging and rewarding activity is a team field trip. To have a successful field trip, read the guidelines outlined in Chapter 4. Also, use the reproducibles from the same chapter (pages 254–257).

The major difference between conducting a class field trip and a team field trip is the size of the student body. Therefore, careful planning is necessary. In a team of around 150 students, there might be about 25 who have to stay behind because of academic or behavioral problems. One teacher will be left behind to watch the nonparticipants. The other five teachers will supervise the trip. Recruit enough parents to provide a seven-to-one student-adult ratio. Give students and parent volunteers a guide to the field trip, with maps, diagrams, and important scheduling information.

On the following pages are samples of a bus organization chart and an orientation map to be included in the packet for each person. These were developed for an interdisciplinary unit on the Greco-Romans. Each bus was organized as a cohort with one teacher and six parents supervising. The diagram shows the location and floor layout for the Classical History Museum.

Also included should be a map showing the exact route from the school to the destination and a schedule showing times for departure from school, estimated arrival at destination, departure from destination, and estimated return arrival at the school. Procedures for lunch must be explained, of course, as well as standards of behavior.

An important last reminder: All students should have an emergency phone number along with specific instructions about what to do if they are ever separated from the group.

Teaming *(cont.)*

Dream Team
Greco-Roman Field Trip

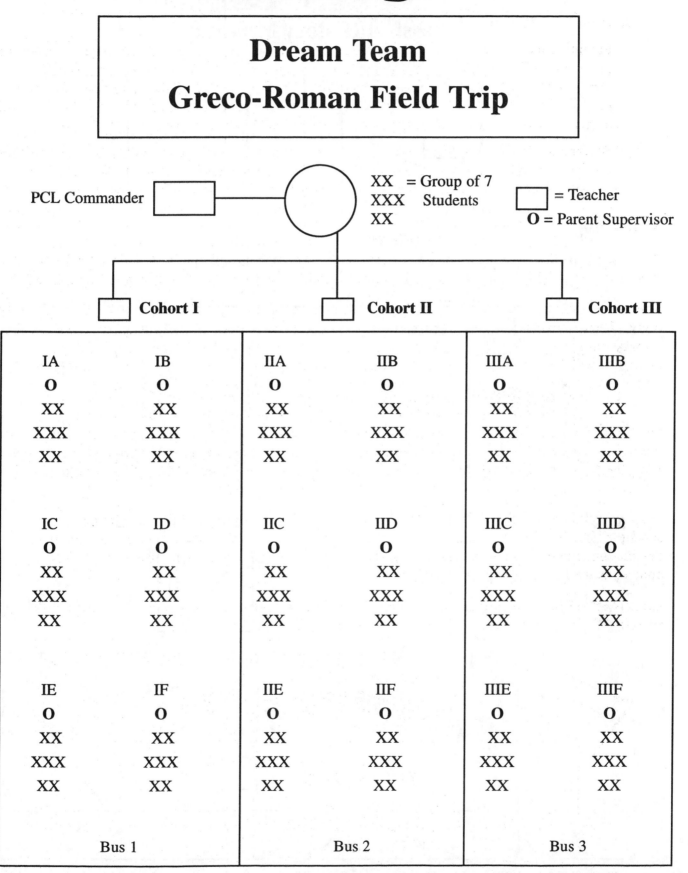

PCL Commander

XX = Group of 7
XXX   Students
XX

□ = Teacher
O = Parent Supervisor

Cohort I   Cohort II   Cohort III

IA	IB	IIA	IIB	IIIA	IIIB
O	O	O	O	O	O
XX	XX	XX	XX	XX	XX
XXX	XXX	XXX	XXX	XXX	XXX
XX	XX	XX	XX	XX	XX

IC	ID	IIC	IID	IIIC	IIID
O	O	O	O	O	O
XX	XX	XX	XX	XX	XX
XXX	XXX	XXX	XXX	XXX	XXX
XX	XX	XX	XX	XX	XX

IE	IF	IIE	IIF	IIIE	IIIF
O	O	O	O	O	O
XX	XX	XX	XX	XX	XX
XXX	XXX	XXX	XXX	XXX	XXX
XX	XX	XX	XX	XX	XX

Bus 1   Bus 2   Bus 3

Teaming *(cont.)*

Classical History Museum

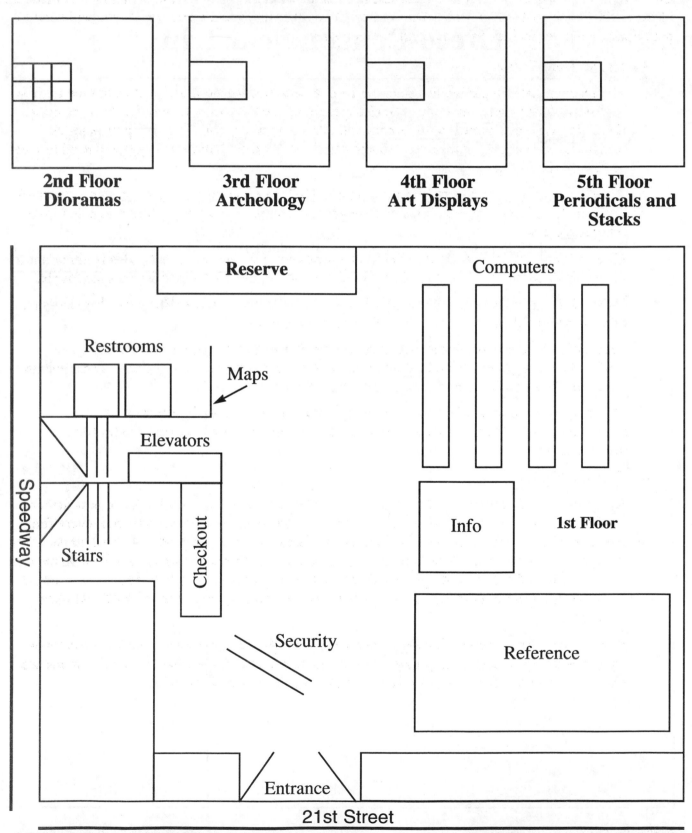

**2nd Floor
Dioramas**

**3rd Floor
Archeology**

**4th Floor
Art Displays**

**5th Floor
Periodicals and
Stacks**

21st Street

Teaming *(cont.)*

VIII. Other Types of Teams

The regular team which we have been discussing is called a core academic team, meaning it is made up of the basic subjects which all students must take. Two other important teams which you will need to participate in are vertical teams and departmental teams.

A. Department Teams

The teachers in your particular discipline form a department who must meet from time to time to discuss departmental matters. The chairperson of each department will decide on meeting times, location, and agenda with teacher and administrative input. The chairperson might designate formal or informal structure and roles. At the most basic level, you will need to meet to discuss the following items:

Funding: Many departments fund themselves. Under site based management, this is required. Teachers have input into what kinds of things they want in classrooms—books, supplies, and other resources.

Curriculum: Departments need to line their curriculum just like the teams. This is important to prevent redundancy and to let teachers know what the students have previously been taught.

Policy: It is a good idea to formulate policies which bind the entire department. For example, uniform rules for the computer lab make a more efficient lab.

Upcoming Events: Important announcements are disseminated through these meetings— conferences, computer workshops, and other opportunities valuable to teachers. Other events might be class-related, like plays to which other teachers are invited.

Miscellaneous Matters: Many other matters should be brought to the attention of the department, like administrative decisions, teacher announcements, contests, community resources, etc.

B. Vertical Teams

A vertical team is composed of teachers in separate grade levels, regardless of subject matter. For instance, vertical teams composed of 6th, 7th, and 8th grade teachers can meet every four weeks to discuss curriculum and to share ideas. Thus, they become more informed on the other grade levels. Multi-grade level activities are encouraged. Mentor programs can be instituted, in which responsible 7th and 8th graders share quality time with 6th graders. In general, vertical teams tie the loose ends of school-wide curriculum to create a more united school and more effective faculty.

By opening the communication lines between grades, the school is empowered to create even more relevance and meaning. Taking vertical teams one step further, some school systems are organizing vertical teams of elementary, middle, and high school teachers.

The Counselor and Other Support Services

Outline of Chapter 8

I. The Many Roles of the Counselor

    A. Administrative

    B. Counseling

    C. Evaluating

    D. Special Support Programs

    E. Career Advocacy

II. The Counselor's Staff

    A. Grade Reports

    B. Progress Reports

III. Outside Support

    A. Educational Psychologists

    B. Other Professionals

    C. Independent Diagnostic/Tutorial Centers

IV. Special Education Staff

    A. Background

    B. Special Education Classrooms

    C. Tutoring Centers

    D. Other-Language Teachers

    E. Gifted and Talented

V. The School Library

    A. Effective Use of the Library

    B. Managing Library Privileges

VI. The School Nurse

Reproducibles for Chapter 8 (See pages 274–280.)

1. *Counselor Referral Form*

2. *College Plans Form*

3. *Grade Change Form*

4. *Progress Report Form*

5. *Tutoring Center Matrix*

6. *Library Rules Poster*

7. *Library Passes*

The Counselor and Other Support Services *(cont.)*

I. The Many Roles of the Counselor

A. Administrative

The counselor is an important member of the school team who can make life easier for teachers. Counselors are usually intelligent, caring people in touch with the feelings and dynamics of school children. You might think their main task is counseling, but they are often required to be administrators. Many schools have given counselors responsibilities in the areas of planning and administration. The two most important administrative tasks for some counselors are scheduling and reporting grades. It is important to understand how this is done.

Scheduling

In the past, scheduling was easier, conforming to the old factory model of efficiency. However, since scheduling now is seen as a process involving teams, heterogeneity, and other complex factors, many schools think the counselors are best suited to provide optimum schedules for individual students.

Each state has different admission procedures. The concept of school "choice" is changing many district enrollment procedures, as well as the schools themselves. For instance, areas like Cambridge, Massachusetts, allow all students to pick their own schools. Minnesota has gone further with their "open choice" system, leading the country in innovative enrollment procedures. In many Midwest states, as in Texas, rigid boundaries enforce strict attendance laws. If you live in a certain area, you are required to attend a certain school. Other states have mixed procedures, but school choice is becoming popular.

Other factors to affect scheduling criteria are districting and desegregation. In the 1980s schools were required by federal law to bus many parts of a city to other parts to integrate schools racially. These cut-up districts have changed, especially in elementary schools, where community schools are seen as more beneficial. But in middle school and high school, ethnic districting still prevails.

Still other considerations that the counselors must contend with to create master schedules are the following:

- Students may be teamed, having the same core group of teachers.
- Classes must contain gender balance.
- Some classes are based on academic ability (honors class).
- Classes need to be as racially heterogeneous as possible.
- Applications for admission must be answered.
- Students who move into the district must be added.
- Immunization records must be completed for admission.

The Counselor and Other Support Services *(cont.)*

Scheduling (cont.)

To add to this list, one important feature that complicates scheduling is teacher-student ratio. Many states are serious about keeping this ratio low to provide more individual learning opportunities. Also, professional organizations and advocacy groups lobby intensely for this ratio to be as low as possible. The counselors must conform to state law on this matter.

The master schedule is simply a high powered spreadsheet, able to sort, calculate, and re-sort millions of bits of information. This software is one of the biggest applications in technology that your school possesses.

All in all, counselors will probably tell you that scheduling is their biggest headache. Many times, teachers may not get their class rosters until the first day of school. But if you ever have any scheduling problems, counselors will be glad to help you.

Reporting Grades

The other major administrative function that has fallen into the counselor's lap is reporting grades. This is a major undertaking done on the same spreadsheets that produce the schedules. Most schools give out bubble sheets for the teachers to fill out at every grading period. These sheets are then read by computers and entered appropriately, although they can be typed in by hand for special circumstances.

The counselors' main job is to see to the well-being of the children, so grades are an important feature which the counselor reviews and stores. If parents are concerned about a grade, counselors are often the first to hear. Counselors keep extensive records of all grades, test scores, and other evaluative materials.

B. Counseling

The original task of a counselor remains the most important: caring for the mental health and well-being of the children. This process involves group or direct one-on-one discussions, leading to solutions and plans for improvement.

Following are reasons students may need to see the counselor:

Emotional Distress

In middle school, students may suffer bouts of anxiety, mood swings, feelings of loneliness, anger, and other psychological maladies that result from children becoming adults. Many times, students are unable to talk to their parents, especially about serious matters like drugs or sex. The counselor offers a non-threatening area where students can confide in someone without being judged or reprimanded. Expressing feelings and discussing options can be a welcome outlet for confused emotions. Counselors are trained in psychological techniques and methods of reducing mental stress.

The Counselor and Other Support Services *(cont.)*

Behavioral Problems

Many times, teachers will rely on the counselor to help in a behavioral matter. Counselors might be able to get to the core of the problem. Students might be willing to open up to a counselor and reveal family problems or peer problems that are affecting the student's behavior. At the very least, the counselor is able to suggest programs or other referrals that might help the student.

Sending students to the counselor for behavioral therapy is considered these days more productive and healthy than sending them to the principal's office.

Academic Problems

Grades are important to parents, students, and teachers, so counselors try to direct the student into productive channels where grades can be raised. Working with all parties, counselors can often help improve performance. Frequently a counselor can be a source of learning activities and ideas. Most of them have been classroom teachers and still understand the classroom experience.

Participation in Special Programs

Sometimes students will need to leave class to attend a special counseling program. Depending on the school, there are a large variety of special programs for youth. Such programs are designed for the students' health, a number one priority. They may even help raise academic performance in your class.

Method of Counseling

How do counselors "counsel"? Most of them agree that the main goal is for students to understand themselves and empower themselves to make positive change. Some counselors have a natural gift for bringing this about, and all have had years of study and training. Their background involves familiarity and knowledge of the psychological contributions of major figures like Freud, Pavlov, Watson, Skinner, Piaget, Maslow, Carl Rogers, and Howard Gardner.

Human Effectiveness

In most schools throughout the country, counselors approach student sessions with the following intentions:

1. To assist students in vocational and educational planning
2. To motivate pupils to seek counseling when needed
3. To enable pupils to learn how to make positive change
4. To help students achieve self-awareness and understanding
5. To enable students to become more effective people

The Counselor and Other Support Services *(cont.)*

Human Effectiveness (cont.)

Counselors teach human effectiveness, identifying five levels.

Level 1—*Panic:* Some students react in panic to threatening situations. A common panic scene in a middle school classroom is a student frozen in terror to get up and speak in front of peers.

Level 2—*Inertia:* Students in the inertia stage are only partially effective. They are very apprehensive about trying anything new.

Level 3—*Coping:* At level 3, a student will get up and make that speech, having learned to cope with fears and be adequately effective.

Level 4—*Striving:* After learning to cope with anxieties, students strive to go beyond average performance. The speech now involves poster boards with visual aids and extra-credit materials. At this level, the student is excited about the speech and showing off talent and hard work.

Level 5—*Mastery:* Mastery over self and ability to influence others is the key to effectiveness. This student will go beyond the speech, using the principles of the assignment to engage more than just the class.

Background of Psychological Counseling

Trends in the psychological field have been changing and developing since Freud's first ground-breaking efforts in the late 19th century. Among other things, Freud asserted that people's actions can be related strongly to previous experiences, especially at infancy. Many of his specifics are seen as defunct today, especially since most of his patients were very ill. However, his broad concepts of the unconscious mind and dream analysis are valued by many.

Taking a more rigid scientific approach, B. F. Skinner developed his form of behaviorism, modifying work done by Pavlov and Watson. Based on stimulus-reaction, Skinner's theories hold many truths about external motivation. For instance, have you ever used an enticing food item to motivate a child? If so, you have used behavioral psychology. Many educators see Skinner's principles as limited because of their emphasis on external motivation.

Among the most influential developments have been Piaget's developmental psychology theories, which have powerful implications for teachers. Originally a biologist, Piaget chronicled how children learn by watching his own offspring grow. In this way, Piaget is seen as a seminal leader in developmental psychology, explaining how humans process, remember, and retrieve information.

A strong set of ideas in the past 30 years has been the "human potential" theory, led by Abraham Maslow and Carl Rogers. Closely aligned with this school of thought, Howard Gardner's multi-intelligence theories are making an impact on educational practice.

The Counselor and Other Support Services *(cont.)*

C. Evaluating

Another role the counseling office frequently plays is test giver. Every state mandates that standardized tests be given to their students. This acts as a yardstick for their own educational system. If test scores are high, the state can brag that its inhabitants are exceptionally intelligent and their schools are exceptionally qualified. In addition, the state can receive federal dollars for special innovative programs. These bragging rights and fund allocations make standardized tests a serious business. Each state assigns an entire office staff (measurement and evaluation) to develop tests, formulate policy, and determine testing procedures. It is usually the counseling office which acts as the charge d'affaires of state test administration.

A standardized test may not be the most valid form of measuring student learning. However, the advantage of these tests is that they yield real numbers that can be calculated, sorted, and compared. Many times, students are judged solely on these numbers. Many voices criticize this type of measure, but until we can agree on something better, these tests are here to stay. Educators do realize that test scores are only one factor in approaching the whole student. But since much of the world is based on such tests (SAT, bar exams, teacher competency tests, etc.), it is only responsible to prepare students for these occasions.

The counselor's job is to administer the tests as a school-wide affair. Because some middle schools have more than 1,000 students, the job can be particularly complex. Basically, the counselor delegates the testing procedures to the teachers, entrusting them to give exact instructions. However, it is not that easy. Special considerations have to be made. Other-language instructions, special needs students testing, and a host of other variables make overseeing standardized testing difficult. In addition, if any teacher errs seriously, the whole school can be sanctioned.

D. Special Support Programs

Along with giving state tests, counseling, and formulating scheduling and grade reports, the counselor also plays the role of support program coordinator. Such programs are called "outreach" programs when coming from local universities or civic groups. Their main goal is to help certain students by group counseling. Varying tremendously across the nation, some types of support programs are the following:

Mentor/Buddy

Mentor programs are used to pair students. One student acts as a mentor, and the other acts as the mentor's buddy. Used for at-risk students especially, this program gets results. Sharing time with an older, caring person can make a tremendous difference in some lives. The biggest program of its kind, Big Brothers/Big Sisters of America, relies on local volunteers to help.

The Counselor and Other Support Services *(cont.)*

Emotional Needs

Many counselors create a special staff or bring in experts to help children deal with different emotional problems. For instance, "Anger Management" programs help students prone to get frustrated easily and take it out on others. Also, a range of programs for shy students, emotionally disturbed, and other emotionally needy students has been developed. The focus of these groups is support and understanding. It is easier to fight battles together than alone.

Special Populations

Counselors often encourage special groups, like minorities or females, to join programs for enrichment. Historically, minorities and females have not been encouraged to be successful, consequently developing low self-esteem. Programs like "Hispanics Tomorrow," "Successful Women," and "African-American Alliance" give these students support and information to raise their awareness of their own potential. Programs like these frequently involve field trips, guest speakers and other activities.

Leadership Teams

Many counselors have developed programs for eager and outgoing students. Those who show a high aptitude for responsible leadership are grouped and given various tasks. Being mentors, tutoring, improving the campus, and helping others through modeling and doing are the main goals of these programs.

Many counselors have found that by putting at-risk students into leadership positions, attitudes and work quality improve.

E. Career Advocacy

Traditionally, the middle school has been thought of as the time when counselors should ready students for high school and deal with their emotional needs. This set of values is being reexamined. The idea that students should be thinking of careers as early as middle school has led many counselors to form career-related programs and activities. Counselors do many things to help this process. Bringing in university staff and career speakers is a popular procedure. Representatives from the military, local business persons, and other careers, professions, and trades are powerful helps in this procedure.

College choices is another important field. Familiarizing students with colleges and collegiate procedures across the country can never be done too early. It is generally understood that children who can visualize themselves in college are the ones who naturally go on to higher learning. Use your College Plans form (page 275) to help students think about their future plans.

An effective way to help students visualize going to college is by administering the classroom activity "When I Go to College . . ." which appears on the next page.

The Counselor and Other Support Services *(cont.)*

"When I Go to College . . ."

In this exercise, you can help students start or continue to reflect on their collegiate future. Try to coordinate this activity with the counselor present or as part of an ongoing career unit. Follow this easy procedure:

Materials

- College Plans worksheets (page 275)
- construction paper (all colors), glue, tape, and scissors
- college brochures, banners, or any other materials which portray university logos

Gather Information

Discussion: Provide a background for this exercise by asking students what they know about college. You might want to talk about your experience of going to college. Try to show them all the possible majors, subjects, and schools there are. Explain the differences between a big university and a small college. Ask the students how many colleges they can name. You will receive a lot of football team associations, but work with that enthusiasm.

You might want to stimulate enthusiasm by showing a video about college or part of a movie where college is the focus. You will find that students know very little about the realities of higher education.

Listing: Next, list all the general majors one can follow in college and briefly explain what they involve. Since there are many majors, it might take you a while to explain all. Do not be afraid to use one or even two class periods to give students an overview of their potential future. You may use the partial listing on the following page as a model.

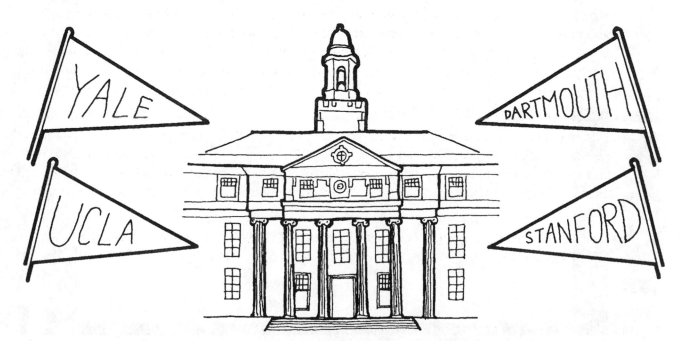

The Counselor and Other Support Services *(cont.)*

Major Fields of Study in College

Liberal Arts
English
history
political science
government
economics
philosophy
anthropology
archaeology
linguistics
foreign languages
geography
humanities
Latin American studies
sociology
religious studies
classics—Greek/Latin,
  mythology

Sciences
biology
chemistry
geology
astronomy
botany
oceanography
mathematics
physics
zoology

Communications
speech
radio/TV/film
advertising
journalism

Fine Arts
art
music
theater
dance

Professional Schools
Nursing
Pharmacy
Social Work
Computer Sciences
Architecture
Education
Engineering
Kinesiology (sports)

Post Graduate
Law
Medicine
Masters
Doctorate

The Counselor and Other Support Services *(cont.)*

Next, have students fill out their prospective majors and minors, using their College Plan forms. If they already know what college they want to go to and the mascot, colors, or symbol for that college, have them write that down as well. It is a good idea to discuss and bring into their vocabulary the following concepts: *tuition, scholarship, grant,* and *financial aid/loan.*

Construct

After gathering the information, the fun begins. Have students begin constructing their college banners. They should contain the school colors and be triangular. There are many ways to make these. Cutting and pasting letter shapes, logos, designs, and mascots onto the banners is the general idea. To better manage this portion, assign students in groups to share the resources.

Make sure each name and major is on the owner's banner.

Display

After the students are finished, tape the banners to the walls or tie string across the room and hang them. When finished, you should have a very colorful classroom.

Extras

Bring in guest speakers like college students or celebrities who attended a local college. Field trips to local colleges and universities can be a learning experience for the students. Also, these facilities usually have large food service centers for lunch.

II. The Counselor's Staff

The counselors are not alone in the counseling division. There are other important persons—indispensable aides—in the office. These are the counselor's staff members. Sometimes they are actually more active in getting things done than the counselors. Depending on the size of the school, there can be 1–4 staff members. Teachers will usually deal with the counseling staff when submitting grade reports and progress reports.

A. Grade Reports

It is important to be very accurate and double check your numbers. The most efficient grading calculations can be done with computer grade books. Apart from regular A–F grades, there is also the "I" grade. "I" stands for incomplete. This grade is given typically when a student has a long absence. Also, this grade may be given in anticipation for late work. "I's" should be given very rarely. Moreover, you must change the "I" to a regular grade within a few weeks.

After you have turned in your grades, the staff will usually send them to be processed in the main computer. This will generate a list of grades for the entire school. You may receive proof sheets to compare with your grade book. If there are any changes to be made, fill out a change form and give it to the counseling staff.

The Counselor and Other Support Services *(cont.)*

B. Progress Reports

Many schools also send progress reports home. This is also done electronically and is handled the same way as grade reports. But instead of filling in numbers, teachers fill in the appropriate comments. Often, progress reports are meant to warn parents of impending doom. This is necessary because a student should never be failed without prior notification to parents.

Progress reports do not have to be negative. You might find positive comments such as these:

❑ good attendance   ❑ prompt

❑ courteous   ❑ effective study habits

❑ excellent achievement   ❑ attentive in class

❑ participated well in class   ❑ completes assignments well

❑ dependable   ❑ cooperative

Parents like to see these comments. Sending home positive remarks can go a long way to bringing parents into the learning process. If your school does not provide progress reports, you may want to send a progress report home on your own.

III. Outside Support

Your district may use other specialists to aid the counselor in diagnoses and treatment. Common outside experts are educational psychologists, behavioral therapists, and physical therapists.

A. Educational Psychologists

Educational psychologists usually hold doctorates in psychology, focusing on learning and development. Instead of practicing in an office or clinic, they are hired by school districts to go to various schools when needed. In some schools there is a waiting list just to see them. They act as scientists and doctors, giving expert analysis and suggestions for problem students.

The main job of the psychologists is to diagnose learning disabilities like dyslexia, ADD, and general disabilities. A diagnosis might result in one of the following actions:

- change in classes
- medication
- referral to support services
- recommendations for teachers
- modifications for learning
- development or change in Individualized Education Plan

The Counselor and Other Support Services *(cont.)*

B. Other Professionals

Behavioral Therapists: Like the educational psychologists, behavioral therapists come to schools and work from the counselor's office. They are trained specifically in adolescent behavior and treatment. Their suggestions or work with the students can make a tremendous difference. Frequently they diagnose problems as well.

Behavioral therapists usually can make excellent recommendations concerning seating arrangements, discipline management, contract criteria, and group counseling.

Physical Therapists: These experts concentrate on students with physical ailments, handicaps, or general problems. For instance, you might have a student with a bone structure problem that makes it hard to write. The physical therapist can suggest how to teach that child to write differently. Other helpful advice may concern field trips, class activities, and simple matters like walking down the hall.

Speech Therapists: These professionals help students with speaking disorders. Through training and coaching, a speech therapist can make life much easier for a middle school student with a speech impediment.

C. Independent Diagnostic/Tutorial Centers

It is clear that many school systems are overburdened. Independent professional centers are places where parents can take their children for specialized one-on-one care. It is a good idea to make a list of the centers around your neighborhood so you can point these out to parents when appropriate.

The best way to find the centers around you is to ask a counselor or look in the yellow pages under "tutoring." You'll probably find a host of centers advertising the following skills and elements:

    . . . language and study skills!   . . . reading improvement!

    . . . individualized study skills!   . . . complete diagnostic testing!

    . . . regular and special needs students!   . . . building math skills!

Basically, these centers do two things which can greatly aid the classroom teacher: tutor and diagnose ability. Many centers are able to provide excellent tutoring opportunities by having one-on-one instruction. Professional tutors usually hold at least a bachelors degree in the subject which they are tutoring. They also can diagnose skills and abilities. A student reading well below grade level in your class can get strong support and build undeveloped skills with personal tutoring help on a regular basis. Your own teaching will be more effective with this kind of help.

Working closely with the private tutoring centers in your area can greatly help the success of your own students.

The Counselor and Other Support Services *(cont.)*

IV. Special Education Staff

A. Background

Over the last fifty years, the federal courts have been ruling for more inclusion and heterogeneity in classrooms. This means racial, ethnic, and socioeconomic factors, as well as students with learning disabilities. Public Law 94-142 states that all students, regardless of disability, have the right to be included in regular classrooms as much as possible. The reasoning is sound; how can we get all children to develop into productive citizens by isolating them? Including them in regular situations not only will give them opportunities to adjust and understand the real world but will also give other students an appreciation for diversity.

As more and more such students have entered the schools, a new teacher has appeared—the special education teacher. When it became clear that keeping special education students in regular classrooms all the time was not working, new systems were created. In these new systems, more special education teachers were needed until soon the special education department became an entity in itself. Today, most schools have an entire special education department, replete with teachers, assistants, secretaries, and specialists. In fact, the field is one of the fastest growing and most in demand.

B. Special Education Classrooms

For students who suffer from milder learning disabilities and medical disorders, a special classroom where they can be provided with more individual care is available. The types of students in these classrooms are varied and previously discussed in Chapter 3. Usually, the special education classroom tries to get students academically up to par so they can rejoin their peers in regular classrooms.

The dilemma that faces the special education teachers is to teach academics while instilling basic life and behavioral skills. Many times, students go to these classrooms only for a particular subject in which they are deficient. The regular and special education teachers need to work closely together to ensure consistency and development. It is a good idea to invite special education teachers to team meetings and to observe them in action.

A responsible move was made by Mr. Rockler, who invited the special education teacher, Mrs O'Brien, to a team meeting. After an initial discussion, Mrs. O'Brien offered many insights into some of the students who were enrolled in the team but came to her for certain subjects and special help. She was also able to supply some special materials appropriate for the teaching units. These materials enabled some of their special needs students to participate more fully in activities that had previously been out of reach for them. Also the team teachers were able to alert Mrs. O'Brien to some upcoming studies and activities which she could help them with.

The Counselor and Other Support Services *(cont.)*

C. Tutoring Centers

Many schools have been inspired to create special tutoring centers for students who need extra time and attention. These students must qualify for this care. Usually the system works on a walk-in basis. A teacher sees that an eligible student needs more practice on pronouns, so she sends him to the tutoring center for mastery of the material. In other words, this is not a classroom; it is a resource for teachers and students to gain mastery over material.

Many students like the tutoring center because of the individual attention. Sometimes, it can get so overcrowded that it becomes unmanageable. Use the tutoring center wisely and stay in touch with the director of the center. Working together can create quality learning.

D. Other-Language Teachers

Most schools in the nation contain teachers and classrooms where students can learn English as a second language (ESL). Spanish speakers comprise the largest population of these students. Other languages include Portuguese, Haitian, Vietnamese, Russian, and many more. Since America has an open door policy for immigrants, we receive people of all nations. Our responsibility to these newcomers is to educate them for the greater good of society.

To perform this task in most schools, teachers are staffed who are bilingual. Their main task is to teach English and other academic skills while providing a friendly introduction to a strange new land. Usually, bilingual teachers can prepare foreign students with sufficient English skills to integrate them into most classes within a year.

E. Gifted and Talented

Most states have a special designation for students who possess advanced thinking skills. Often referred to as gifted and talented, these programs go by various titles. Many districts require that teachers of these students have additional training in understanding the gifted child. Most teachers would agree that teaching these special students includes the following:

- giving more options
- going faster through material
- letting students explore their interests
- using cooperative learning
- accepting student input in curriculum development
- challenging students to go above and beyond the "call of duty"

V. The School Library

One of the greatest sources of support for any school is the library—certainly a treasure house of information and resources. However, there is a large measure of responsibility that accompanies the use of the library. Knowing how to effectively use the library and manage library privileges is essential for the classroom teacher.

The Counselor and Other Support Services *(cont.)*

A. Effective Use of the Library

Using the library effectively means knowing what is available, how to find materials, and how that can help your class.

Periodicals: All libraries have a periodical section, some more extensive than others. Many students enjoy flipping through interesting magazines like *Teen,* made specifically for young people. Low-level readers can build interest and motivation by reading magazines. Teach your students to use magazines for research by using the periodical index, a catalog of all the library's articles, organized by subject.

Book Selection: Fiction can be used for pleasure and class-related reading. Paperbacks are usually on the carousels, and hardbacks are usually on shelves, organized by author's last name.

Nonfiction includes biographies, histories, science, social issues, and other topics. Popular among middle schoolers are strange phenomena like UFO's, Bigfoot, and the Loch Ness Monster. Biographies help students identify with heroes as role models.

Reference books include encyclopedias, almanacs, atlases, and dictionaries. The underused almanacs and atlases are rich sources for research, providing statistics, facts, and visuals.

Whatever books your students look for, the most important thing is knowing how to find them. A card catalog is the usual system of book listings, although many libraries use computer catalogs as well. Be sure to teach your students the specifics of your library system. Remind students to take pencil and paper for writing specific catalog numbers and for notes.

Audio-Video: Usually available only for teacher checkout, audio and video tapes can be extremely beneficial. If you use books-on-tape for remedial work, remember to have the student(s) read along with the tape. Create exercises and activities to go with the tapes. Other audio tapes contain music with educational applications. Store this material in the learning center of your classroom. Let a student helper be the custodian of this equipment.

Video tapes can be strong learning tools to enrich class activities. Teachers can normally check out audio equipment, like tape players and headphones, for an extended period of time. Uses for the video camera are endless: taping presentations, making movies, taping mock commercials or newscasts, and making class records or video portfolios.

Computer/On-line: Many libraries now include computer services. Having whole reference shelves on one disc makes this particularly attractive. Along with CD-ROM encyclopedia, almanacs, and atlases, the computer in the library is also useful for on-line services. Talk to your librarian about this exciting privilege.

The Counselor and Other Support Services *(cont.)*

B. Managing Library Privileges

Going to the library is a privilege students must respect.

Teachers often wish to take a whole class into the library and also to let individuals go alone from time to time.

Library Rules: It is imperative that the teacher lay down a strict set of rules for students to follow. This will ensure productive habits in the library and build a positive working relationship with the librarian. For a list of five effective rules for the library, see Library Rules poster (page 279). If students break these rules, provide logical consequences like losing library or other privileges.

The main reason teachers take a whole class into the library is for research. You should arrange library time with your librarian ahead of time. When doing research, the librarian will probably request that your class stay in a particular area of the library. Another reason to take the whole class to the library is for a special presentation like a video or guest speaker. Still another reason for whole-class assembly is library "book fairs" where students are allowed to buy books, posters, and other educational items. When your classes return from a book fair, make certain that students mark their names in ink on front cover flaps.

Library Passes: If you choose to let students go individually to the library, provide a pass. Always follow up on student behavior in the library by chatting with the librarian from time to time. The best reasons for students to go the library are the following:

- earned reward
- specific purpose (researching the mountain lion)
- casual reading privileges
- quiet work, catch-up work

Keeping Tabs on Overdue Books: When students check out books, they are expected to take care of them and return them within the due date period. If they need a longer time for good reasons, they are often allowed to recheck the book, as long as it has not been requested by another student or teacher.

As a teacher you may need to help with the overdues and care of the library books. Middle schoolers in general are forgetful of due dates. An efficient way to handle this is to assign student helpers as "librarian aides." Their job is to collect overdue information and report it back to you. Keeping a running list of this information is recommended. Remind students that overdue books can cost them library privileges and fines.

If a book is reported lost or stolen, the responsible student must pay for the item. Contact parents so they can look for the book also. It might be in a locker, under a desk, or at home in the sometimes frightening adolescent closet. After a reasonable time the student should remit payment for any lost items.

The Counselor and Other Support Services *(cont.)*

VI. The School Nurse

The final support agency for the classroom teacher is the health unit. Your students' health care is addressed in Chapter 5, "Administering Health Care." The usual public school nurse generally services many schools in the district. Find out when your nurse is on the grounds so you can make proper referrals. Along with common ailments, the school nurse is usually responsible for the following:

- eye and ear testing
- administering medications
- scoliosis diagnosis
- treating serious illnesses or injuries
- referrals to other medical specialists
- general health care and information services

Your school nurse is most likely a loving, caring individual who likes working with children and improving health for all people. Many times, especially in urban districts, the nurse is also the director of a health center. Acting as a guide and specialist in areas such as drug abuse, teenage pregnancy, child abuse, and other maladies which can destroy families, they provide support and referral services to needy families.

Special Note on Child Abuse: **Suspected victims of child abuse must be reported by law.**

Teachers who ignore obvious examples of abuse can be prosecuted under federal law. The best way to approach this delicate matter is to refer the suspected abuse victim to the school nurse. Also, you should inform the school administration and counselors in writing. Of course, never talk about your concerns to other students. Under certain circumstances, you might want to talk to the suspected abuse victim first. Without being obvious, you can tell much from the answers to simple, indirect questions.

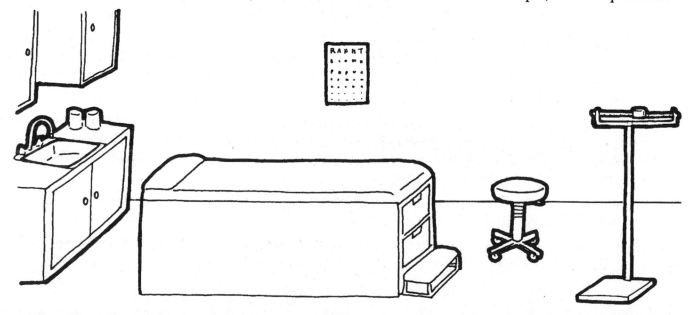

Campus Administration

Outline of Chapter 9

I. Organization of a Typical Middle School Campus

II. New Paradigms of Power: Site Based Management (SBM)
    A. Campus Leadership Committee
    B. Tasks of the Leadership Committee

III. The Principal

IV. The Vice Principals
    A. Discipline
    B. Administrative Responsibilities

V. The Office Staff
    A. Attendance
    B. Student Records
    C. Supplies
    D. Communication Services

VI. Custodial Staff/Food Services
    A. Custodians
    B. Building Personnel
    C. Food Services

VII. Receiving an Observation/Appraisal

Reproducibles for Chapter 9 (See pages 281–286.)

1. *Memo to the Principal Form*
2. *Memo to the Vice Principal Form*
3. *Attendance Change Form*
4. *Supplies Order Form*
5. *School Fax Form*
6. *Furniture Request/Equipment Repair Form*

I. Organization of a Typical Middle School Campus

In today's educational paradigm, the individual campus is going through many changes. In many ways these changes deal with the fundamental way we see education operating. Although the actual structure of the campus administration may have remained unchanged, the philosophy and style have not.

On the following page is a diagram of the organization of a typical middle school in the United States. Notice that the faculty interacts with all parts of the school, from the principal to the students to the janitorial staff. The teacher is the connection that makes everything happen in the school. On any given day, the average classroom teacher will interact with students, principals, counselors, food service, building staff, office staff, and parents. The teacher is the vital cog in the wheel of education.

Also important to note is the chain of command. Under site-based management, the principal shares decision-making with a leadership council but is still technically the site supervisor.

Organization of a Typical Middle School Campus

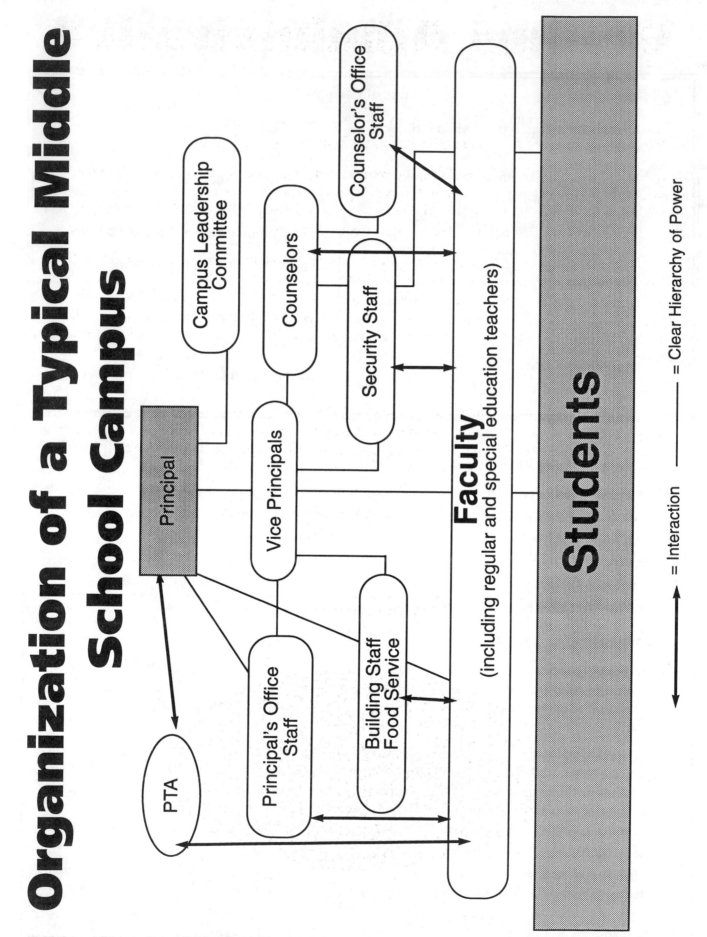

Campus Administration

(cont.)

II. New Paradigms of Power: Site-Based Management (SBM)

The concept of site-based management shifts power from the top levels (state and district) to the campus itself. The reasoning is that only the specific campus knows its real needs. Closely aligned with this power shift is the practice of participatory decision making. Shared decision making brings in the teachers, parents, and community leaders who have a direct stake in the decisions being made.

Usually, school districts and states follow a model that has worked somewhere else. The first school system to implement site-based management on a district-wide scale was Dade County, Florida, in the late 1980s. One of the biggest ethnically diverse school districts in the country, Dade County set a standard which most campuses employ today—a management committee composed of many different people who have a direct stake in the campus. We will refer to this committee as the campus leadership committee.

A. Campus Leadership Committee

Also called "steering committees," "cadres," "SBM teams," "campus improvement councils," and other local variations, this committee is the main vehicle for the implementation of site-based management. These teams usually contain a wide-ranging representation of the school and community, like the following:

- the principal
- other administrators
- teachers
- parents
- other building staff
- community leaders
- students

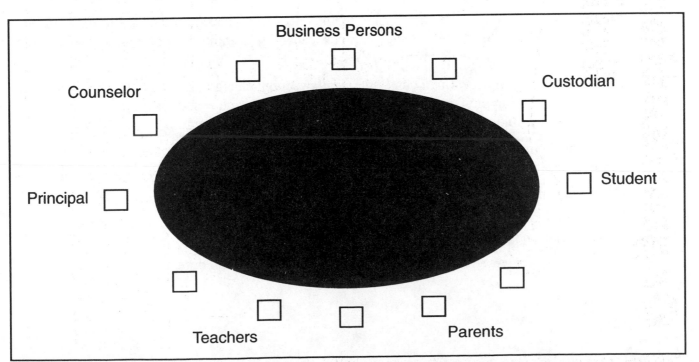

Campus Administration

(cont.)

B. Tasks of the Leadership Committee

The tasks of the leadership committee are usually divided among three major categories: budget, staffing, and curriculum.

Budget: Members must decide how to spend their funds. The district and state give each school a budget based on average daily attendance and other special factors. Under SBM, the campus receives funding to be allocated as they see fit. The biggest expense is salaries of faculty and staff, which are not set by the committee. Other budgetary concerns are these:

- technologies—computers, software, laser discs, audio-video
- professional development—consultants, instructional materials
- office equipment—copiers, paper, supplies, etc.
- teaching supplies—construction paper, pens, tape, glue, etc.
- classroom equipment—furniture, overheads, boards, chairs, etc.
- special projects/promotions
- emergency fund

Staffing: When hired, you probably were interviewed by the principal, who made the recommendation for your employment. This process is changing. Many SBM schools are letting the leadership councils conduct interviews and make recommendations. The theory is that the ones closest to the classrooms, mainly teachers, know how to judge potential teachers.

Staffing decisions also occur when positions are shuffled to meet the needs of the campus. For instance, at Pine Oaks, the leadership council looked at the staffing report and found they could eliminate two cafeteria monitor positions and hire another teacher for the tutoring center.

The hardest staffing task for a leadership team is deciding which positions to eliminate in the event of a budget crunch. However, a campus leadership committee is more likely to be a fair judge of staffing needs than any single individual.

Curriculum: A campus council can implement sweeping changes in a school. The two most popular are teaming the faculty and block scheduling. We addressed teaming in Chapter 7. One successful schedule using the block concept is on the following page.

Notice how simple it can be to switch the old schedule, which was formulated in the 19th century, to a block schedule. The eight periods are still there; they are just twice as long.

Other curriculum matters for the council might be these:

- reading lists
- school-wide units
- student-centered programs
- interdisciplinary units
- special presentations
- disciplinary procedures

Block Scheduling—Four 90-Minute Periods Per Day

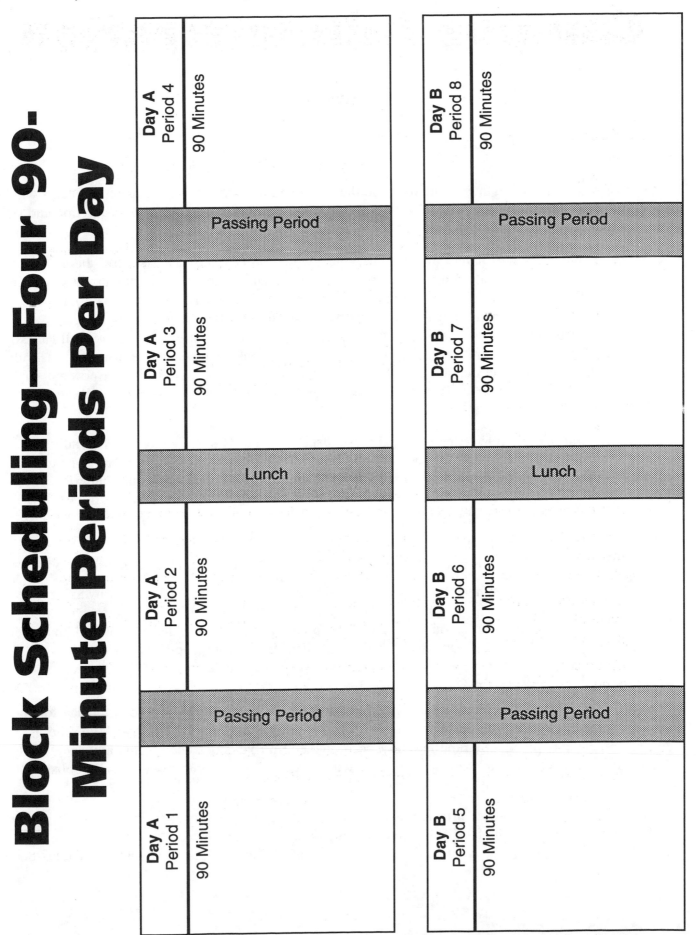

Day A Period 1 90 Minutes	Passing Period	Day A Period 2 90 Minutes	Lunch	Day A Period 3 90 Minutes	Passing Period	Day A Period 4 90 Minutes

Day B Period 5 90 Minutes	Passing Period	Day B Period 6 90 Minutes	Lunch	Day B Period 7 90 Minutes	Passing Period	Day B Period 8 90 Minutes

Campus Administration

(cont.)

III. The Principal

Traditionally the monarch of the school, the principal's role is changing. As leadership committees take much work off their hands, principals find they are freed from many management problems which limit their effectiveness. Principals of today are more likely to spend time planning instruction and professional development.

However, the principal is still very much an individual who can make or break a school. In the past, it was thought that the principal should mainly be an efficient manager and should "run a tight ship." In matters of discipline, the principal would have final say, acting like a sheriff in a lawless frontier community. In addition, the principal would supervise the building staff, inspect work by the custodians, and be available for district or state personnel. Encouraging attendance at football games and building school spirit were also important jobs of the principal. In essence, the principal was truly the "Moses" of the school community, the law giver who communicates with the higher powers. In this old paradigm, the teachers were given their textbooks and basal readers and expected to follow instructions.

Today, it is clear that the role of the principal must adapt to the needs of a society which is falling behind in academic and life skills. Especially at a time when more powers than ever are given to the principal under SBM, a fresh outlook is needed. Phil Schlechty, the President of the Center for Leadership in School Reform, thinks that the principal's role is not that of monarch, but one of colleague and facilitator. He opines,

> *And if teachers are leaders, then the principal is the leader of leaders. I don't consider the principal as instructional leader; instead, I see the principal as leader of instructors.*

Teachers will need to communicate with the principal often. The best way to do this is by using your Memo to the Principal form (page 281). On the form indicate whether you need a response or are simply writing to supply information. You should keep your principal up to date on curriculum matters, ideas for campus improvement, samples of student excellence, and emergency matters.

IV. The Vice Principals

The vice principals, also called assistant principals, are usually involved much more in the day-to-day operations than the principals, and they wield substantial power on a campus. In large high schools, vice principals may practically run the school because the principal is detached from daily operations. This relationship is similar to the aloof professor who concerns himself with research and publishing and lets the teaching assistant run the course.

Acting in the capacity of a vice principal is not an easy task. Their concern is mainly that of discipline. In this way, they act like chiefs of police, maintaining order and peace in society. Along with discipline, however, they also concern themselves with many other administrative matters, like textbook distribution.

Campus Administration

(cont.)

A. Discipline

The following account of a typical day in the life of a vice principal, although fictional, is quite realistic.

✉ A Day in the Life of Mr. Marquez ✉

It is 8:05 AM at Pine Oaks Middle School, and already Mr. Marquez, the vice principal, has a minor crisis. Two girls were fighting on school grounds. Now, they are waiting in the vice principal's office. After Mr. Marquez documents their stories, assigns appropriate consequences, calls their parents, and makes other necessary arrangements, it is 8:41 AM.

Two boys are waiting to see Mr. Marquez with referrals. On the walkie-talkie, a hall monitor reports a student cutting class, apprehends the suspect, and brings him into the office. At 9:12 AM Mr. Marquez finally has time to check his box. It is loaded with paperwork and referrals.

At 9:26, a pair of students are brought in for writing on bathroom walls. A check of the records indicates these students have a long history of misbehavior. What should Mr. Marquez do with them now? A stern warning and a day of in-school suspension will not make a difference. Suddenly, a fire alarm goes off; the whole school must evacuate the building immediately. At 10:35 AM, it is found that a student has tripped the alarm as a joke.

At 11:20 AM, Mr. Marquez starts his daily rounds supervising lunch periods. Taking names, giving warnings, stopping mid-air food missiles, and directing outside recess activities is normal for this part of his day.

By 12:45 PM, Mr. Marquez sees five more students lined up by his office with referrals. AT 1:45 PM, he meets with a team of teachers. By 2:45, he sees more referrals. At 3:05, an administrator's meeting is called. It is 3:25, and Mr. Marquez must get ready to supervise loading and transportation of over 1,000 students.

At 3:45, he can't rest because several teachers want to talk about a particularly offensive student; it seems that "nothing is being done about him." At 4:30, Mr. Marquez starts planning for the next day, and by 5:15, he is out of the office. Leaving, he feels like a rat jumping off a sinking ship; maybe tomorrow will be better.

As this fictional account of the day in the life of Mr. Marquez illustrates, the vice principal's role is one of putting out grass fires all day. The hectic schedule is usually tolerated because vice principals hope to move into a higher position in the district. Very few vice principals "love" their jobs.

Campus Administration

(cont.)

Corrective Discipline

Vice principals must administer justice on a daily basis. Usually, the cause for the action is a disruptive student. Five common consequences the assistant principals prescribe are the following:

Warning/Mediator: Used for a first time offense to explain exactly why behavior was unacceptable.

Detention: Used for many common discipline problems. Detention is given commonly after school, although some schools use a "Saturday School" technique where tutoring is also available.

In-School Suspension (ISS): Used for more serious offense or repeat offense. ISS assignments are usually for a day or two, but not longer than three days.

Home Suspension: Used for very serious offenses, like fighting.

Expulsion/Assignment to Alternative Learning Setting: The most extreme measure to correct behavior, students are taken out of school and placed in "alternative schools" for a lengthly period of time, usually six months. Given for drug/weapons possession or extreme violence.

Other: Many schools are trying new approaches to solving misbehavior. In a process known as "shadowing," schools bring in students' parents to follow them around for a day. In general, schools are trying to activate the parents to help control student behavior.

Preventive Discipline

Monitoring: The vice principals make the rounds during passing periods and lunch times to monitor and correct misbehavior.

Security Staff: Under the vice principal, a security staff is usually hired, consisting of hall monitors and/or school police staff.

School Rules: Most schools have strict rules regarding behavior, dress codes, language, and other activities that aim at halting poor behavioral patterns before they start.

Parent Communications: Most schools institute regular parent orientation meetings concerning student behavior, requesting parent support and cooperation in making and enforcing standards for the school campus.

Community Involvement: Many schools participate in district-wide councils whose responsibility is to maintain community newsletters and awareness of ongoing programs aimed at forming positive behavior standards.

Campus Administration

(cont.)

B. Administrative Responsibilities

In addition to discipline, the assistant principals are involved in a host of administrative responsibilities. These commonly include:

- textbook accounting
- building security
- building maintenance
- teacher complaints
- coordinating athletics
- master activities schedule
- supply coordination
- scheduling
- teacher absence/substitutes
- emergency drills
- club organizations
- bus and field trip arrangements
- any other duty assigned by the principal
- supervision of special events—dances, sports, etc.

You will want to keep the vice principals apprised of all major discipline matters. Use your Memo to the Vice Principal (page 282) for effective communication. When planning extra-curricular activities, check with the vice principal first.

In summary, a good vice principal is a powerful force for good on a campus. This person will be omnipresent and energetic, shouldering all responsibilities delegated by the principal. It is a demanding job, entailing all the responsibilities of a principal but lacking that person's ultimate authority. It serves as a genuine trial by fire for the candidate in training to become a school principal.

V. The Office Staff

The staff working in the main office is composed of the office manager and two to five clerks. These professionals ensure that the vital task of running the school is done smoothly. They must be accurate and well versed in office duties. Teachers need to interact with the office staff in attendance, student records, supplies, and communication services.

A. Attendance

Attendance accounting is taken in most schools daily. Most likely, one of the clerks in the office specializes in attendance. The vital nature of accurate attendance accounting is addressed in Chapter 5. The main reason you will deal with the attendance clerk is to change the attendance marking. Use your Attendance Change Form (page 283), if your school does not provide a form.

Many attendance offices communicate directly with parents about absentees and truants. It is most important for community relations that their information be accurate, as one might imagine.

Few events can be more embarrassing to a school than communicating to a family that their child is absent when, in fact, the student is in class. The school appears both negligent and incompetent while simultaneously causing worry and distress to parents.

Campus Administration

(cont.)

B. Student Records

There will be many occasions when you need access to student records to find a home phone number or determine a student's schedule. These records are generally kept on file in the main office where a clerk will help you find them. Many schools are using computers to file this information. On student records, you will probably find the following items:

- name of student
- home address
- work phones
- name of family physician

- name of parents
- home phone
- work addresses
- other personal information (immunization record, health documentation)

In addition to these records, a master schedule of every student is also available. Used by the clerks regularly to locate students for appointments, office summons, special circumstances, or emergencies, this master schedule will tell you where any given student is at any given time. You might need this information for finding certain students. It is important to apprise the office staff of all extra-classroom situations, like "class outside," or team assemblies. Otherwise, the office will assume you are in your room, and an embarrassing situation might ensue.

C. Supplies

Usually, the office manager is responsible for ordering and disseminating teaching supplies. There should be no excuse for you not to be well provisioned as a teacher. Supplies found in the supply room are usually the following:

- chalk
- pencils/pens
- tape
- scissors
- special media supplies (video tapes, audio tapes, computer discs)

- transparencies/pens
- staples
- paper
- art supplies

Put orders for supplies in writing. It is unprofessional to bother the office manager with oral requests. Use your Supplies Order Form (page 284) to make your requests.

D. Communication Services

During the year, you will need to make use of basic communication tools, like stamping letters or sending a fax. In most schools, stamps for official school business are provided for the teacher at no cost. In addition, most school districts provide an interschool mail system to transfer messages. The envelopes are available through the main office.

A facsimile, popularly known as a "fax," is a copy of a document that can be sent over phone lines. The difference between a fax machine and a mail carrier is like the difference between a jet airliner and a wagon train.

Campus Administration

(cont.)

IV. Custodial Staff/Food Services

Other staff in the building are the custodians, building personnel, and food service workers.

A. Custodians

Schools usually employ a head custodian who manages quite a large custodial staff. In some large inner-city schools, there might upwards of 15 custodians. Specifically, they are responsible for the following maintenance:

- floors
- cafeteria
- classrooms and offices (trash, blackboards, and floors)
- bathrooms
- grounds

It is important to develop a good working relationship with the custodial staff. These workers are hard working individuals in the school, and they receive little thanks. Most teachers come into a clean classroom every day, owing to the diligence of these workers.

On the other hand, if custodians are not doing their job in your classroom, confront them personally and ask why. If you get an unsatisfactory response, alert the head custodian, who will most likely solve the problem.

In general, custodians are hard working individuals who take pride in their work. Some are so good at treating floors with waxes and buffing machines, they can practically turn the floor into a mirror. A clean school is a boon to the day-to-day work of the classroom teacher.

One way you can help the custodians is by expressing your appreciation through vocal comments, written communication, prizes, awards, gift certificates, etc. Have a drive to get all the teachers to pitch in a few dollars and buy the custodians presents or certificates. This is a guaranteed way to improve job morale and performance.

All teachers should follow the practice of having students clean up after themselves. Always allow a few minutes before class is over to check the classroom thoroughly. A teacher in middle school should dismiss the class one row or group at a time when all trash on the floor is picked up. An efficient method to do this is by getting the student helpers to inspect and approve rows or sections of the room.

It is most important to instill in students a habit of respect for custodians, as opposed to an attitude of regarding them as servants hired to clean up after students' litter. Self-respect and a decent regard for all persons in a school organization are strong elements in the development of good citizens. Students raised in this type of environment are not likely to become careless litterers, graffiti scrawlers, or destructive vandals.

Campus Administration

(cont.)

B. Building Personnel

Along with the custodians, there are specialists who operate the building. These workers are usually technicians trained in maintenance. There are also some floating specialists who service many schools on an as-needed basis. They are usually air conditioning repairmen, electricians, carpenters, painters, flooring personnel, and other technicians trained in upkeep.

Usually the building personnel double as furniture/equipment repairmen and movers. If you have a specific furniture or equipment-repair request, use your Furniture Request/Equipment Repair form (page 286).

C. Food Services

Other important people in the building are the food service personnel. If you eat in the cafeteria, then you know the value of these coworkers. Make sure your students respect them like all other adults, and be friendly with them yourself.

Another occasion for interacting with food service is planning field trips. Since many students eat reduced-priced lunches, planning a cafeteria lunch is necessary for them on field trips. Alert the food service manager of your field trip plans, and give him or her the names of students who eat reduced-priced lunches if that information is available to you. Also, the cafeteria food service personnel will fill your coolers with ice as necessary.

VII. Receiving an Observation/Appraisal

The final element of understanding your campus is realizing that your principal needs to have something on paper telling his superior that you are doing your job. This need has manifested itself in teacher observations, also called appraisals. This accountability system is seen as almost ludicrous to many educators. How can you base teachers' performance on seeing them for 45 minutes in a whole year? Teacher observation systems have come under full fire from many education professionals. A typical scene of teacher appraisal was humorously documented by two elementary teachers. They wrote the following:

On Monday morning, the principal enters your classroom and asks if Thursday is a good day to schedule your appraisal. "Sure! Thursday is fine," you answer.

On Tuesday, you frantically gather materials. Wednesday is spent reviewing those Madeline Hunter notes that you have had buried since your last evaluation. On Wednesday evening, a pit begins to form in your stomach. By the time Thursday rolls around, you're so nervous you can barely think clearly. Yet, once again, you pull it off. You breathe a sigh of relief and figure out when you will have to go through this again.

Campus Administration

(cont.)

Legitimately, educators are asking what impact, if any, is produced by this system. Many teachers get nervous, however, when new methods are suggested to evaluate teachers. A successful alternative to principal appraisals is peer appraisals, where a committee of teachers evaluates their own, based on democratically selected criteria.

For the most part, however, the traditional principal evaluations exist for better or worse. This system is important to understand because it hits at your number one priority—job security. In order to understand what you are being graded on, check with your principal to get a copy of your district's appraisal criteria. Most criteria are extremely specific. Here is an example of one small part of the Texas Teacher Appraisal System which is used statewide.

Presentation of Subject Matter
- ❏ uses effective communication skills
- ❏ makes no significant errors
- ❏ explains assignment clearly
- ❏ stresses important points/dimensions
- ❏ uses correct grammar
- ❏ uses accurate language

Learning Environment
- ❏ uses strategies to motivate student learning
- ❏ relates content to interests/experiences
- ❏ emphasizes value/importance of activity
- ❏ reinforces/praises efforts
- ❏ challenges students

Maintains Supportive Environment
- ❏ avoids sarcasm/negative criticism
- ❏ establishes climate of courtesy
- ❏ encourages slow/reluctant students
- ❏ establishes and maintains positive support

Professional Growth and Responsibilities
- ❏ plans for and engages in professional development
- ❏ progressive in growth requirements
- ❏ stays current in content taught
- ❏ stays current in instructional metholodology

You can see why most teachers are nervous about living up to such high standards when there are so many variables that can make a normal day of teaching completely unpredictable. Add to that the point of view of the appraiser. Some principals mold their own criteria, regardless of district or state guidelines. In one appraisal in a small town, a teacher who was administrating a cooperative learning activity was told by the principal that he would "come back when she taught a real lesson."

Understanding both the point of view of your appraiser and the criteria which you are theoretically graded on is the only balanced approach to getting a fair appraisal.

Districts, Regions, and States

Outline of Chapter 10

I. The Organization of Districts, Regions, and States

II. Districts

    A. Salaries and Other Payments

    B. Benefits

    C. Professional Development

III. Regions

IV. States

V. Federal Case Law Affecting Teachers

VI. Professional Organizations List

I. The Organization of Districts, Regions, and States

Your state is probably organized in the following fashion:

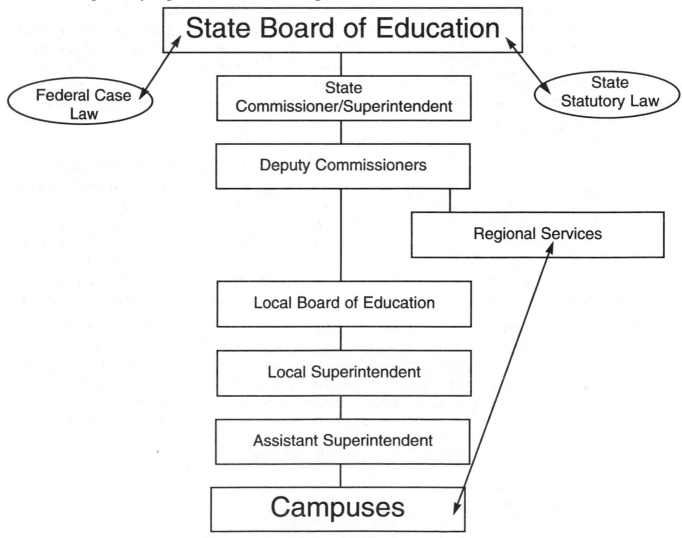

Districts, Regions, and States *(cont.)*

Although this diagram is overly simplified and many variations exist, it gives the average teacher a model to follow. Over all else is the ruling state board of education. These trustees are citizens elected by the people. They appoint a state superintendent, also called a state commissioner, to run the executive duties of the education office. The state commissioner's deputies control regions of the state. Each school district has a board of education that is elected by the people. Like the state board, they appoint an executive officer, also known as the district superintendent. The superintendent and his or her assistants administer the district campuses.

II. Districts

Your school and the others around you comprise a school district. Large metropolitan cities, like New York and Los Angeles, have one giant district that unifies all the small districts into one entity. However, other large cities, like San Antonio, choose to balkanize their districts into smaller, self-supporting units. The district has direct influence on the classroom teacher.

A. Salaries and Other Payments

The main influence your district has on you is your paycheck. Most districts in the nation have power of taxation and are labeled "independent school districts." These taxes on all citizens in the district go directly for educational purposes. The large majority goes for teacher salaries. Some districts can offer high salaries because they are wealthier than others. Your local board of education sets the salary schedules each year. Most salary schedules are based on the experience ladder, where each year of experience brings a higher salary. The district may also make arrangements for teacher retirement funds.

In addition to salaries, your school district makes other forms of payment, stipends, and reimbursements. A stipend is a sum of money which is paid for going above the required salary hours. For instance, most athletic coaches receive a flat salary with a coaching stipend tacked on. At Pine Oaks, the athletic coordinator, Coach Greenlawn, makes a salary of $28,500, as a six-year physical education teacher. Because he coordinates all the sports and coaches football, basketball, and track after school, the district pays Coach Greenlawn a stipend of $6,000, making his total yearly earnings $34,500. Stipends are also given for any extra-curricular activities where teachers are forced to work long after-school hours, like preparing a yearbook.

Districts have also been known to pay reimbursements for teacher participation in extra classroom activities. Such extra jobs as conducting workshops in the summer, working on district projects, and helping other schools are considered qualifiable for reimbursement. For example, Mrs. Clay gave a workshop in the summer on cooperative learning which paid her $500. It is widely recognized, nonetheless, that teachers do not receive adequate compensation for all the overtime work they put in. Sometimes this can be a source of frustration and disappointment.

Districts, Regions, and States

(cont.)

B. Benefits

Your district also handles your security benefits as well. Health care is usually provided at very reasonable rates to teachers. Child care, life insurance, and other benefits are available. In general, teachers are usually well taken care of. It is important to look over your benefits package in detail. Usually, districts allow many different options and choices for health coverage. Contact your district benefits office and arrange a meeting to go over these specifics.

C. Professional Development

Still another influence that a district has on its employees is professional development. Workshops and seminars are made available to teachers to improve their teaching techniques and also to establish contact and relations with other teachers and schools. The importance of professional development cannot be overstated. It is true that some workshops are poorly prepared, but for every one of those, there are three more that are useful for you as a teacher.

Commonly, professional development opportunities offer training or experience in these areas:

- new technologies—how to use different computer software and resources, like on-line systems

- pedagogical training—cooperative learning, writing instruction, developing interdisciplinary units, discipline management, teaching study skills

- child development education—information about how adolescents learn and develop

- teacher empowerment—how to become an effective communicator, how to be a leader

III. Regions

Larger states sectionalize themselves into regions to better serve their campuses. Regions are usually more of a service-oriented designation, rather than a governing structure. Regional service centers are fairly common. These service centers are places for supplies, media services, and other teaching resources. It is wise to make full use of the regional service centers.

Usually, the service center will have a check-out procedure like that of a library. The teacher simply fills out a request form and sends it through school mail. A day later the materials come with the date when the material is due. Common services from regional outlets are these:

- teaching supplies
- audio-video
- computer software/services
- books/manuals/guides

Districts, Regions, and States *(cont.)*

IV. States

The State Board of Education

Our United States Constitution never mentions education, so according to the 10th Amendment, the power of administering education is the responsibility of each state. The state board of education is elected to oversee the education in its own state. The characteristics of the board are the following:

- serves as policy-making body for public education
- appoints superintendent of education (Some states elect the superintendent.)
- holds meetings open to the public and reviews staff reports of work under way
- debates proposals for new programs and hears suggestions for improvement
- develops committees to formulate policy
- develops standards for teachers, certification
- approves textbooks for adoption

State Curriculum Requirements

The primary influence that a state has on a teacher is through its education guidelines. For instance, most states require that students learn the history, geography, culture, and literature of that state's past and present. States also contribute a large percentage of funds to run each campus.

Reciprocity

Because states develop their own unique standards for teacher certification, it is not easy to cross state lines and start teaching. However, each state has a system known as *teacher reciprocity*. This system allows for teachers who have recently come into the state to receive emergency certification while they take the courses which they lack.

State Law

State statutory law is also relevant to teachers. Although each state has different laws, a set of Federal statutory laws has been adopted by all states. The core of these laws follows:

- **Civil Rights Act of 1964**: prohibits discrimination on the basis of race, color, or creed on public property or private businesses.
- **Education Amendments of 1972**: prohibits discrimination in any school on the basis of race, color, national origin, religion, or sex.
- **Family Educational Rights and Privacy Act of 1972**: parents and students have a right to see student school records.
- **Public Law 94-142 (Handicapped Children Act of 1975)**: provides for a free education for all children, regardless of disability, and provides that each school create a individual education plan suited to each disabled child.

Districts, Regions, and States *(cont.)*

V. Federal Case Law Affecting Teachers

Although the highest authority of education rests with the state, there are constitutional matters which directly affect all teachers working in the United States. Case law is the ruling by judges which set standards and practices appropriate to the case which they rule upon. Federal case law is the highest law in the nation, equal to the Constitution in jurisdiction, and usually pronounced by the United States Supreme Court.

In Loco Parentis

This term is a Latin phrase meaning "in the place of the parents." This concept refers to the responsibility of the teachers. All teachers are expected to care for their students. This means you as a teacher are technically responsible for the well-being of all students while they are in your care. Any form of gross negligence, corruption, abuse, or other damaging action on your part is a violation of students' constitutional rights.

Students' Rights

Most courts have agreed with school officials regarding dress codes and behavior. However, students are free to express themselves symbolically with labels, buttons, arm bands, and T-shirts with signs and symbols. This freedom of expression is allowable only if no substantial disruption in the educational program is likely to be caused by wearing or displaying such items. In terms of written expression, most courts have sided with school officials who restricted certain offensive written articles or remarks. The reasoning is that the school newspaper or journal is not considered a "public forum" and can be restricted by the proper school officials.

Teachers' Rights

Teachers get involved in the legal system usually when their jobs are endangered. School districts have fired many teachers based on misconduct. Many states' laws back the firing of teachers for public acts of homosexuality or other private acts considered substantially harmful to the credibility of the teacher's effectiveness in the classroom. In general, courts do not look upon deviance, especially sexual, and teachers as a good combination.

In terms of free expression, the courts have overwhelmingly ruled in favor of teachers who speak out or criticize their school systems outside of the school. This is considered freedom of speech and protected under our Bill of Rights.

Due Process

Due process refers to the formal procedure for legal action. The courts have ruled in favor of a long "due process" procedure for both teachers and students. If a student is going to be expelled, hearings, documentation, and other forms of evidence are required to make absolutely sure that the student must go. In the same vein, if teachers are going to be fired, a long, lengthy process must be followed as well. This due process concept is meant to protect the rights of the individual.

Districts, Regions, and States *(cont.)*

Church and State

The courts have been very rigid about religion in the school. The Bible and other religious works cannot be studied unless they are part of a history or literature component. School prayer is still illegal, and until recently (1990), no religious club could meet on school property or enjoy school patronage. In general, the courts do not allow religious dogma to invade public schools.

A teacher can be released for violation of this principle. It is important to remember, however, that religious clubs, like Christians in Action, The Judaic League, and Students for Mohammed, are perfectly allowable as long as they do not meet during regular school hours.

VI. Professional Organizations

As a teacher, it is important that you belong to a group where you can identify and get support. In the United States, there are over 11,000 educational organizations. Many national organizations also have state and local branches. The following pages list of some of the most popular educational organizations in the country. It is strongly recommended that you find information on some that interest you. In some districts, organizations affiliated with NEA or AFT may act as bargaining unions and have strong influence over education personnel.

Belonging to a professional organization can open a world of exciting opportunities for you and give you a larger forum to contribute your own ideas. For a small yearly fee, you can become a member of any of these associations. Members usually receive newsletters or other regular communication. Almost all such organizations hold yearly conventions, generally moving them around the country from year to year. In addition, these organizations provide professional opportunities, like seminars and advanced training, for their members.

Moreover, most professional associations issue quarterly journals of general and scholarly interest. Members not only enjoy the opportunity to avail themselves of the monographs and announcements contained but also may submit articles of their own. As an introduction to scholarly publication, these journals provide teachers with excellent opportunities. It is strongly recommended that all teachers submit ideas, projects, units, analyses, essays, and other reasoned proposals to at least one professional journal. The experience provides one with invaluable experience in organizing one's ideas and connecting professionally with others in one's field. Furthermore, few other activities serve to publicly validate one's professionalism and prestige. Other services and resources are also provided by professional organizations.

Some organizations are also for the students to join and participate in. These student-centered organizations will be designated with an asterisk (*).

Associations which are strongly recommended for leadership-minded teachers are designated with a double asterisk (**).

Districts, Regions, and States *(cont.)*

Professional Organizations List

Administration

American Association of School Administrators, Arlington, Virginia

Business

Future Business Leaders of America, Dulles, Washington, D.C. *

Junior Achievement Incorporated, Stamford, Connecticut *

Communications and Speech

Speech Communication Association, Annadale, Virginia

Computer Technology

Association for Computers in Mathematics and Science Teaching, Austin, Texas

Association for Educational Communications and Technology, Washington, D.C.

International Council for Computers in Education, Eugene, Oregon

Educational Research/Philosophy/Leadership

American Education Research Association, Washington, D.C. **

Carnegie Foundation for the Advancement of Teaching, Lawrenceville, New Jersey **

Coalition of Essential Schools, Providence, Rhode Island **

Association for Supervision and Curriculum Development, Alexandria, Virginia **

Covey Leadership Center, Provo, Utah **

English

Modern Language Association of America, New York City, New York

National Council of Teachers of English, Urbana, Illinois

Sigma Tau Delta, Dekalb, Illinois

Exceptional Children

American Association for Gifted Children, New York City, New York

National Association for Gifted Children, St. Paul, Minnesota

Districts, Regions, and States *(cont.)*

Fine Arts

American College of Musicians, Austin, Texas

American String Teachers Association, Athens, Georgia

Delta Omicron International Music Fraternity, Columbus, Ohio

International Thespian Society, Cincinnati, Ohio

Music Teachers National Association, Cincinnati, Ohio

National Art Education Association, Reston, Virginia

National Band Association, Ada, Ohio

Secondary School Theater Association, Washington, D.C.

Foreign Languages

American Association of Teachers of French, Champaign, Illinois

American Association of Teachers of Spanish and Portuguese, Mississippi State, Mississippi

Journalism

Association for Education in Journalism and Mass Communication, Columbia, South Carolina

Kappa Tau Alpha, Columbia, Missouri

Quill & Scroll Society, Iowa City, Iowa

Society of Student Publications, Norman, Oklahoma *

Library

Association for Library and Information Science Education, State College, Pennsylvania

Math

Mu Alpha Theta, Norman, Oklahoma

National Council for Teachers in Mathematics, Reston, Virginia

Middle School

National Middle School Association, PO Box 968, Fairborn, Ohio, 45324

Society for the Advancement of Middle School Teaching, 3700 Convict Hill, Austin, Texas, 78749, ATTN: J. Williams

National Teacher Organizations

American Federation of Teachers (AFT), Washington, D.C. **

National Alliance of Black School Educators, Washington, D.C.

National Education Association (NEA), Washington, D.C. **

Districts, Regions, and States *(cont.)*

Parent and Volunteer
The National PTA, Chicago, Illinois

The National Committee for Citizens in Education, Columbia, Maryland

Physical Education/Health
American Alliance for Health, P.E., Recreation, and Dance, Reston, Virginia

American School Health Association, Kent, Ohio

Association for the Advancement of Health Education, Reston, Virginia

Religious and Independent Schools
Christian Schools International, Dallas, Texas

Jewish Teachers Association, New York City, New York

National Catholic Educators, Washington, D.C.

Association of Christian Schools, International, La Habra, CA

Science
American Association of Physics Teachers, College Park, Maryland

National Association of Geology Teachers, Lawrence, Kansas

National Science Teachers Association, Washington, D.C.

School Science & Mathematics Association, Bowling Green, Ohio

Sigma Zeta, Canton, Ohio

Society of Sigma Gamma Epsilon, Norman, Oklahoma

Social Studies
American Economics Association, Nashville, Tennessee

Association of American Geographers, Washington, D.C.

National Council for Geographic Education, Macomb, Illinois

National Council for Social Studies, Washington, D.C.

Organization of American Historians, Washington, D.C.

Vocational, Industrial, and Agricultural
American Industrial Arts Student Association, Reston, Virginia

Future Farmers of America, Alexandria, Virginia

International Technology Education Association, Reston, Virginia

Parental Involvement

Outline of Chapter 11

I. The Education Triangle

II. Effectively Communicating with Parents

    A. Written Communication

    B. Telephoning Parents

    C. Conferences

    D. School-Home Contracts

III. Bringing Parents into the Classroom

    A. Back-to-School Night

    B. Volunteerism

    C. Parents on School Advisory Committees

IV. The PTA

Reproducibles for Chapter 11 (See pages 287–295.)

1. General Letter Home

2. Parent Phone Record

3. Parent Conference Log

4. School-Home Contract (Daily)

5. School-Home Contract (Weekly)

6. Parent Conference Sign-Up Form

7. Parent Volunteer Sign-Up Form

8. Parent Volunteer Call

9. Parent Thank You Letter

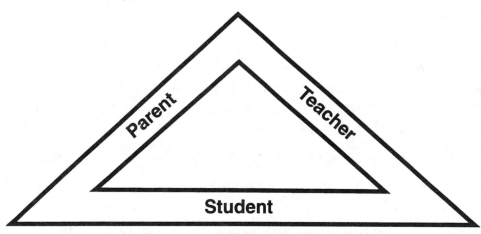

I. The Education Triangle

This book so far has been concentrating on you as a teacher and the world around you that you interact with every day, like the students, other teachers, the administrators, and the governing personnel on local and state levels. There is one giant piece of the structure, however, that we have not addressed—the parents. Without the parents' help, our job is exponentially more difficult. In an age when the parents are often missing in their role as supports and guides, teachers must use proven methods and find new ways to bring parents into the learning process. Education for our children is truly governed by a triangular law: the student, the teacher, and the parent.

Parental Involvement *(cont.)*

II. Effectively Communicating with Parents

The first step to getting active in the learning process is to communicate effectively with parents. Parental communication should take place on a regular basis. This can be done easily and efficiently through written means, by telephone, or face-to-face meetings. Each of these modes has its own advantages, and each requires its own set of skills for maximum effectiveness. The enduring thread of constancy that runs through all forms, however, is sincerity.

As in any form of communication between people, there really is no substitute for honesty and sincere respect. Parents can detect defensiveness, falseness, and insincerity very easily; and their reaction to such elements is sure to erode the strong cooperation needed among parent, teacher, and student. Above all else, then, keep your communication lines open, sincere, friendly, and honest. If these principles are followed, there is really no secret to good community-school relations. Moreover, there will follow an almost direct one-to-one relationship in classroom success for the student. Conversely, ineffective communication with parents can reduce the finest classroom planning and procedure to little more than misunderstanding, mistrust, and in the worst case, active resistance. Never underestimate the importance of effective communication with the home.

A. Written Communication

General Letter Home

At the beginning of the year, start parental communication on the right foot by sending home a letter explaining the various information which parents need to know about your course. A General Letter Home (page 287) is provided for you to fill in. Give your first name as well as your last and provide a brief background of your education and certification areas. Parents want to know that their children are in qualified hands. To make the letter even friendlier, provide a small description of your family as well. This will make you seem real to the parents, instead of some educational automaton that teaches their child somewhere in a large building. In addition, knowing that you have a family too encourages parents to relate to you as a fellow child raiser. Parenthetically, swapping parent stories (like the time your son crashed the family car into the house) is an effective way to gain parent confidence.

Also on the general letter, give your daily schedule with the school phone numbers. This will give parents an idea how and when to contact you or arrange a conference with you. Other important information to send home is a list of materials that students need for your class. Also, advise the parents on how their child can be successful in your class. Suggestions such as daily time allotment for homework, obtaining a library card, making an "office," and providing study strategies are relevant and useful information that the parents may not have thought of. To ensure proper delivery of your letter, you might want to seal the letters in envelopes and have parents sign the envelopes for a homework grade.

Parental Involvement *(cont.)*

Other Written Communication

Throughout the year, you will want to make brief comments about student progress. This can be done on memos, letters, or notes. A detailed Progress Report (page 277) that you can copy and send home was already mentioned in Chapter 8. It is a good idea to express the good news about the students at least as much as the negative developments. In fact, there are few actions that will increase your esteem with parents as much as regular personal notes home, commenting on a student's achievements and good qualities.

Such praise, of course, filters back to the student via the parents and serves as strong motivation for the student to strive even more. Obviously, the student's self-esteem is positively affected. The attendant influence on behavior and accomplishment is marked and enduring.

A less formal, and even quicker, form to send home was discussed in Chapter 5, Teacher-Parent Warning forms (page 260). This is easy for the teacher because it takes no more than a minute to fill out and provides quality information for the parent. Have parents sign the notice to provide for accountability. An efficient way to keep up with this written communication is to mark a "C" or other designation in your grade book on the date which the communication was given. By circling this designation, you can indicate no signed slip was returned.

Receiving Parent Communication

Every now and then, a parent will write you a letter for some purpose. Make sure you provide a file for "Parent Communications" to store this important information. It is also imperative that you respond immediately in writing or by telephone.

B. Telephoning Parents

The best time to communicate with parents by phone is during business hours because this increases everybody's quality time at home. However, some parents insist on being contacted in the home only. When teachers and parents talk on the phone, there often is a problem in the classroom, either behavioral or academic. Whatever the case, the most important thing to remember is to document these calls. Use your Parent Phone Record (page 288) to make careful documentation. Then store the notes about the call in your parent communication file. If you do not document this oral communication, it might come back to haunt you. A parent may not remember the conversation the same way you do, and a dated written record of your notes goes a long way toward helping with mutual understanding.

The advantage to phone conversations with parents is that they are immediate and usually quite effective. When parents and teachers can touch base, then things can start happening. Another advantage is that many times parents hear a different story from the child, and a phone call can shock the parents into reality.

Parental Involvement *(cont.)*

B. Telephoning Parents *(cont.)*

When talking to parents about their children, always start off with a positive comment about the child. Following are some sample starting ideas:

- "Mr. Kelso, I really enjoy your son's creativity in the classroom. His creative stories are magnificent! However, there are areas where he needs some improvement . . ."

- "Mrs. Purdell, Amy is a delightful child, very courteous and sweet. I'm calling because I'm worried about her homework grades . . ."

- "Mr. Genoa, let me tell you that Brandon is quite the socialite in the classroom. He has very effective interpersonal skills. The reason I'm calling is because his behavior is sometimes a bit too extroverted for a classroom situation . . ."

- "Mrs. Livingston, first let me say that Jeanie is a great person and a thrill to have in the classroom. Her enthusiasm spills over to everybody else. However, lately I notice she might be getting into bad habits . . ."

With these calming initial sentences, parents are less likely to put up the shield of defense, and a more productive phone conversation can ensue.

C. Conferences

Conducting a parent conference is usually not high on the list of thrilling things for the classroom teacher. This is because it is hard to tell parents to their faces that their child has major problems. Unfortunately, parent conferences are almost always called as a serious measure because the child in question has been having difficulties in school. Of course, conferences to discuss general progress are not unheard of, but those are always easier to participate in—for both teachers and parents.

The good news is that parent conferences can often change things around for the better. This is especially true, of course, if there is a culminating unity of opinion and intent between the parent and the teacher. The student almost always feels the strength of these two influences on his/her life as a positive force. When the student can be made to experience that unified concern as a shared force designed to help—not punish—then the conference has every chance of being successful, and the student has a strong chance to improve.

There are good and bad ways to conduct parent conferences. Here is an eight-step approach for an effective parent conference.

1. **Persons Present**: Decide on who will be at the conference. Obviously, it will include you and the parent(s). You might want to include other team members, the counselor, or other administrators as necessary. It is often recommended to bring the student in to be faced with the decisions and also so he/she can participate and share in the thinking.

Parental Involvement *(cont.)*

2. **Set a Time:** Schedule a date and time when the conference will take place. Write this on your own calendar and on the team calendar as well.

   Most parent conferences last 30 minutes to an hour. Contact parents and arrange the meeting.

3. **Gather Documentation:** In parent conferences, it is essential that you present hard evidence. Grade books are a must, as well as examples of student work, any parent-teacher communication, and any discipline notices. If you have students keep a notebook, then have that available for the parents to look at. Some parents are amazed at their child's academic work—or lack thereof. Hard evidence is the ultimate persuasion. Also, make sure you document the meeting with your Parent Conference Log (page 289).

4. **Greet Parents Warmly:** When parents show up, offer them a drink—coffee, tea, soft drink, or fruit juice. They will appreciate your kindness and know immediately that you must be a courteous, concerned teacher. Ask them if they had any trouble finding the classroom and what their thoughts are of the school. A little small talk is always an effective icebreaker.

5. **Begin Conference:** When all persons are present, get right down to business. As always, begin your communication with parents on a positive note. Explain the positive aspects of their child's progress. Go into detail about what you find are their beneficial aspects.

   For example,

   > *"Thank you for coming, Mrs. Austin. I really appreciate your involvement in your son's education. Without parents like you, we would really be stuck! Let me start by saying a few things about Tray's positive side. Tray is very active; he gets involved, especially with hands-on learning. His intelligence is very high when he sees relevance and meaning in what he is doing. In addition, Tray is an impressive artist. He draws with true inspiration. Here is an illustration Tray drew for me one day—I truly treasure it.*

6. **Explain Concerns:** Next, begin explaining what your concerns are about the student in question. Back up your assertions with hard evidence so that there is no mistaking the genuine nature of your case. Continue with the discussion . . .

   > *"The reason I wanted to talk to your personally was because of Tray's motivation and bad grades. Many times Tray stares out the window and daydreams when he is not interested in the lesson. Consequently, his grades are sinking below average, and I think he is getting into bad habits. This is an essay on the slave trade that Tray turned in a week ago. You can see that he is not even writing in complete sentences. Furthermore, his facts are all garbled. I'm afraid Tray is going to slip through the cracks if we don't find some solution."*

Parental Involvement *(cont.)*

7. **Listen to Reaction:** Listen closely to the parents' reactions to your concerns. They might shed valuable light onto a dark situation. Tray's mother, Mrs. Austin, had this to say . . .

> *"This work is really beneath Tray, and it is frankly embarrassing. I'm afraid Tray is falling behind in all of his subjects. I don't know what to do. I know that the divorce is really hitting him hard. Tray's father just is not there anymore, and I work all day. To tell you the truth, I don't spend enough time with him, and I think he resents me. He argues with me much more now; I just don't know what to do."*

8. **Find Solutions:** The next step is to bring the student in and hear his or her side of the story. Sometimes this can be productive, but often their answers are cloaked in the "I-don't-know" school of thought. Explain to the student what you and the parents have been talking about. Offer several solutions. Maybe the student will agree to follow the desired behavior if given more reading or computer time. Often, continuous misbehavior is a signal that the student simply needs more attention. If the problem runs deeper, the counselor should get involved. There might be a beneficial program or support group that can help.

If you feel that the student does not seem to feel the gravity of the situation, it is a good idea to prepare a school-home contract. A conference in itself is not likely to change behavior immediately. That is why the contract is so useful; it monitors the student every day and gives feedback to the parents.

Quiet—Tray is coming in . . .

Teacher: Tray, your mother and I have been talking about your progress. We both agree that you are an exceptionally smart young man, your drawings are beautiful, and I want to thank you personally for giving one of them to me. The reason I'm concerned is that lately, you seem to be slacking off. Remember this essay on the slave trade? Now, you tell me if you think you could have done better than that.

Tray: Yeah, I kinda goofed up on that.

Teacher: I know, but that's OK, because we all goof up now and then. The important thing is that we learn from our mistakes, right?

Tray: Yeah, right.

Mother: Tray, your teacher and I want to know why your work is falling behind. We are going to work together to help you do the best you can. Lately, we have noticed you don't seem to be doing your best. What do you have to say for yourself?

Tray: I dunno.

Teacher: Is there something bothering you that you can tell us?

Tray: (starting to whimper) No . . . I mean, I guess . . . I dunno!

Teacher: Tray, here's a tissue. I think you feel confused; is that right?

Tray: Yeah.

Parental Involvement *(cont.)*

Mother: I bet you want your father back, too.

Tray: No! I hate him for leaving us! I never want to see him again! (more crying)

Mother: Tray! Don't ever say that! Your father loves you, Tray, and he wants the best for you—starting here in the classroom.

Teacher: Tray, I sense that your feelings for your father are getting in the way of your school work. Would you say that's a fair assumption? Remember that word *assumption* from your vocabulary list? (smiling)

Tray: (smiling) Yeah, I guess—something that's not said, but felt.

Teacher: That's right! See, you can't hide your intelligence from me; now answer that question.

Tray: Yes, that's a fair unsumshun.

Teacher: You know, Tray, it's hard to learn when your mind is bothering you with things like that. I'm going to talk to our counselor and see if I can get you in the Right Track Club.

Tray: What's that?

Teacher: It's a fun group where kids like you can talk about things and help each other. You even get to have ice cream parties. How does that sound?

Tray: OK, I guess . . . I still get to be in your class, right?

Teacher: Of course, you're stuck with me all year. What I will require you to do, though, is get on a contract so we can ensure your success with all teachers. I'll talk to your other teachers and counselor to let you make up work which you didn't try very hard on. Sound like a deal? (smiling)

Tray: Yeah, OK.

Teacher: Now, the conditions of the contract are that every day, you do the following things: come to class prepared, turn in homework, and stay tuned in class.

Now, if all of these conditions are met, Tray, you will receive the following rewards: at home—computer privileges and other privileges decided by your mother; and at school—library visits.

Does that sound good Tray? Fair enough?

Tray: Umm, yeah

Teacher: Tray, I know how you like computer games, but if you get an X in any of those categories, the following consequences will result: at home—no TV or computer games, and at school—lose creative time/lose computer time.

That would be no fun, would it? But either way, we're going to get you in Right Track. I think you will enjoy it, don't you agree?

Tray: I guess so.

Parental Involvement *(cont.)*

Teacher: OK, it's a deal then! Just sign right here after you read this paragraph. Read it out loud for us, can you? As an advance for signing the contract, I'll let you take my computer game "Road Soldiers" home for this weekend.

Tray: Really? *I, Tray Henderson, understand the terms of this contract and pledge to do my best to live up to its guidelines. I know that this contract is meant to help me be the best I can be. I also understand that if I break the rules of the contract I will have consequences at home and at school. If I live up its expectations, I will be rewarded.*

(signing of contract)

Teacher: I'll expect you to live up to its conditions starting Monday morning.

Mother: Tray, Mrs. Springer is doing all she can to help you. Isn't there something you want to tell her?

Tray: Thank you, Mrs. Springer.

Mother: Come on Tray, we have a lot to talk about. (Turning towards teacher) Thank you again for all your help. You've really made a difference.

Teacher: That's my job! I hope the contract will work; we'll be in touch if it doesn't.

D. School-Home Contracts

An effective weapon for continued misconduct is a school-home contract. You have just seen how Mrs. Springer used a set of consequences and rewards to make up a school-home contract. You will find a School-Home Contract (Daily) and a School-Home Contract (Weekly) on pages 290–291. This contract will spell out the desired behaviors which are lacking. The student is expected to live up to these usually simple requirements.

Desired behaviors are unique to the individual student but usually follow these types of outcomes:

- ❑ comes prepared to class
- ❑ is on time to class
- ❑ has homework completed
- ❑ works diligently and tries hard
- ❑ completes class assignment
- ❑ follows class rules
- ❑ is respectful to teacher
- ❑ is respectful to other students
- ❑ has good attitude and is positive about self

If the school-home contract does not work and the student continues to get X's, then either of two things will happen: more pressure at home or more pressure at school. More pressure at home usually means grounding. At school, the step beyond a contract means the vice principal interviews the student and determines an appropriate path of action for the future.

Parental Involvement *(cont.)*

III. Bringing Parents into the Classroom

Besides communicating with parents, it is also a worthwhile endeavor to try to bring them physically into the classroom or school. Three ways of doing this are back-to-school night, volunteerism, and having parents join campus decision-making committees.

A. Back-to-School Night

Most schools conduct an exercise where parents are invited into the school, toured through classrooms, and given the chance to see and hear the teachers of their children. Of course, this is done in many ways. The most traditional way is for the parents to come to the school and follow a mock "day at school," using their child's schedule. Other ways are having whole teams of teachers address a large audience. Another method is to have departments set up their own sections while parents breeze in and out at will. Whatever strategy that your school employs, it is recommended that you follow these basic guidelines:

1. *Decorate your room if you intend to use it.* Put up students' work, projects, and pictures.

2. *Prepare a presentation.* If you are required to give a speech to the parents, take some time to make a thoughtful presentation. Remember that this will be the only time to leave any impression on many of the parents. Since you are representing your school, you must do a professional job in this activity. Good parent presentations contain the following elements:

   - List of Credentials: Tell the parents your educational background and area of certification to give them a sense of your accomplishment and professionalism. Parents want to know that their children are in good hands. Do not, however, go into every workshop you ever attended. Be brief enough so that everyone is still awake for the next teacher's class.

   - Outline of Skills Covered: Give a general outline of the skills you will teach to their children and the methods that you employ. An excellent idea is to have a mini-quiz which the parents can take (see how many parents remember what a metaphor is!). This is sure to provoke a humorous scene and will set the parents at ease while revealing academics of your class.

   - Outline Materials/Special Requirements: List any special items that students need to be successful in your class. Reveal any strategies which you think are necessary for optimum student performance.

   - Question and Answer: Try to leave time for questions and answers.

   This can be a most important and fruitful period for the evening, for it is at this time that there is real interplay between parents and teachers. It is really important to set a friendly tone and cooperative atmosphere—both elements that allow a positive bonding between school and home.

3. *Be professional.* Dress appropriately and conduct yourself in a manner befitting the professional status that you hold.

Parental Involvement *(cont.)*

A. Back-to-School Night *(cont.)*

4. *Provide greetings and a conference sign up.* Try to greet as many parents as possible. If they want to talk at length, suggest that they sign up for a parent conference when you can spend quality time discussing the education of their child. Use your Parent Conference Sign Up sheet (page 292) to have parents sign up for a conference by writing their names and phone numbers. It is a good idea to have them indicate whether they would like to have a teleconference or a sit-down conference. With all the demands on the teacher's time these days, it is almost absurd to think you can personally meet with every parent. Having a teleconference can be a more efficient way to get information and give feedback.

5. *The last thing you want to mention is to call for volunteers.* Use your Parent Volunteer Sign Up form (page 293) for parents to attest to their willingness to participate. Depending on the circumstances and demographics of your school district, the large majority of parents are house mothers. But some parents are working professionals who could take personal leave to attend special activities or field trips. Let the parents know that the volunteer sign-up form is non-obligatory; it is just to give you a basic idea of the numbers of volunteers interested.

By following these simple guidelines, you can rest assured that your parents will be aware of your professionalism as well as your personal concern. This will encourage them to help you with special projects and tightly bind the three sides of the education triangle.

B. Volunteerism

Throughout the year, you will want to call on parents to volunteer their time or funds for special purposes. Parent volunteerism involves basically two concepts: time and material. Use your Parent Volunteer Call (page 294) when the necessary time comes to call forth extra help.

Time

When parents volunteer time, they help supervise activities, accompany students on field trips, work concession stands, manage games or sports, and just help out in general. Any person can see how having five or six parent volunteers opens up whole new possibilities. For instance, the Medieval Festival mentioned in Chapter 4 would be impossible if parents were not there to help serve food and drinks, supervise the students, and manage other activities.

Material

Material can be defined as anything purchased. This means food and drinks, supplies, sports equipment, theatrical costumes, books, and whatever else that you need or request. Because there are so many demands on working parents, donating their money to a worthy cause gives them a sense of helping out when ordinarily they could not.

For example, if you use your Parent Volunteer Call, indicating a need for cups, soft drinks, and snacks for a thematic celebration, your room will be filled with soft drinks, cookies, chips, and paper cups in a few days.

Parental Involvement *(cont.)*

Thank You Letters

It is imperative that you write thank you letters to all volunteer parents. Otherwise, they will feel slighted or uncertain of the help their contribution made. This can be done quickly with three things: student helpers, Student ID Sheets (from Chapter 2), and Parent Thank You Letters (page 295). First fill out the date and sign the Parent Thank You form—do not put any parent names on the form yet. Next, have all the students sign the document, adding personal comments as necessary. Now, make copies for all the parents. This is when your student helpers come in handy; have them write in each parent name and address the envelopes according to the information on the Student ID Sheets. Next, obtain the required number of stamps and mail the letters. The whole process might take five minutes of your time.

C. Parents on School Advisory Committees

Besides back-to-school night and volunteerism, there is another way that parents are being persuaded to join the school. Because the concept of site-based management is growing stronger every day in our nation's schools, parents are being asked to help govern and manage the school as sitting members on campus leadership teams (see Chapter 9). The results of this new and exciting development, of course, have yet to be well documented.

If you want to know more about parents on school councils or if your school needs more information on this developing movement, contact the following organizations:

> National Committee for Citizens in Education, a parent advocacy group
>
> 10840 Little Patuxent Parkway, Suite 301, Columbia, MD, 21044

The NCCE has two manuals about school-based management and shared decision making:

> School-Based Improvement, *A Manual for Training School Councils* by Barbara J. Hansen and Carl L. Marburger (1989); $39.95
>
> *A Workbook on Parent Involvement for District Leaders* by Anne T. Henderson and Carl L. Marburger (1990); $39.95

IV. The PTA

The Parent-Teachers Association is the largest parent organization in the country, touching almost all schools in the nation. The national PTA headquarters is located in Chicago. The main goal in your local PTA is to stress parental involvement for the good of the school. Each year, elections are held among members to determine the PTA officers. The typical governing structure looks like this:

President—directs the overall PTA program

Vice President—involved with management of the program, helps the president

Treasurer—collects and banks funds raised

Secretary—types PTA communication and minutes from PTA meetings

Other Members—serve in various utilitarian functions

Parental Involvement *(cont.)*

The chief ways the PTA helps the school and gets parents involved is through fund-raising and services.

Fund-Raising

Fund-raising is a big part of the PTA program. Through funds which are raised in various ways, the PTA can help improve the school in many areas. For instance, funds can be used to buy more computers, or more books, or maybe to plant new trees on the campus; an endless range of possibilities is present. Although there are many ways to raise money, some of the most common are the following:

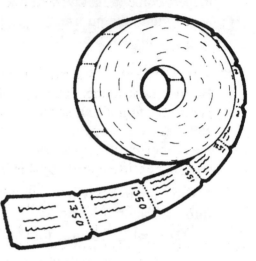

Raffles: Raffles are contests where one or a few people get a big prize. Usually, this prize, like a boom box, is donated. Then, the PTA sells raffle tickets to everyone who is interested in winning the prize or in donating to the cause. The tickets are usually very inexpensive, commonly no more than a dollar. If you get a thousand people to buy tickets, you have just made $1,000. Since the prize was donated and there is no tax on school fund-raising, the school receives a clear profit.

Dances: Dances require more organization, but the profit potential is much higher, and the fun and participation that students receive makes them quite worthwhile. All that is needed for a dance is volunteer supervisors, a musical component, and the students themselves.

A good idea is to contact the local law enforcement agencies who will usually help supervise. The presence of police officers discourages the possibility of any unsavory elements making an appearance at a dance. In fact, these days it is almost imperative to have abundant securtity at such affairs.

Tickets to a dance can be sold these days for anywhere from five to ten dollars. Again, the profit from having 500 students attend a dance is substantial. The best thing about a dance, though, is that it gives the kids a forum to meet, joke, and have fun together.

Dinners: Conducting dinner parties is another favorite of PTA officials. To do this, they get a local sponsor to donate food and supplies or reduce the price of a large catering service. Parents, friends, and students are all invited to attend. The plates can range from five to ten dollars. The trick to the dinner fund-raising is advertising to prepay plates. Other ways to entice buyers are by having a special feature attraction, like a student show, dance, or play after the dinner. If you multiply 10 times 100, you get a whopping $1,000! Of course, this method is a famous political fund-raising technique as well. As we know, Presidential dinners are known to cost $1,000 per plate and more.

Auctions: A great way to get many people involved is to conduct an auction. Parents and teachers donate valuable items, and then they are sold to the highest bidder. This is especially enjoyable when combined with food sales, box suppers, etc.

Parental Involvement *(cont.)*

Fund-Raising (cont.)

Presentations/Shows: Charging admission for special presentations like student plays or talent shows can also raise hundreds of dollars.

Athletic Events: A popular and easy way to raise a few hundred dollars is to organize faculty versus student athletic contests where parents and other students are charged admission. This is always guaranteed to bring out a big audience of parents and relatives. Both boys and girls can participate. Again, combining this with booths for food sales is effective.

Bake Sale: The traditional bake sale is still very popular. Profits from bake sales can soar into the hundreds.

Teachers have always participated in PTA fund-raising and joined the organization by paying the small membership fee. Through the years this organization has proven to be the strongest local support for our nation's schools, well-deserving of its reputation as a pillar of education.

PTA Services

The other way PTA helps the school is by providing services. Usually services include helping with office duties, serving as teaching aides, providing library assistance, supplementing campus supervision, chaperoning dances, conducting community surveys, and helping out wherever needed. If you see parents in the building who are serving in the capacity of volunteers, be sure to take time to introduce yourself. Chat with them about the school and welcome them as you would a strong friend and colleague. This friendliness will reverberate through the community, and more parents will likely become involved with the school in positive, supportive ways.

Builders of bridges and geodesic domes know that the triangle is the strongest architectural support form. Similarly, builders of community social structures seek a strongly welded education triangle of student, parent, and teacher. The PTA has provided solid support for this endeavor.

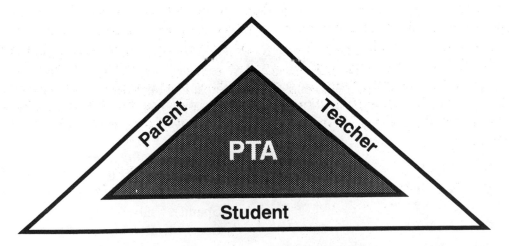

Organizing a School Club

Reproducibles for Chapter 12 (See pages 296–304.)

1. *Club Members Matrix*
2. *Club Passes*
3. *Club Activities Planner*
4. *Intent of Fund-Raising Form*
5. *Bake Sale Form*

6. *Community/Business Request for Help Form*
7. *Accounting Log*
8. *Club Contacts Matrix*
9. *Club Event Organizer*

I. Beginning a Club

A. What Are Your Interests/Talents?

Take a minute to fill out the interest survey on the following page. After you have finished, look at your responses. What did you answer? Any of these interests could easily be turned into a club where you and students who share your interest can take part in enjoyable, enriching activities. In fact, schools all over the country have clubs based on just those interests. For instance,

if you picked:	*the corresponding club is:*
take photos	Photography Club
draw/paint/art	Art Club
study Spanish	Spanish Club
play soccer	Soccer Club
investigate scientific phenomena	Science Club

Organizing a School Club *(cont.)*

Interest Survey
(Check the appropriate boxes.)

I like to . . .

❏ Read

❏ Write Stories

❏ Use Computers

❏ Act in Plays

❏ Write Journalism

❏ Take Photos

❏ Draw/Paint/Art

❏ Study Science

❏ Hike/Camp

❏ Listen to/Play Music

❏ Study Religion

❏ Play Sports

    ❏ Football

    ❏ Basketball

    ❏ Soccer

    ❏ Tennis

    ❏ Other

❏ Study Politics

❏ Work on Mechanical Items

❏ Grow Gardens

❏ Study Foreign Languages

    ❏ Spanish

    ❏ French

    ❏ Latin

    ❏ German

    ❏ Russian

    ❏ Japanese

    ❏ Other

❏ Study History

❏ Study Mythology

❏ Help the Community

❏ Other

Organizing a School Club *(cont.)*

B. Finding the Time

The main reason teachers do not follow up on their interests is that there is so little time to create a new program, replete with new responsibilities and tasks. To compound the problem, many schools do not provide for club time. However, most middle schools do provide a homeroom or advisory period. This is your key to starting a club.

If your school provides no time at all for any extra-classroom activities, the first thing you should do is bring this up to the principal. It is not only healthy but completely necessary for middle school children to develop their interests and motivations with positive role models. The school system with no club or homeroom time is missing an opportunity to help students develop a sense of belonging and accomplishment. This sense of security might be more necessary in middle school than anywhere else.

II. The Efficient Administration of a Club

A. Determining Membership

❑ *Sign Up*

The first element of starting a club is to determine who is going to be in it. Everybody who wants to be in the club should be able to get in. (One reason you may have to deny membership is because of failing grades. Some schools feel that students who are not passing their courses need extra time for tutoring and should not be granted extra-curricular privileges. Check with your administration and make sure you are apprised of any other regulations regarding club membership.)

Normally, you have to turn away members only when response is so large that it would make running the club impossible.

What do you do if such a response occurs? The fairest way to narrow the membership is to pick names randomly. You might want to call all candidates together and have them put their names in a hat. Then, using some assistants, pick the lucky winners! (Also pick alternates in case the winners are unable to be in the club or they drop out.)

Another way to handle an overcrowding situation is to ask other teachers to co-sponsor the club with you. This method could double the enrollment, building a sense of camaraderie among you, the students, and the other sponsors. Sharing the good times with your colleagues will make for a better work environment.

❑ *Recording Members*

After you know exactly who will be in your club, enter their names on your Club Members Matrix (page 296). Also on this matrix, you might want to record which classes they attend before the club meeting time, their phone numbers, and their addresses.

Organizing a School Club *(cont.)*

B. Deciding Club Times

Your school might set all club times, or you might have to develop your own time. Whichever the case, make sure all members are informed of when the club meets. In some schools, club times are at the end of the day or during homeroom, one or two times a week. Other schools might have clubs in the morning or after lunch.

When you have set exact club times, make passes for your members (see page 297). Make one normal copy of the passes first. On this master copy, write in the name of your club and the times that it meets. Write your name as the sponsor and the room number of where the meetings will take place. Write in any other information that should appear the same on every pass. Next, take this master copy and make color copies enough for all your members. On these color copies, write in the names of the individual members and names of the classes they will leave for the club meeting.

For example, let's say Mrs. Orangetree has a theater club which meets every Friday during advisory (3:15 PM–4:00 PM). Since Pine Oaks does not let students run around the building without authorization, giving a pass to her members is the only way she can legally get them out of their advisory class. Let's say one of her members is Darren Dumont, and every Friday he has advisory with Mrs. Doolittle in room 210. His pass, then, would look like this illustration:

Theater Club Pass

For	*Darren Dumont*
Club Times	*Fridays 3:15–4:00 in theater*
Sponsor	*Orangetree*
Depart	*Doolittle, 210*

Once you have all your members' passes completed, then the next step is to laminate them for protection. After lamination, cut them out and store appropriately.

The next decision you must make is how to distribute them. One way is to place them in the teachers' boxes to give to members. Unfortunately, this causes inconvenience for those teachers, and they commonly lose the passes or don't check their boxes.

A better way is to have student messengers distribute the passes to the teachers about 30 minutes before club times. This method takes a load off the teachers and ensures that all members get passes. Moreover, it can be a great motivator for students who enjoy "courier" privileges, the one condition being that they must have finished all classroom requirements.

A third method is simply to give the passes to the members permanently. Some students are very responsible and can keep their passes the whole year, but some are unable to do this.

Organizing a School Club *(cont.)*

C. Developing Club Activities

It is stimulating to think about, design, and develop club activities. Obviously, the type of club you sponsor immediately suggests some activities. It wouldn't be a shock, for instance, if you see a basketball club play basketball. But there are many elements other than the obvious which make a club interesting. Clubs are best when students are learning, and the best activities for clubs center around the concept of learning by doing.

When forming a club, jot down all the ideas you can think of to generate interest and enthusiasm. Mrs. Orangetree, excited about her new theater club, brainstormed ideas on club activities; here are her results.

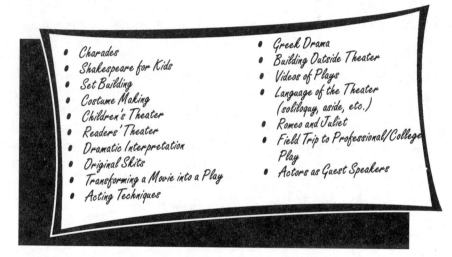

- Charades
- Shakespeare for Kids
- Set Building
- Costume Making
- Children's Theater
- Readers' Theater
- Dramatic Interpretation
- Original Skits
- Transforming a Movie into a Play
- Acting Techniques
- Greek Drama
- Building Outside Theater
- Videos of Plays
- Language of the Theater (soliloquy, aside, etc.)
- Romeo and Juliet
- Field Trip to Professional/College Play
- Actors as Guest Speakers

From this brainstorming session, Mrs. Orangetree has a whole year of interesting activity ideas. Now, from her file cabinet, she takes out her Club Activities Planner (page 298). Because her club meets once a week, she can plan for a six-week period. Here are her results:

Meetings and Activities

1. Introduction to the theater, Greek drama, get acquainted, mini skits—"My Life"
2. Acting techniques: voice projection, gesture
3. Vote on play performance, distribute script, decide on roles
4. Start rehearsing, building set, making costumes
5. Rehearsal
6. Rehearsal, watch play on video if available

Special Materials Needed
- Costuming Materials
- Prop Materials
- Set Materials

Upcoming Events
- Field Trip to *Julius Caesar* (high school production)
- Visiting Speaker (professional or high school actor)
- Scripts

From this planner, Mrs. Orangetree will know what her club will be doing in the next six weeks.

Organizing a School Club *(cont.)*

D. Delegating Club Responsibilities

Managing a club can be a chore if you choose to put it all on your own back. The best ways to delegate club management are the following:

- **Other Teachers:** Find another teacher to help sponsor the club with you. This can make club activities twice as easy and twice as much fun. Sharing a club together can be a rewarding professional and personal experience. We teachers are so used to teaching by ourselves (the "monastery effect") that we forget there is no law against having more than one teacher in a classroom—or a clubroom, in this case.

- **Other Parents:** There are probably many parents who would welcome the chance to help out a club, especially if their child is a member. Send out a parent volunteer form with all the members and see how much response you can get. At the very least, parents will probably supply materials and transportation for field trips. If you can secure transportation from parents, this can save everybody the trouble of getting a bus.

  The parents of your club members will most likely be impressed and excited that you are getting their children involved. Students genuinely enjoy being in clubs because they feel accepted and develop a sense of belongingness. You can be sure this radiates back to the parents during dinner table conversation. This positive feeling, incidentally, will radiate to community and school administrators as well. It is simply exhilarating to know that your extra efforts can influence surrounding communities in a positive fashion.

- **Other Students:** Have club members vote on a leader or captain. You may want to hand-pick the leader. Give the leader the responsibility of informing others of changes in scheduling, upcoming events, recent development, etc. You might want to give your club leader a copy of the Club Members Matrix so he or she can call from home. Other responsibilities that a club leader can shoulder are organizing and participating in the fund-raising activities, conducting after-school club activities, and being the liaison between the club sponsor and the club members.

III. Fund Raising/Accounting

How will Mrs. Orangetree pay for all the extra materials she needs to build sets and make costumes? A way to pay for necessary club expenses is to raise money. This money will go toward improving the club with goods or services. Also, this is a way to keep the costs from coming out of parents' pockets. As a club sponsor, there are two main items you need to be aware of: ways to raise money and how to account for the money you raise.

Organizing a School Club

(cont.)

A. Ways to Raise Money

As mentioned in the preceding chapter, there are many ways to raise necessary funds. First of all, it is necessary that you get approval from your principal if you plan to do any fund-raising. The administration can get very touchy about fund-raising, so it is a good idea to inform them of your every move. Many schools and districts will actually cap the number of club fund-raisers allowed.

Use your Intent of Fund-Raising form (page 299) to get approval for your money-making attempts. Remember, fund-raising is not only economically helpful, but a learning experience as well. Learning the value and responsibility of raising money is a life skill that will serve all students well in the future. Following is a list of some successful methods to raise money.

Bake Sale

The old fashioned bake sale is still very effective. Use your Bake Sale form (page 300) to solicit baked items from club member parents. You will receive cookies, brownies, cakes, Rice Krispie treats, and other delicious baked goods. Determine the price and sell them during lunch. Even, round figures, like $.50 or $1.00, are the best prices because they ease accounting procedures.

It is a good idea to advertise over the public address system, the bulletin or on the walls in high traffic areas with attractive signs and posters. A cash box can be acquired from the office. Have club members help with the selling. Depending on how many baked items you have, a good day at a bake sale can fetch $100.

Raffle

Raffles are an easy way to make large profits. Many states fill their general treasuries with billions of dollars each year from lottery sales. The key to a good raffle is the prize(s). If you can get a good prize, people will be willing to pay a small fee for the chance to win. To secure a lucrative prize, contact some local businesses. Through your Community/Business Request for Help form (page 301), you can see if local businesses will help you. They are usually willing to donate items as a means of advertising. Some companies have a whole department that does nothing but process requests like these (public relations, community relations, etc.). If you can build a relationship with these people, it will be a lasting investment.

After you have your prize(s), the next thing to do is to obtain a roll of small tickets. General admission tickets work well. Actually, any tickets will do, as long as they all have a unique identification number on them. The easiest way to "register" for the prize is to sell students the tickets (before or after school or at lunch) and then write their names on the back. The tickets then should be kept securely in a container. When the time comes to draw the winning tickets, all the tickets will be there, and the lucky winners can easily be revealed over the intercom during announcements.

Organizing a School Club *(cont.)*

Car Wash

Undoubtedly, the fund-raising activity that students seem most enthusiastic about is having a car wash. A strange combination of the kid-like instinct to get wet and the sense of financial rewards can make a car wash an event to remember.

There are really only a few things to do for a successful car wash. First, contact a gas station owner willing to donate the water and space. Next, make posters that read . . .

Free Car Wash!
Donations Accepted
Benefiting Pine Oaks Theater Club!

Position students in a safe but visible part of the property. It is usually effective to have one or two sign bearers, six to eight washers and driers, and a designated money taker. The money taker should be the most charismatic and should ask "Would you care to donate any money for the club?"

Usually, you can get a few parents to supervise. All you have to do is bring a chair, a book, and a place to store the money. Just make sure you have plenty of soap, buckets, and wash rags. Also, don't be afraid to get wet! You might want to take color snapshots of action during the day. Such a record will provide some humorous memories of an always-popular event. Post them on the club bulletin board, and there will be no shortage of students clustered around!

Handicrafts Sale

Often, students will make handcrafted jewelry, beads, necklaces, friendship bracelets, paintings, handmade T-shirts, etc. Setting up a small table or booth during lunch period can be a profitable enterprise as well as a lot of fun for the students.

Special Events

Charging admission to a special event which relates to your club can be fun for everybody who attends. For instance, a basketball club can stage a "club-versus-faculty" game. Mrs. Orangetree's theater club could put on a special play fund-raiser.

B. Accounting Procedures

When you make money for a nonprofit institution like a public school, it must be properly accounted for. Any mistake or indiscretion can be seen as financial impropriety by you as a teacher, and that has severe repercussions—from closing your club to filing a lawsuit against you. Therefore, it is imperative that you account properly for the money you make.

Organizing a School Club *(cont.)*

Proper Accounting Flow

Following this introduction, there is a diagram of how funds that are raised for a public school go from source to school and then back again to pay for goods or services. Once the money has been collected, it must be counted carefully. At this time a deposit slip must be filled out, just as when you make a deposit in your bank, except that there will be many more "coin" entries. Deposit slips are held with the office manager.

The next thing to consider is whether your funds are large enough to make a separate account in the school treasury. Consult the office manager about this possibility. If not, then the funds will be deposited in the "general accounts" of the school's treasury. To keep track of all your money earned, deposits, and other financial matters, create an Accounting File. In this file put the carbon copies of your deposit slips and keep your Accounting Log (page 302) so you have a running total of money earned and spent, as if it were a checkbook.

When you are ready to pay for goods or services, determine the exact total (remember that there is no tax on schools). Then determine the business name and address of the payee. If you are paying an individual, you may be required to get personal information, like social security number, phone number, etc. After this is done, obtain a check request form from the office manager and fill out the proper information. In turn the office manager will get it approved by the principal (who already knows your plans, thanks to the Intent of Fund-Raising form). The office then will issue a check for you.

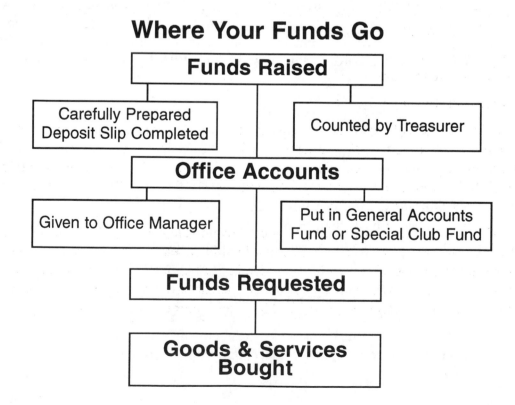

Where Your Funds Go

Funds Raised

Carefully Prepared Deposit Slip Completed

Counted by Treasurer

Office Accounts

Given to Office Manager

Put in General Accounts Fund or Special Club Fund

Funds Requested

Goods & Services Bought

Organizing a School Club *(cont.)*

IV. Club Trips and Competitions

Through club trips and competitions, you can expand your positive influence into other schools and communities. It does not take important connections to move into this arena—anyone can do it! Many times, the principal will allow club trips for a worthwhile cause.

A. Making the Contacts

Making contacts at other schools is the first step to planning multi-school competitions. Just get on the telephone and call schools. For instance, Mrs. Orangetree is calling other schools in her district right now . . .

Office Clerk: Good morning, Rosa Parks Middle School.

Orangetree: Hello, My name is Loretta Orangetree from Pine Oaks Middle School. I was wondering if your school has a drama or theater club.

Clerk: I know Mr. Van Dam runs the drama club.

Orangetree: Great! Can you leave him my name and number? I would like to see if he would be interested in combining our clubs for a theater festival.

(later, a call to another school)

Clerk: Good afternoon, Lewis & Clark Middle School, this is Rosetta. Can I help you?

Orangetree: Yes, I'm Loretta Orangetree from Pine Oaks Middle School. Do you know if I can get in touch with the drama club sponsor?

Clerk: I didn't know we had a drama club, ma'am. Mrs. Peabody is the drama instructor. Would you like to leave a message for her?

Orangetree: Yes, it couldn't hurt.

After six more calls like these, Mrs. Orangetree got two that were favorable—Rosa Parks Middle School and Susan B. Anthony Middle School. Her contacts there—Hans Van Dam and Anastasia Bellarosa, respectively—were excited that Mrs. Orangetree was organizing an inter-school theater movement. On her Club Contacts Matrix (page 303), Mrs. Orangetree wrote their names, phone numbers, and fax numbers.

Mrs. Orangetree could have called the local private schools as well. Building bridges between public schools and private schools is a worthwhile endeavor, especially for the students, who get to see the other sides of the worlds they live in. Other options for contacts are schools in other districts and even in other cities. Extending student horizons beyond their own school builds self-confidence, understanding, social skills, and maturity—central concerns for every teacher.

Organizing a School Club *(cont.)*

B. Planning Events

Once contacts are made and recorded, it is time to plan the events which the clubs will participate in. Possibilities usually revolve around the nature of the club. For instance, the theater clubs can get together and have a play competition, featuring the best scenes from a Greek tragedy, a Shakespearean comedy, and an original skit. The judges will be selected teachers, and an audience of students can also be assembled. The winner can receive a trophy or other valuable prize, but everybody gets to celebrate at the "cast party" afterwards.

Sports clubs are easy to plan competitions for, because it is fairly evident what the nature of the competition will be. In other words, sports clubs act as school teams. The chance to represent their school on a "field of battle" is exciting and an honorable vocation for both boys and girls, regardless of who wins. Your school probably already participates in interscholastic league sports, so talk to the athletic director before starting any sports activities. Most likely, the athletic personnel will be appreciative that you are conducting extracurricular sports activities.

Other clubs could have a variety of activities—art showcases, science fairs, Mexican fiestas (Spanish clubs), and other exhibitions and galleries. Students can learn a great deal by just seeing others in their field.

The next step is to plan when and where the event will take place. First, see if your principal will allow school time for competition. Explain the benefits and rewards of the experiences, as well as the learning value attached. Next, show how this trip can mean better interscholastic relations and more cooperation between communities. Last, show that the students will be responsible for all work missed. If you are going on school time, make sure you arrange for the smooth transition of your regular classes into other rooms. (See Chapter 4, Field Trips.)

If you cannot get any school time, then the event must be held after school. This time may actually be better because the entire school is at your disposal. The disadvantage, of course, is that you have to stay after school.

C. Securing Equipment/Materials/Personnel

After confirming contacts and planning events, the next steps involve the practical aspects. Make a list of equipment, materials, and any personnel needed on your Club Event Organizer (page 304).

Mrs. Orangetree knows that she will need to get a few costumes and a trophy. From the money raised by the bake sale, she will easily have enough. Also, for the cast party afterwards, she knows she will need tables, food, drinks, trash cans, plates, and napkins. English teachers and their classes can serve as judges and audiences at no cost.

Sports clubs might have to hire a referee. Using your Business Request form, you can often get T-shirts as uniforms, donated by local businesses.

Organizing a School Club *(cont.)*

C. Securing Equipment/Materials/Personnel *(cont.)*

For any competition, you will probably want trophies and ribbons. If you provide something for everybody, you will honor excellence as well as participation. If planning a food activity, use your Parent Volunteer form (Chapter 11) to request soda, chips, baked foods, etc.

D. Transportation

If you can get enough parents to transport the students, that saves everybody the trouble of securing a bus. If not, call the transportation office for a bus. Whatever method you use, it is of extreme importance that everybody get there safely. Providing detailed maps is a must.

E. Have Fun!

You have made it to the event location, and everybody is accounted for. If you did your planning, then all you have to do is set the wheels in motion and enjoy the ride. Sure, there will be a few discrepancies, but the fun that the students will have and the cooperative nature of a multischool operation will outweigh any small technical difficulties. Let's drop in on Mrs. Orangetree's theater festival, but try to keep it down because her students are performing an emotional scene from *Julius Caesar* . . .

Antony: (emotional) *Come I to speak at Caesar's funeral.*

He was my friend, faithful and just to me;

But Brutus says he was ambitious,

And Brutus is an honorable man.

He hath brought many captives home to Rome,

Whose ransoms did the general coffers fill.

(loudly, angrily) *Did this in Caesar seem ambitious?* (silence)

(crying) *When the poor had cried, Caesar hath wept;*

Ambition should be made of sterner stuff—

Van Dam: (whispering) Wow, Loretta, this is really good. I hope my kids can pull off their scene from *Medea* as well as this.

Orangetree: Oh, I'm sure they will be great, Hans. I'm surprised they remember their lines; they were so nervous before the show.

Bellarosa: My kids had a bad case of stage fright too, but I can understand it. However, I know how excited they are to be performing. This is so much fun, Loretta; thanks again for doing all this.

Orangetree: I couldn't have done it without you two. It is so gratifying to know that other teachers out there care about experiencing performance theater with the kids!

Bellarosa: Oh, it looks like my troubadours are ready—get prepared for our selection from *Pygmalion.*

Organizing a School Club *(cont.)*

After all scenes had been performed, the judges agreed that the best performance went to *Medea*. Afterwards, all the members had their party, making new friends they would keep all through high school.

This example is one of thousands that go on in our nation's schools every year. These unsung heroes make education come alive for young people, enrich their lives, give a sense of belonging, and expand their vision beyond their own sidewalks and hallways into new communities. This cultivates a sense of civic responsibility and mission that is missing in a large part of our society. Chief among all others, teachers have the high privilege of fostering these qualities.

F. Follow Up

To ensure proper follow up, create a club folder or notebook to organize all the club documents. On file, you should have the following:

1. Club Members Matrix
2. Club Passes
3. Club Activities Planner
4. Intent of Fund-Raising Form
5. Bake Sale Form
6. Community/Business Request for Help Form
7. Accounting Log
8. Club Contacts Matrix
9. Club Event Organizer

Be certain to store any related documents in the proper place. A good idea is to call your local newspapers and television stations about the event you are planning. Most likely, they have a community beat reporter who will be interested in covering the event.

When contacting the media, make sure you record their names and numbers on your Club Contacts Matrix. This will be an important reference. Building relationships and bridging communities gets easier every year. The initial outlay of energy and courage required to build this network is what stops most people from doing things they really want to do.

V. Creating an Interscholastic League

Contact Superintendent

Contact your superintendent in writing to apprise him or her of your interest in forming an interscholastic club. Describe your success in the club you founded and lay out your plans for an organization. Ask for approval to address the school board.

Organizing a School Club *(cont.)*

Address the Trustees

Find out when the board of trustees (local school board) meets. Contact the board clerk and get on the board's agenda. Tell the board of your plans and provide them with pictures, documents, letters, and other evidence to convince them of your sincerity. They will be all ears if they hear no financial requests. Ask them to recognize your league and promote it.

Consolidate Organization

When you get the board to recognize your organization and support it, then send a letter to all your contacts, telling them of your success. Indicate that you expect them or their representatives to participate and support the league. Send another letter to all the schools in your area, soliciting participation. Next, delegate power by assigning certain functions to trusted officers.

For instance, in Mrs. Orangetree's Theater Interscholastic Club, she assigns the following officers:

- commissioner of transportation
- commissioner of judging criteria
- commissioner of food/drink
- commissioner of prizes

By delegating these powers, Mrs. Orangetree is able to concentrate on the task of management and coordination.

Create Schedule

Next, look at the year as a whole. Competitions or activities should happen at least two or three times a semester to keep students involved. Make a tentative calendar and pass it along to your officers. After confirmation, supply copies to all participating schools, giving them ample notice. Have all participants confirm or modify the schedule. Forward schedules to your officers and district personnel.

Manage League

Overseeing an interscholastic activity that you have created provides a real sense of accomplishment. When problems arise, call a conference with your officers to have a problem-solving session. Together, you should be able to smooth out the difficulties. When you have established a broad network to make the league run, you will find management much easier. Do not forget your management tools—fax machine and club contacts sheet.

The Sky Is the Limit

There is really no end of what you can accomplish if you put your mind and will power behind it. The more good you do for your community, the more that will come back to you in kind. A former school teacher who later became President of the United States once framed the idea this way:

> *It is far better to carve your name in the heart of a person than on a granite wall.*
>
> —Lyndon Baines Johnson

Writing Grants

I. Background

There is actually no magic formula for successfully winning grants. All it takes is a good idea that benefits your students or community and a sponsor who sees the value.

A. Two Approaches for Seeking a Grant

There are basically two ways to seek grants. First, you can research grant companies and try to find the right one which suits your needs. This is done by consulting a grant agency index. The second method involves watching the grant bulletins and seeing which agencies are ready and waiting for proposals. Then tailor your proposal to that company.

For example, let's say you want to win a grant to provide for more computers in your school. If you follow the first method, then you will look up grant agencies which cater to giving technology-related services to schools. Using the second method, you would read the grant bulletins to see what agencies are ready to grant computer services, and then you target those organizations. (See pages 223–225 for some listings.)

B. Where to Find Grant Monies

The best way to start looking for grant agencies is to contact your district grant coordinator. Giant volumes of grant agencies are updated every year. Your grant coordinator will be able to tell you where this literature is. Usually, your grant coordinator has copies of all major grant publications. The amount of information that surrounds the grant process is quite formidable. Unfortunately, this stops most people from realizing their dreams. Having a specialist, like your district grant coordinator, makes the grant process flow smoothly.

You can also research grants on your own. Your public library also has in stock the grant reference volumes. Ask your librarian where you can find this material. Make copies or notes of the agencies that you would like to target. Although the grant information will probably seem overwhelming, it is good to get exposed to this technical literature.

II. Proposal Writing

Once you have established who you will write to, the next step is to send them a letter requesting grant guidelines and other pertinent information. Some government agencies have generic applications. On a grant application, you simply follow the directions and send the application with other relevant materials back to the agency. Eventually, you will get a response. However, most grant agencies will request that you write a proposal according to their guidelines. On the following page begins a list of eight steps which are fairly standard guidelines to writing a proposal.

Writing Grants *(cont.)*

A. Eight Steps to an Effective Proposal

1. Summary

A summary of your entire proposal is a good way to start the request. You can write your summary after you have finished all the rest of the steps to mold it better to your content, or you can write your summary first to provide an outline for the rest of your proposal. It serves the purpose of being brief and concise, as well as persuasive and attractive.

The main goal of the summary is to capture the attention of the reader while explaining the merit of your cause. A good summary does the following things:

- Introduces the Grant Applicant: You must explain your organization and tell briefly your background.
- Reveals Credibility: You must answer the question of why your organization is legitimate. A good way to do this is by providing a statistic or quote backing up your organization.
- Identifies the Problem or Goals or Project: You need to highlight what you want to accomplish in a concise manner.
- Specifies a Summary Budget Proposal: Specify the main figures regarding the amount of money you are requesting.

Good summaries are usually no more than a half of a page long.

2. Introduction/Background

This first part of your proposal should lay the foundation for your situation. It should contain the following:

- The kinds of activities that you have done: What has your organization been doing?
- Statistics of credibility for the company/club: Go into detail on specific numbers which justify the legitimacy of your program. "We involved over 400 students from a multi-district region."
- Brief history of your organization: How did your program get off the ground?
- Letters of support and endorsement: Provide for letters from parents, businesses, or anyone else who supports your cause. You can reference these letters by writing "see attached letter."
- Description of your constituents: Who are the people you serve? Are they Hispanics, gifted, underprivileged, at-risk, or other populations?
- Evidence of your accomplishment: Explain the activities your organization did that were successful. Add any newspaper clippings or write-ups.

3. Problem Statement/Needs Assessment

In this section, you must be careful to explain your needs. For instance, if you want to win a grant for 50 extra computers, your need is not to have 50 computers. Your need is to have children learning about technology, etc. At all times, keep in mind that the money you win goes for a greater purpose.

Writing Grants *(cont.)*

3. Problem Statement/Needs Assessment *(cont.)*

Also, be mindful of the difference between a problem and a need. A problem is localized. For instance, a problem for your campus might be lack of playground area. If you win a grant to build a playground, you have solved the problem. A need, on the other hand, is much wider in scope. It is known that many at-risk youth do not prepare for college, clearly a widespread need. A need-based grant is better than a problem-based grant because fulfilling needs has the potential to influence society at a higher level.

A thorough problem statement/needs assessment contains the following items:

- Reason Behind the Proposal: What made you seek a grant?
- Relation of Problem/Need to Purposes of the Organization: Does your need correlate with what your organization does? How?
- Practical Application: Is your need or problem one of reasonable dimensions? Is it possible to solve the it in a practical way?
- Statistical Support: What facts and figures can you provide that show the need or problem in an obvious fashion?
- Statements from Authorities: What do experts say about your problem or need? Does it agree with your assessment of the problem? How?

4. Program Objectives

You must list the objectives your program seeks to accomplish. For instance, if you are writing that grant for 50 computers, your goal is "to make our youth computer-literate for the 21st century." Program objectives should relate to the improvement of society as a whole. Keep your objectives realistic and down to earth. Some grant agencies want to see objectives in numerical or measurable terms. Examples of program objectives are the following:

- to have 500 youths participate in an interscholastic league
- to train all students on word processing programs
- to improve the grade average of all at-risk students
- to facilitate the communication between teachers and students
- to improve the citizenship values of all students

5. Methods

The next step is to explain how you will attain your program objectives. Powerful descriptions of methods usually . . .

- flow naturally from problems and objectives.
- clearly describe problems and objectives.
- give a calendar or sequence of activities/methods.
- describe staffing needs.
- detail clients and describe method of client selection.
- present a reasonable scope of activities.

Writing Grants *(cont.)*

6. Evaluation Plan

After you have explained the reasons for your program, your objectives, and how you reach those objectives, you must describe how all this will be evaluated. In other words, the grant agency is interested in knowing whether their money will go into something that works. Therefore, it is essential that you provide a plan which outlines how your outcomes will be measured. This section might be the hardest section to complete, depending on the program. Finding ways to evaluate performance is complex and susceptible to bias.

For example, an ineffective evaluation plan would be a write-up by you as the program director of program effectiveness after the program is completed. You may see the program working differently than others will.

A more balanced evaluation plan would be write ups from not only you as the director but from parents, students, community people and others who were affected by the program. Providing for a questionnaire that expresses anonymous reactions and evaluations of your program is another balanced approach. Other methods to develop evaluation plans are the following:

- cost effectiveness analysis
- data analysis
- assigning an evaluation committee
- hiring an independent consultant/evaluator
- letters from constituents

The benefits of a well-thought-out evaluation plan are that it gives evidence of success. Also, it targets areas of improvement or redirection. In addition, a solid evaluation plan will make it easier to get funding in the future.

7. Future Funding

It is necessary to think beyond the proposed grant period. Will your program just die after the grant runs out? If so, it is not likely that a grant agency will look on your proposal very seriously. Therefore, you must describe how your program will continue after the grant runs out.

It could be that your grant will start up a program which will run itself. This kind of grant is called "seed money." If this is the case, then describe how it will operate. If your program will still need funding after the grant period, list ways that you will obtain that funding.

Remember from Chapter 12 all the ways you can raise funds? Those methods are legitimate ways of future funding. Other methods of future funding are the following:

- fees from members or others involved
- patronage from local organizations
- providing profitable services
- other grants

Writing Grants *(cont.)*

8. Proposed Budget

In the last section of your proposal, you need to give a detailed list of funds needed. On your proposed budget, indicate how much money has already been donated according to the item. Make a list of all your program's expenses and organize it in the following fashion:

Item	Total Requested	Total Donated
1. Personnel		
a. salaries and wages	$	$
b. fringe benefits	$	$
c. consultants and contact services	$	$
2. Non-personnel		
a. space		
- rent	$	$
- utilities	$	$
- upkeep	$	$
b. other costs		
- equipment	$	$
- telephone	$	$
- consumable supplies	$	$
- travel/mileage	$	$

Your budget might not be this detailed. For instance, if you propose getting 50 computers, the only cost will be equipment and consultant/repair fees. If you are providing a service, then there are mainly salary/wage expenses. Be as reasonable and detailed as possible.

B. Putting It All Together

When you put all this together, the whole proposal should not exceed five typed pages. Grant coordinators usually like to see three pages plus the budget. Edit it carefully before you submit the final copy. Have a colleague read it over and provide suggestions. Copy the letter on school letterhead or your organization's letterhead. Add any clippings, letters, write ups or other documents which are referenced in the proposal. Send the proposal in a large envelope that cannot be folded or mangled. Make sure that your principal knows about your grant-seeking adventures and give copies of all communication to your district.

Next, wait patiently for the letter of acceptance or denial. If you get a denial, send it to other grant agencies. You may be surprised at how easy it is to win a grant for a good cause. Think large, prepare thoroughly, and you can help your students, school, and community in ways that you never thought possible.

Writing Grants *(cont.)*

The most commonly asked question concerning educational technology is "How do we pay for all of this?" With shrinking school budgets and the increasing demand for current innovation in the classroom, how can schools keep up? There are resources available for teachers and schools, and it is quite frequently just a matter of expressing a need, submitting an application, and formulating a technology plan. The following is a list of foundations, coalitions, technology educational funds and the like, which offer financial assistance to schools seeking technology.

1. **Foundation Center** has published a directory listing over 6,000 large foundations which donated over $9 billion dollars last year. This publication is called the *Foundation Directory*. It includes descriptions of grants, fund-raising examples, and grant makers' priorities in addition to listings of these foundations. The cost is $195 for hard cover and $170 for soft cover. It may be available in your public library. There are other helpful publications available as well.

   Contact: The Foundation Center

   Dept. PR35

   79 Fifth Avenue

   New York, NY 10003-3076

   (800) 424-9836

2. **The U.S. Department of Education** offers a listing of national educational technology groups and other resources through its Goals 2000 Resource Center. For more information call (800) USA-LEARN.

   Also from the U.S. Department of Education is an annual listing of grants and fellowships offered by various offices of education. There are a variety of deadlines, levels of support, and eligibility requirements. The publication, *The Federal Register*, costs $4.50.

   Contact: Superintendent of Documents

   U.S. Government Printing Office

   Washington, D.C. 20402

Writing Grants *(cont.)*

3. **Nike** has a funding program called the "Just Do It" fund which supports disadvantaged youth. Grants range from $5,000 to $25,000. Grants are administered through the National Foundation for the Improvement of Education.

   Contact: NFIE

   Just Do It Teacher Grants

   1201 16th Street NW

   Washington, D.C. 20036

4. **CompuMentor** is a nonprofit group which offers corporation-donated software and computer books at low cost to nonprofit groups and schools. DOS software is $25 and MAC is $6.

   Contact: CompuMentor

   89 Stillman Street

   San Francisco, CA 94107

5. **Kraft General Foods** offers grants to K-12 programs focusing on educational achievement. Priority is given to programs operating where company facilities are located.

   Contact: Director, Corporate Contribution

   Kraft General Foods

   Three Lakes Drive N3C

   Northfield, IL 60093

6. **Sony Electronics** supports programs encouraging the learning of technical and scientific skills required for tomorrow's work force.

   Contact: Corporate Communications

   Sony Electronics, Inc.

   One Sony Drive MD 3E2

   Park Ridge, NJ 07656

Writing Grants *(cont.)*

7. **Pew Charitable Trusts** provides grants in several areas, including the restructuring of American education for higher performance, supporting the 21st century classroom, and strengthening the quality of teaching and learning in America's schools.

   Contact: The Pew Charitable Trusts

   One Commerce Square

   2005 Market Street #1700

   Philadelphia, PA 19103

8. **The Software Publishers Association** and **Gifts in Kind America** are working together to collect donations of software for schools and nonprofit organizations nation wide. In 1993 over $16 million dollars worth of software was donated by groups such as Microsoft, Lotus, Egghead, Claris, Aldus, and WordPerfect.

   Contact: Gifts in Kind America

   700 North Fairfax Street #300

   Alexandria, VA 22314

9. Last year the **Ford Foundation** contributed over $50 million to education and cultural projects. If your technology projects can coincide with the promotion of cultural diversity and the preservation of cultural traditions, contact the Foundation for further information.

   Contact: Secretary

   Ford Foundation

   320 East 43rd Street

   New York, NY 10017

10. **The Prudential Foundation** focuses mainly on educational projects that enrich the lives of disadvantaged and minority young children. Promotion of conflict-resolution projects is largely supported.

    Contact: The Prudential Foundation

    751 Broad Street, 15th Floor

    Newark, NJ 07102

Resource Library

Outline of Chapter 14

I. Further Reading   II. Reproducibles

Chapter 14 provides practical and immediate reference for all occasions. First, a list of related literature is provided for you by chapter and topic. After each chapter is read, the list may be checked for further interests. Note that periodicals are especially relevant for current topics. At present, for example, no authoritative books on teaming are available, although many periodicals address the topic. Staying abreast of the crucial literature in education is a key element in becoming a good teacher. Practical books like Canter's *Assertive Discipline* and Johnson and Johnson's *Cooperation in the Classroom* are especially helpful to every classroom teacher.

The second part of the chapter is a library of almost every form you will need as a classroom teacher. These "reproducibles," intended for your use, are arranged by chapter and cross-referenced in the text. On the opening page of each chapter, you may recall, the reproducibles mentioned in that chapter are listed in bold-faced italic type directly under the chapter outline. There are many ways to use reproducibles:

1. For most of the forms, you should make an appropriate number of copies and store them in your file cabinet.

2. For the matrices, you will want to record valuable names and numbers, making sure to guard against loss.

3. Some forms, like the mediators (Chapter 2) and the library poster (Chapter 8), you will want to laminate and store appropriately.

4. The passes (Chapters 5,7,8, and 12) should be copied on differently colored paper to stand out. The club passes from Chapter 12 should be laminated for protection.

5. Some reproducibles are meant to give to the students, like the Matching Game (Chapter 2), Conflict Resolution form (Chapter 2), Student Award form (Chapter 4), College Plans worksheet (Chapter 8), and School-Home Contracts (Chapter 11). Make copies appropriately.

6. Lastly, some forms are intended to go home to parents. These are located in Chapters 4, 5, 7, 8, 11, and 12. You might wish to send these home in envelopes and have students return the envelopes signed to ensure accountability.

Resource Library *(cont.)*

I. Further Reading

Following is a list of seminal literature to improve professional awareness. It is organized by chapter and topic. The book titles are represented first, and then the author, publisher, and year first published. Starred works are highly recommended by the author.

Chapter I: The Micro/Macro Worlds of Middle School

Adolescent Issues

Adolescent Sex Roles and Social Change. George Lawry. Year Book Medical, 1978.

The Biology of the Adolescent. Herant Katchadourian. Freeman, 1977.

Child Abuse. Kempe/Kempe. Harvard University Press, 1984.

The Developing Person Through the Life Span. K. Berger. Worth, 1988.

The Divorce Revolution: The Unexpected Social and Economic Consequences for Women and Children in America. Lenore Weitzman. Free Press, 1985.

Girls at Puberty: Biological and Psychosocial Perspectives. Karen Paige. Plenum, 1983.

The Nature of Adolescent Judgment. E. A. Peel. Wiley, 1971.

The Philosophy of Moral Development. Lawrence Kohlberg. Harper & Row, 1981.*

Periodicals:

American Psychologist
Journal of Early Adolescence
Psychology Today

Reform Issues

The Fifth Discipline, the Art and Practice of Learning Organization. Peter Senge. Doubleday, 1990.

High School: A Report on Secondary Education in America. Ernest Boyer. Harper & Row, 1983.*

The Mismeasure of Man. S. J. Gould. W. W. Thornton, 1981.

A Nation at Risk. National Commission on Excellence in Education. U. S. Government Printing Office, 1983.

Schools for the 21st Century: Leadership Imperatives for Educational Reform. Phillip C. Schlechty. Jossey-Bass, 1990.

Schools of Quality, an Introduction to Total Quality Management in Education. John Jay Bonstingle. ASCD, 1992.

Resource Library *(cont.)*

Chapter 1 *(cont.)*

Schools We Deserve: Reflections of the Educational Crisis of Our Time. Diane Ravitch. Basic Books, 1985.

Smart Schools, Smart Kids: Why Do Some Schools Work? Edward B. Fiske. Touchstone Books, 1991.*

Periodicals:

Educational Leadership*

Chapter 2: Creating Order in the Classroom

Assertive Discipline, a Take Charge Approach for Today's Educator. Canter/Canter. Lee Canter & Assc., 1976* (See also video tapes, workshops, and other Canter manuals.)

Building Classroom Discipline. C. M. Charles. Longman, 1992.*

Control Theory in the Classroom. W. Glasser. Perennial Library, 1986.

Discipline with Dignity. Curwin/Mendler. ASCD, 1988.

Juvenile Delinquency: Trends and Perspectives. Rutter/Giller, 1984.

RX Improved Instruction. Madeline Hunter. Tip, 1976.

Chapter 3: Teaching the Basics

Cognitive Instructional Psychology: Components of Classroom Learning. J. Snowman. Academic Press, 1989.

Dyslexia, an Appraisal of Current Knowledge. Satz/Taylor/Friel/Fletcher, Oxford University Press, 1987.

Educating Mentally Retarded Persons in the Mainstream. Baker/Gottlieb. University Park Press, 1980.

Frames of Mind, the Theory of Multiple Intelligences. Howard Gardener. Harper Collins, 1983.*

Handbook of Special Education. Sprague/Ullman. Prentice Hall, 1981.

The Hyperactive Child, Adolescent and Adult: Attention Deficit Disorder Through the Life Span. Oxford Press, 1987.

Hyperactivity: Current Issues, Research, and Theory. Ross/Ross. Wiley, 1982.

In Their Own Way: Discovering and Learning Your Child's Personal Learning Style. T. Armstrong. J. P. Tarcher, 1987.

Mainstream Education for Hearing Impaired Children and Youth. Gary Nix (ed.). Grune & Stratton , 1976.

Resource Library *(cont.)*

Chapter 3 *(cont.)*

Seven Ways of Knowing: Teaching for Multiple Intelligences. David Lazear. Skylight pub., 1991.

Taxonomy of Educational Objectives. Benjamin Bloom. David McKay, 1956*

Chapter 4: Curriculum Development

Awareness Through Movement: Health Exercises for Personal Growth. M. Feldenkrais. Harper & Row, 1977.

Circles of Learning. Johnson/Johnson/Holubec. International Books Co., 1988.*

Cooperation in the Classroom. Johnson/Johnson/Holubec. International Books Co., 1988.*

Cooperative Learning. R. Slavin. Longman Press, 1983.

Cooperative Learning Resources for Teachers. S. Kagan. Resources for Teachers, 1990.

Curriculum: Foundation, Principles, and Issues. Ornstein/Hunkins. Prentice Hall, 1988.

Curriculum Planning: A New Approach. Glen Hass (ed.). Allyin & Bacon, 1987.

Developing Minds. A. Costa (ed.). ASCD, 1991.

Instruction: A Models Approach. Gunter/Estes/Swab. Allyn & Bacon, 1990.

Using Literature to Teach Middle Grades About War. P. Kennemer. Oryx Press, 1993.

Chapter 6: Incorporating Technology in the Classroom

Information Age

Future Shock. A. Toffler. Random House, 1970.

Megatrends. John Naisbit. Warner Books, 1984.

Micro Millennium. T. Evans. Washington Square Press, 1979.

Third Wave. A. Toffler. William Morrow, 1980.

Classroom Applications

Classroom Applications of Microcomputers. Beatty/Bullough. Macmillan, 1991.

Computer Based Instruction: Methods and Development. Alessi/Trollip. Prentice Hall, 1985.

Computers in Education. J. Hirschbuhl. Dushkin, 1988.

Computer in the School: Tutor, Tool, Tutee. R. Taylor. Teacher's College Press, 1980.

Resource Library *(cont.)*

Chapter 6 *(cont.)*

The Illustrated Computer Dictionary. D. Spenser. Merril, 1986.

Integrating Computers into the Elementary Middle School. Roberts/Carter/Friel/Miller. Prentice Hall, 1987.

Power On! New Tools for Teaching and Learning. U.S. Office of Technology Assessment, 1988.

Periodicals:

A+
Apple Educator's Newsletter
Classroom Computer Learning
The Computing Teacher
Educational Technology
inCider
Macazine
PC World
School Microcomputer Bulletin
Technology Review

Chapter 7: Teaming

Periodicals:

Childhood Education (Summer 1994)
Education Digest (Feb. 1989, May 1987)
Educational Leadership (Oct. 1991)
Education Week (March 9, 1988)
Phi Delta Kappan (May 1993)

Chapter 8: The Counselor and Other Support Services

Behavioralism. John Watson. University of Chicago Press, 1967.

The Developmental Psychology of Jean Piaget. Flavell. Van Nostrand, 1963.

The Essential Piaget. Gruber/Vonech *(eds.).* Basic Books, 1977.

Farther Reaches of Human Nature. Abraham Maslow. Viking Press, 1971.*

Interpretation of Dreams. Sigmund Freud. Basic Books, 1965 (1899).

On Becoming a Person. Carl Rogers. Houghton Mifflin, 1961.

Science and Human Behavior. B. F. Skinner. Macmillan, 1953. (See also *Verbal Behavior* and *Beyond Freedom and Dignity*.)

Resource Library *(cont.)*

Chapter 8 *(cont.)*

Seven Habits of Highly Effective People. Stephen Covey. Simon & Schuster, 1990.*

Toward a Psychology of Learning. Abraham Maslow. Van Nostrand Reinhold, 1982.

Chapter 9: Campus Administration

Principals in Action. Morris/Crowson/Porter-Gehrie/Hurwitz. Merrial Books, 1984.

Periodicals:

Education Evaluation & Policy Analysis (vol. 14, no. 1)

Educational Leadership (Oct. 1993)

Chapter 10: Districts, Regions, and States

Ella Flagg Young: Portrait of a Leader. Joan Smith. Iowa State Press, 1979.

A History of Thought and Practice in Education Administration. Cabell/Fleming/Newell/Bennion. Teacher's College Press, 1987.

The Law of Public Education. E. Reutter. Foundation Press, 1985.

Public School Law, Teacher's and Student's Rights. Allyn & Bacon, 1992.

School Law: Cases and Concepts. M. LaMorte. Allyn & Bacon, 1991.

Teachers and the Law. Fischer/Schimmel/Kelly. Longman Press, 1991.

Chapter 11: Parental Involvement

The Third Side of the Desk: How Parents Can Change the Schools. Charles Scribner's Sons, 1973.

Chapter 13: Writing Grants

Grantsmanship. Armand Lauffer. Sage Publications, 1983.

How to Write Proposals that Produce. Joel Bowman, Oryx Press, 1992.

Resource Library

II. Reproducibles

from Chapter 2: Creating Order in the Classroom

1. Matching Game
2. Personary Activity Sheet
3. Personal ID Sheets
4. Student Helpers Form
5. Syllabus Unit Planner
6. Mediators—Tardiness, Not Following Directions, Talking, Rudeness, and Silliness
7. Conflict Resolution Form

from Chapter 3: Teaching the Basics

1. Book Check-Out List
2. Textbook Record Sheet
3. Cognitive Map Form

from Chapter 4: Curriculum Development

1. Instructional Unit Planning Sheet
2. Lesson Plan Sheet
3. Home Groups Cooperative Learning
4. Lesson Plan Form Cooperative Learning
5. Presentation Evaluation
6. Guest Speakers Matrix
7. Field Trip Form
8. Field Trip Checklist
9. Field Trip Letter to Parents Form
10. Field Trip Nonparticipant Form
11. Student Award Form

from Chapter 5: Effective Classroom Administration

1. Class Grid (all purpose)
2. Teacher Parent Warning Form
3. Homework Weekly Planner
4. Self-Evaluation Form
5. Hall Passes
6. Health Notice to Parents
7. Substitute Record Form

from Chapter 7: Teaming

1. Team Procedures Checklist
2. Team Calendar
3. D-Hall Passes
4. Team Instructional Unit Form
5. Team Meeting Record
6. Team-Student Conference Form
7. Team Assembly Form
8. Team Assembly Notice

from Chapter 8: The Counselor and Other Support Services

1. Counselor Referral Form
2. College Plans Worksheet
3. Grade Change Form
4. Progress Report Form
5. Tutoring Center Matrix
6. Library Rules Poster
7. Library Passes

from Chapter 9: Campus Administration

1. Memo to Principal Form
2. Memo to Vice Principal Form
3. Attendance Change Form
4. Supplies Order Form
5. School Fax Form
6. Furniture Request/Equipment Repair Form

from Chapter 11: Parental Involvement

1. General Letter Home
2. Parent Phone Record
3. Parent Conference Log
4. School-Home Contract (Daily)
5. School-Home Contract (Weekly)
6. Parent Conference Sign Up Sheet
7. Parent Volunteer Sign Up Form
8. Parent Volunteer Call
9. Parent Thank You Letter

from Chapter 12: Organizing a School Club

1. Club Members Matrix
2. Club Passes
3. Club Activities Planner
4. Intent of Fund-Raising
5. Bake Sale Form
6. Community/Business Request for Help
7. Accounting Log
8. Club Contacts Matrix
9. Club Event Organizer

Matching Game

What is your favorite. . .

animal?

book?

song?

color?

food?

place to visit?

movie?

type of shoe?

instrument?

Directions: Write your answers to the questions in the boxes. When your teacher tells you to, check around the room to see how many students wrote the same responses. If you find a match with another student, have that person sign his\her name in the box. Be prepared to speak about your experience.

Personary Activity Sheet

Name:

_____

Pronunciation Key:

(_____)

Part of Speech:

_____

Definitions:

1. _____
_____

2. _____
_____

3. _____
_____

Synonym: _____

Antonym: _____

Name Used in a Sentence: _____

Picture _____

Personal ID Sheet

Name: _____

Address: _____

Home phone: _____

Parents' names: _____

Parents' work phones: _____

Schedule

Period	Teacher	Room #	Subject

Student Helpers!

Attendance _____

_____

Scribes/Recorders _____

_____

Passers/Collectors _____

_____

Organizers _____

_____

Messengers _____

_____

Cleaners _____

_____

Officers of the Class _____

_____

Other _____

_____

_____

_____

Syllabus Unit Planner

Teacher _____   Subject _____

School _____

Dates _____

Unit	Projects	Other

Month_____   **Activities**

M _____

_____

T _____

W _____

Th _____

F _____

M _____

T _____

W _____

Th _____

F _____

Syllabus Unit Planner *(cont.)*

Month_____   **Activities**

M
_____

T
_____

W
_____

Th
_____

F
_____

M
_____

T
_____

W
_____

Th
_____

F
_____

M
_____

T
_____

W
_____

Th
_____

F
_____

Special Notes

Tardiness

What Did I Do?

I was late to class.

How Does My Action Affect the Class?

When I am late to class, I interrupt normal activities. The teacher has to stop teaching to deal with my tardiness. In addition, the students who are trying to learn have to be delayed from learning because of my actions.

How Do My Actions Affect Me?

When I am tardy to class, I miss valuable learning time that is intended to help me succeed in life. When I am tardy, I miss warm-ups which are important to my success in class. In addition, I am setting a bad precedent for my life. In the real world, I would probably get fired if I was tardy to my job without a sufficient reason. Tardiness is also a sign of disrespect to the teacher. Above all, tardiness is a negative influence in my life. Tardiness can also make me fail the course.

What Should I Have Done?

I should have taken care of my concerns in the hallway and made it to class on time. If there is a pressing problem, like going to the bathroom, I should ask the teacher ahead of time so I am not tardy to class.

What Will I Do Next Time?

I will make an effort not to be late to class anymore.

Not Following Directions

What Did I Do?

I did not follow directions.

How Does My Action Affect the Class?

When I do not follow directions, I interrupt normal class activities. The teacher has to stop teaching and deal with my situation. In addition, the students who are trying to learn have to be delayed from learning because of my actions.

How Do My Actions Affect Me?

When I do not follow directions, I choose to interrupt the flow of learning. This hurts my grade, and it hurts my potential for future success. In the real world, my boss will expect me to follow company rules too.

What Should I Have Done?

I should have read or listened to the directions carefully and proceeded to followed them like everybody else.

What Will I Do Next Time?

Next time, if I have a question or concern about the directions, I will raise my hand and ask the teacher. The teacher might understand my confusion and explain the directions differently so I can understand.

Certificate of
Award

_____

is awarded this certificate of
Notable Accomplishment in
Recognition of

_____

_____

Signed _____

This ___25^(TH)___ day of _May, 2004_____

Talking

What Did I Do?

I was talking without permission.

How Does My Action Affect the Class?

When I am talking excessively, I interrupt normal class activities. The teacher has to stop teaching and deal with my problem. In addition, the students who are trying to learn have to be delayed from learning because of my actions.

How Do My Actions Affect Me?

By my excessive talk, I show how immaturely I can act. The teacher loses respect for me and has to treat me like a small child. I know I am not a small child, but I will get treated like one when I continue to talk out of turn. The teacher might have to call my parents, and I could be punished.

What Should I Have Done?

I should have raised my hand. The teacher would have called on me, and I could have spoken then. If I needed to communicate to someone else in the classroom, I could have waited until after class.

What Will I Do Next Time?

Next time I will raise my hand to be heard in front of class or wait to speak to my friends after class.

Rudeness

What Did I Do?

I was being rude to another person.

How Does My Action Affect the Class?

Rudeness hurts others' feelings as well as distracts the class from learning. When I am overly rude, I interrupt normal class activities. The teacher has to stop teaching and deal with my rudeness. In addition, the students who are trying to learn have to be delayed from learning because of my actions. The person I was rude to may have hurt feelings.

How Do My Actions Affect Me?

Being rude is a bad reflection on me as a human being. The more badness that I give, the more badness I will get. In addition, rudeness can lower my grade and get me in trouble with my parents.

What Should I Have Done?

If I feel that I should be rude to someone, I should tell the teacher and explain the situation. The teacher will be fair, and I can resolve my conflict peacefully.

What Will I Do Next Time?

I will not be rude to anyone. I know the more love I give, the more love I get.

Silliness

What Did I Do?

I was being annoying by acting silly.

How Does My Action Affect the Class?

When I clown around during a serious part of class, it distracts other members of the class. They have to stop learning and listen to the teacher deal with me. Other students are negatively affected by my actions. They want to learn, but it makes it hard to learn when I am clowning around.

How Do My Actions Affect Me?

By my silliness, I show how immaturely I can act. The teacher loses respect for me and has to treat me like a small child. I know I am not a small child, but I will get treated like one when I continue to be silly. The teacher might have to call my parents, and I could be punished.

What Should I Have Done?

I should keep my silly thoughts and actions to myself or tell a friend during lunch or after school.

What Will I Do Next Time?

I will refrain from annoying the class with my silliness. If I have trouble controlling my silliness, I will tell the teacher so we can resolve the problem.

Conflict Resolution

Persons Involved: _____

Nature of Conflict: _____

Side 1:_____

Side 2:_____

Possible Compromises:

1)

2)

3)

Agreement: Date:_____

_____   _____   _____
Student   Student   Mediator

Book Check-Out List

Teacher _____

Subject _____

Name	Book	Date Checked

Textbook Record Sheet

Text:	Publisher:	Date:

Book Numbers	Student Names	
	Comments:	
	Comments:	
	Comments:	
	Comments:	
	Comments:	
	Comments:	
	Comments:	
	Comments:	

Cognitive Map Form

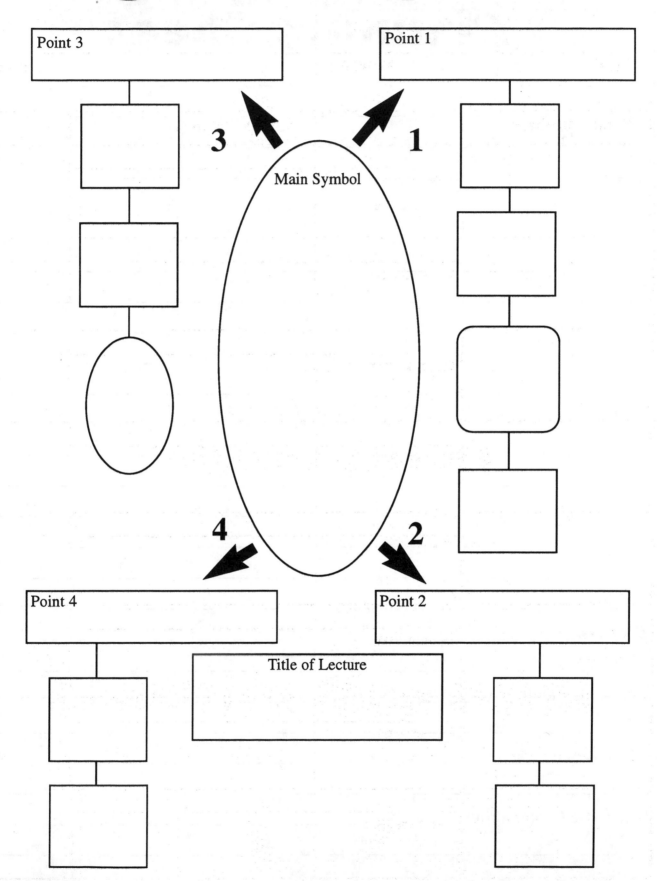

Point 3

Point 1

3

1

Main Symbol

4

2

Point 4

Point 2

Title of Lecture

Instructional Unit Planning Sheet

Unit: _____

Planning Period: _____

Lesson Ideas: _____

_____

_____

_____

_____

_____

_____

_____

Cooperative Learning Ideas: _____

_____

_____

_____

_____

_____

_____

_____

Projects: _____

_____

Guest Speakers: _____

_____

Field Trips: _____

_____

Thematic Celebrations: _____

_____

Lesson Plan

Title of Lesson _____

Objective:

Method:

Assignment:

Materials:

Homework:

Home Groups

Cooperative Learning

CL Lesson Plans

Date:_____

Objective:

Group Size:	Pairs	Triads	Quads	Cinco	Other

Materials:

Student Groups

Directions:

Presentation Evaluation

Student_____

Presentation Title_____ Date_____

1 **not at all**	**2** **a little**	**3** **fair**	**4** **effective**	**5** **superb**

Speaking

☐ voice was clear, commanding

☐ used pauses effectively

☐ varied voice tones, not monotonous

Gestures

☐ used arm gestures

☐ moved appropriately

Vision

☐ made good eye contact

Knowledge

☐ seemed competent in subject matter

☐ answered questions thoroughly

8–14 Needs Major Improvement

15–25 Not Bad

26–34 Good Job

35–40 Excellent Speaking Skills

speaking
gestures
vision
knowledge
total

Presentation Total =

Comments:

Guest Speakers Matrix

Name: _____

Occupation: _____

Phone: Work_____ Home _____

Address: _____

Used for unit:_____ Date: _____

Name: _____

Occupation: _____

Phone: Work_____ Home _____

Address: _____

Used for unit:_____ Date: _____

Name: _____

Occupation: _____

Phone: Work_____ Home _____

Address: _____

Used for unit:_____ Date: _____

Name: _____

Occupation: _____

Phone: Work_____ Home _____

Address: _____

Used for unit:_____ Date: _____

Name: _____

Occupation: _____

Phone: Work_____ Home _____

Address: _____

Used for unit:_____ Date: _____

Field Trip Form

Location:

Unit:

Dates:	**Times:**

Contacts: **Phone:**

House Rules:

Principal Approval: Yes_____   No_____

Conditions for Participation

Grades: **Behavior:**

Field Trip Checklist

Permission slips with parent phone numbers .... ☐

Food

    All student lunches with names .... ☐

    Every student with money for lunch .... ☐

    Cooler with ice and drinks .... ☐

Maps/Information Sheets .... ☐

Attendance .... ☐

Nonparticipants

    Put nonparticipant forms in teachers boxes. .... ☐

    Gave materials to nonparticipants. .... ☐

Students understand rules on bus. .... ☐

Students understand field trip rules .... ☐

Student helpers to move lunches/cooler .... ☐

Special equipment/clothing .... ☐

Students understand what to bring. .... ☐

Keys/Wallet with extra cash .... ☐

Lock your door! .... ☐

Field Trip Letter to Parents Form

Field Trip Alert!

School_____

Date_____

Dear Parents,

Our class is planning a field trip soon.

Place: _____

Address: _____

Date: _____

The purpose of our activity is the following:_____

_____

Students will need the following: _____

_____

_____

_____

Teacher Signature

Please return this letter with your signature if you wish your child to participate in this activity.

_____has my permission to attend this activity.

_____

Signature of parent or guardian

Field Trip Nonparticipant Form

Teacher:_____

The following students are not participating in a class activity:	Teachers receiving students:

Instead, they will be assigned to your class from_____

Their assignment should take them the whole period. Specifically, their assignment is:

Please collect their work and put it in my box.

Names of students who were misbehaving:

Thank you again! I will be glad to return the favor.

Certificate of Award

_____

is awarded this certificate of Notable Accomplishment in Recognition of

_____

_____

Signed _____

This _____ day of _____

Class Grid

Period _____

Teacher _____

Subject_____

	A		B
1			
2			
3			
4			
5			
6			
7			
8			
9			
10			
11			
12			
13			
14			
15			
16			
17			
18			
19			
20			
21			
22			
23			
24			
25			
26			
27			
28			
29			
30			

Teacher-Parent Warning

Teacher-Parent Warning

Your son or daughter has a deficiency in the following area(s):

- ❑ Needs Extra Practice
- ❑ Has Not Turned in Homework
- ❑ Is Currently Failing
- ❑ Is Not Working to Potential

_____

_____

_____

_____

- ❑ Response Needed

Teacher-Parent Warning

Your son or daughter has a deficiency in the following area(s):

- ❑ Needs Extra Practice
- ❑ Has Not Turned in Homework
- ❑ Is Currently Failing
- ❑ Is Not Working to Potential

_____

_____

_____

_____

- ❑ Response Needed

Teacher-Parent Warning

Your son or daughter has a deficiency in the following area(s):

- ❑ Needs Extra Practice
- ❑ Has Not Turned in Homework
- ❑ Is Currently Failing
- ❑ Is Not Working to Potential

_____

_____

_____

_____

- ❑ Response Needed

Teacher-Parent Warning

Your son or daughter has a deficiency in the following area(s):

- ❑ Needs Extra Practice
- ❑ Has Not Turned in Homework
- ❑ Is Currently Failing
- ❑ Is Not Working to Potential

_____

_____

_____

_____

- ❑ Response Needed

Homework Weekly Planner

Name:_____

Monday		Tuesday	

Wednesday		Thursday	

Weekend Homework

Projects:

Self-Evaluation

Answer the following questions thoughtfully on your own paper.

1. What are my strengths in this class?

2. What are the areas that I need to improve?

3. What are the best things about this class?

4. What are the worst things about this class?

5. Did I try as hard as I could have in this class so far? If not, why?

6. Do I think I've learned a lot in the class?

7. What is the most valuable thing I learned? Why?

8. Have I behaved myself in this class? How?

9. Have I treated others with respect? How?

10. What can I do to continuously improve myself?

Hall Passes

Make copies on differently colored paper to distinguish. Cut and use.

Hall Pass	**Hall Pass**	**Hall Pass**
student: _____	student: _____	student: _____
to: _____	to: _____	to: _____
time: _____	time: _____	time: _____
teacher: _____	teacher: _____	teacher: _____
Hall Pass	**Hall Pass**	**Hall Pass**
student: _____	student: _____	student: _____
to: _____	to: _____	to: _____
time: _____	time: _____	time: _____
teacher: _____	teacher: _____	teacher: _____
Hall Pass	**Hall Pass**	**Hall Pass**
student: _____	student: _____	student: _____
to: _____	to: _____	to: _____
time: _____	time: _____	time: _____
teacher: _____	teacher: _____	teacher: _____
Hall Pass	**Hall Pass**	**Hall Pass**
student: _____	student: _____	student: _____
to: _____	to: _____	to: _____
time: _____	time: _____	time: _____
teacher: _____	teacher: _____	teacher: _____

Health Notice to Parents

from_____

In order to provide quality health care for all my students, I request that each parent supply a box of tissue for class use. If every parent donates one box, it will help keep a healthy class all year.

Please fill out the bottom portion of this letter and send it with a box of tissue.

Name of student _____

Name of parents _____

Date on which box of tissue was sent _____

Thank you for your support!

Substitute's Record

Date(s):_____ Subject: _____

Regular Teacher: _____

Substitute Teacher: _____

Message for the substitute . . .

Thank you for teaching my class while I am absent. I want you to know that we appreciate your help and hard work. In my "sub folder" you will find seating charts, lesson plans, mediators, and a list of helpful students. Once again, thank you for everything.

Attendance cards are _____

Hall/restroom privileges are up to your own good judgment. The passes are

_____

If one of my students gives you a problem, please follow this procedure. _____

_____

_____

_____

Please make a record below of the day's events, listing any uncooperative students or other important information.

_____

_____

_____

_____

_____

_____

_____

_____

_____

_____

_____

_____

_____

Team Procedures Checklist

Team Name _____ Colors _____ Symbol _____

Leader _____

Secretary _____

Communications Coordinator _____

Events Coordinator _____

Curriculum Coordinator _____

Parent Coordinator _____

Community Coordinator _____

Treasurer _____

Other _____

Discipline Policies _____

_____

_____

| Substitute folders prepared |
| yes   no |
| Hall/restoom passes |
| yes   no |
| Team Calendar |
| yes   no |

Consequences	**Check if Used**
Warning _____
Mediators _____
Rudeness _____
Talking excessively _____
Tardiness _____
Silliness _____
Not following directions _____
Other _____
Detentions _____
Lunch _____
After School _____
Time-Out Stations _____
Loss of Privileges _____
Outside _____
Activity _____
Other _____
Team Conference _____
Clean-up duty _____
Parent Conference _____
Home contract _____
Referral _____
Other _____

Academic Guidelines
(circle or complete)

Grading standards: **Different   Uniform**

Amount of homework:

  Daily   **Yes   No Sometimes**

  On weekends   **Yes   No Sometimes**

Late work penalty:

  Daily work   _____ a day

  Major projects   _____ a day

  If completed same day _____

Extra credit bonus:

  Assignments available **Yes No**

  Bonus points _____

  For typed work   **Yes No**

Special:_____

_____

_____

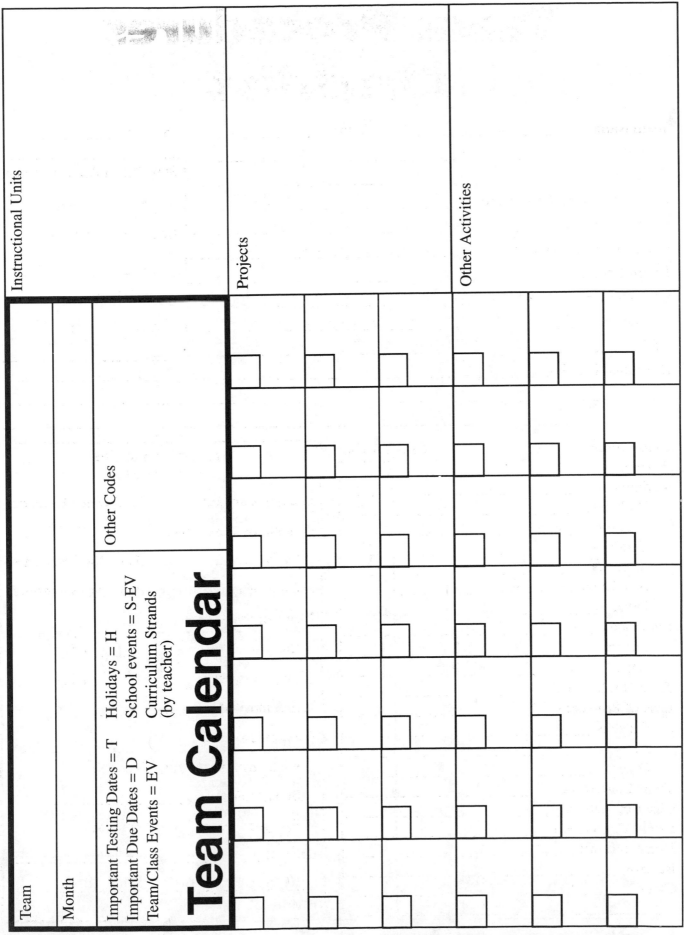

Instructional Units

Projects

Other Activities

Team

Month

Important Testing Dates = T   Holidays = H
Important Due Dates = D   School events = S-EV
Team/Class Events = EV   Curriculum Strands
                                                    (by teacher)

Other Codes

Team Calendar

D-Hall

D-Hall

pass for _____

teacher _____

date signed _____

circle: lunch   after school

in room _____

Bring all books, notebooks, and materials.

D-Hall

pass for _____

teacher _____

date signed _____

circle: lunch   after school

in room _____

Bring all books, notebooks, and materials.

D-Hall

pass for _____

teacher _____

date signed _____

circle: lunch   after school

in room _____

Bring all books, notebooks, and materials.

D-Hall

pass for _____

teacher _____

date signed _____

circle: lunch   after school

in room _____

Bring all books, notebooks, and materials.

D-Hall

pass for _____

teacher _____

date signed _____

circle: lunch   after school

in room _____

Bring all books, notebooks, and materials.

D-Hall

pass for _____

teacher _____

date signed _____

circle: lunch   after school

in room _____

Bring all books, notebooks, and materials.

Team Instructional Unit

Multidisciplinary   Interdisciplinary

Team   Date

Theme

Teachers Involved	Project Ideas

Objectives

_____

_____

_____

Lesson Ideas

Other Activities

Team Meeting Record

Team	Date

Agenda	Visitors/Special Guests	Members Present

Upcoming Events

Team-Student Conference

Team	Date
Student	Members Present
Nature of Concern	Student Feedback

Resolutions Made

Contract Needed   Yes   No
Parents' Names/Phone Numbers
Parent Conference Needed Yes   No

Team Assembly

Team _____

Date of Assembly _____

Type of Assembly _____

Parents Are Invited   yes   no

Location of Assembly _____

Equipment Needed	**Assembly Agenda**
PA System	
Trash Cans	
Extra Tables	
Food/Drink	
_____	
_____	
_____	
_____	
_____	
Other	
_____	
_____	
_____	
_____	
_____	
_____	

Comments

Team Assembly Notice

Dear Parents,

Our team would like to invite you to our assembly.

The date will be _____

The time will be _____

The location will be _____

_____

We want to use this opportunity to bring you into the school and enjoy a casual, relaxing atmosphere where you can participate in your child's learning experiences.

In this assembly, we will specifically be doing the following:

_____

_____

_____

_____

_____

Please come join us if you can!

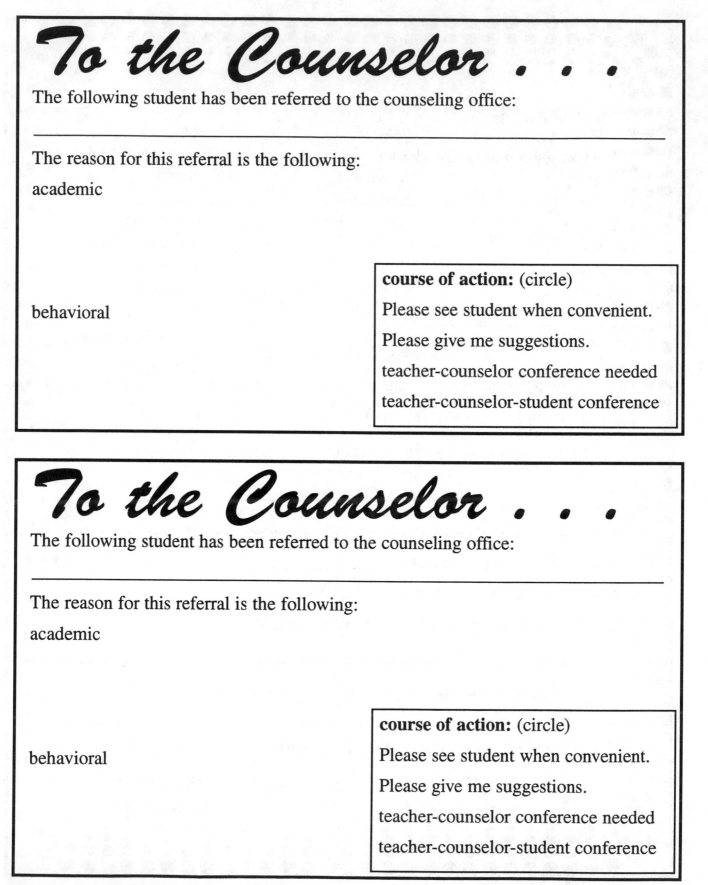

To the Counselor . . .

The following student has been referred to the counseling office:

_____

The reason for this referral is the following:

academic

behavioral

course of action: (circle)

Please see student when convenient.

Please give me suggestions.

teacher-counselor conference needed

teacher-counselor-student conference

To the Counselor . . .

The following student has been referred to the counseling office:

_____

The reason for this referral is the following:

academic

behavioral

course of action: (circle)

Please see student when convenient.

Please give me suggestions.

teacher-counselor conference needed

teacher-counselor-student conference

College Plans

Liberal Arts
-English
-history
-political science
-government
-economics
-philosophy
-anthropology
-archaeology
-linguistics
-foreign languages
-geography
-humanities
-Latin American studies
-sociology
-religious studies
-classics (Greek-
  Latin, mythology)

Science
-biology
-chemistry
-geology
-astronomy
-botany
-oceanography
-mathematics
-physics
-zoology

Business
-accounting
-finance
-management
-marketing

Communications
-speech
-radio/TV-film
-advertising
-journalism

Fine Arts
-art
-music
-theater
-dance

Professional Schools
-Nursing
-Pharmacy
-Social Work
-Computer Sciences
-Architecture
-Education
-Engineering
-Kinesiology (sports)

Post Graduate
Law
Medicine
Masters
Doctorate

The **major** I would like to pursue is_____

The **minor** I would choose to study would be _____

The college or university I would like to attend would be

_____

Their mascot is the _____

Their school colors are _____

I will finance my college education by (circle one):

　　　　Scholarship　　　　　　　　　　　　　School Loan

　　　　　Grant　　　　　　　　　　　　　　My Own Work

Grade Change Form

Teacher _____ Date _____

Student Number	Name	Reporting Period	Previous Grade	New Grade

Comments:

Progress Report

Student _____ Date _____

Teacher _____ Subject _____

Commendations	✓	**Comment Box**
Good Attendance	☐	
Prompt	☐	
Courteous	☐	
Effective Study Habits	☐	
Excellent Achievement......................	☐	
Attentive in Class	☐	
Participates Well in Class	☐	
Dependable	☐	
Cooperative...................................	☐	
Shows Good Leadership....................	☐	
Helpful	☐	

Unsatisfactory Comments	✓	**Comment Box**
Is Currently Failing	☐	
Borderline.....................................	☐	
Ineffective Study Habits	☐	
Lack of Work Ethic	☐	
Uncooperative.................................	☐	
Missing Assignments	☐	
Negative Attitude	☐	
Parent Conference Requested..............	☐	
Lack of Organizational Skills..............	☐	
Other:	☐	

Tutoring Center
Matrix

Name	Contact	Phone	Fax	Comments

Library Rules

The library is a special privilege. You can find magazines, newspapers, books, audio tapes, videos, and even computer services! If you don't observe these simple rules, the library privilege will no longer be an option for you.

1   Use Quiet Voices
Disturbing others is rude.

2   Know How to Find What You Are Looking For
- periodicals index
- card catalog
- reference
- telecommunications
- casual reading

3   Exercise Your Individuality— Do Individual Work
- notes
- worksheets
- bibliographies

4   Know How to Check Out Library Materials
Ask your librarian politely to check out a book and fill out the book card appropriately.

5   Avoid Late Fines—Turn In Books on Time
If you don't return your books, you will be unable to use the library and may have to pay money for being late.

Don't forget these 5 rules, and the wonders of the library will be in your grasp!

Library Pass

Library Pass

For _____

Reason _____

_____

In: _____ AM/PM

Out: _____ AM/PM

Teacher _____

Library Pass

For _____

Reason _____

_____

In: _____ AM/PM

Out: _____ AM/PM

Teacher _____

Library Pass

For _____

Reason _____

_____

In: _____ AM/PM

Out: _____ AM/PM

Teacher _____

Library Pass

For _____

Reason _____

_____

In: _____ AM/PM

Out: _____ AM/PM

Teacher _____

Library Pass

For _____

Reason _____

_____

In: _____ AM/PM

Out: _____ AM/PM

Teacher _____

Library Pass

For _____

Reason _____

_____

In: _____ AM/PM

Out: _____ AM/PM

Teacher _____

Memo to the Principal

☐ Response Requested

☐ FYI   Date:

From: _____

Regarding: _____

_____

_____

_____

_____

_____

_____

_____

_____

Memo to the Principal

☐ Response Requested

☐ FYI   Date:

From: _____

Regarding: _____

_____

_____

_____

_____

_____

_____

_____

_____

Memo to the Vice Principal

☐ Response Requested

☐ FYI   Date:

From: _____

Regarding: _____

_____

_____

_____

_____

_____

_____

_____

_____

Memo to the Vice Principal

☐ Response Requested

☐ FYI   Date:

From: _____

Regarding: _____

_____

_____

_____

_____

_____

_____

_____

_____

Attendance Change Form

Student	Name	Date(s)	Previous Designation	Change To

Comments

Supplies Order Form

To: Office Manager
Date:_____

From:_____

Room: _____

At your convenience, could you please supply me with the following order:

Circle Appropriate Items Needed and Quantity

- **chalk** _____boxes
- **transparencies** quantity_____
- **transparency pens**
  red _____
  black _____
  green _____
  blue _____
  other_____
- **pencils** _____
- **staples** _____
- **paper**_____
- **scissors** _____
- **special media supplies**
  video tapes _____
  audio tapes _____
  computer discs_____

- **stamps** _____
  reason_____
- **stapler** _____
- **construction paper**
  red _____
  yellow _____
  blue _____
  green _____
  other_____
- **glue**
  bottles _____
  glue sticks _____
- **tape**
  scotch _____
  yellow _____
- **other supplies**

  _____

  _____

  _____

  _____

  _____

School Fax Form

To: _____

From: _____

Regarding: _____

Expect _____ Pages to Follow

School _____

FAX # _____

Office Phone Number _____

Special Comments:

Furniture Request/ Equipment Repair

Furniture Request

Item _____

Why Needed _____

Room # _____ Location of Item _____

Teacher Signature _____

Equipment Repair

Item _____

Make _____ Model _____ Serial # _____

Problem _____

_____

_____

Room # _____ Location _____

Teacher Signature _____

Maintenance/Repair Needs

Type of Work	Location in Room	Comments

General Letter Home to Parents

Date: _____

Teacher Name and Subject	**Teacher Background/Education**
Conference Hours	**Family**
School Phone Numbers	
Advice to Succeed in the Course	**Materials Needed**
_____	
_____	**Special Requirements**
_____	
_____	
_____	
_____	
_____	
_____	

Special Comments

Parent Phone Record

Student	Parent Who Was Contacted	Date	Answering Machine?

Summary of Conversation

Student	Parent Who Was Contacted	Date	Answering Machine?

Summary of Conversation

Parent Conference Log

Student _____

Date _____

Parent(s) Present_____

Other Members Present _____

Student's Positive Aspects

Concerns

Possible Solutions

Contract Needed?
Yes   No

Fill out bottom portion, make copies, and have teachers fill out top portion daily. Return contract to home teacher or parent.

School-Home Contract
Daily

Name of Student _____

✔ If Done, **X** If Not Done

Desired Behaviors	Teacher/Subject	Teacher/Subject	Teacher/Subject	Teacher/Subject	Teacher/Subject	Teacher/Subject	Teacher/Subject	Teacher/Subject

School Consequences for Not Meeting Expectations	Rewards

Home Consequences for Not Meeting Expectations	Rewards

I, _____, understand the terms of this contract and pledge to do my best to live up to its guidelines. I know that this contract is meant to help me be the best I can be. I also understand that if I break the rules of this contract, I will have consequences at home and at school. If I live up its expectations, I will be rewarded.

_____
Signature of Student

_____
Signature of Parent

_____
Signature of Teacher

Fill out bottom portion, make copies, and have teachers fill out top portion daily. Return contract to home teacher or parent.

School-Home Contract

Dates _____

Name of Student _____

Teacher _____

Desired Behaviors	✔ If Done, **X** If Not Done						
	M	**T**	**W**	**TH**	**F**		**Comments**

School Consequences for Not Meeting Expectations	Rewards
Home Consequences for Not Meeting Expectations	**Rewards**

I, _____, understand the terms of this contract and pledge to do my best to live up to its guidelines. I know that this contract is meant to help me be the best I can be. I also understand that if I break the rules of this contract, I will have consequences at home and at school. If I live up its expectations, I will be rewarded.

_____
Signature of Student

_____
Signature of Parent

_____
Signature of Teacher

Parent Conference
Sign Up

Teacher_____

Please list your name and phone number and indicate whether you would like to discuss the progress of your child over the telephone or in person.

Parents' names	Student's name	Phone numbers (W/H)	Conference by phone or in person?

Parent Volunteer
Sign Up

Teacher_____

Please list your name, phone number, and the best times during the week you are available. I invite parents to help with activities, games, food, and drinks.

Parents' names	Student's name	Phone numbers (W/H)	Best times of the week when available

Parent Volunteer Call

Teacher_____

I could really use your help in the upcoming event:

_____

    date: _____

    time: _____

Specifically, I need parents to volunteer the following:

    time:

    _____

    _____

    _____

    _____

    materials:

    _____

    _____

    _____

    _____

Please return this portion to the teacher.

Yes, I would like to help by donating my

    time _____

    material _____

    _____

    _____

Parents _____

Parent Thank You Letter!

Date:_____

To:_____

From:_____

I just wanted to take some time and say "thanks" for your help recently!

It is parents like you who make our schools a great place to learn!

I can speak for everybody when I say you really made a quality difference. Don't just take it from me—here are the students:

Club Members Matrix

Club _____ Sponsor_____

Member	Phone	Address	Other

Make color copies, fill in, laminate, cut, and distribute.

club pass

for_____

club times_____

location_____

_____

sponsor _____

depart _____

club pass

for_____

club times_____

location_____

_____

sponsor _____

depart _____

club pass

for_____

club times_____

location_____

_____

sponsor _____

depart _____

club pass

for_____

club times_____

location_____

_____

sponsor _____

depart _____

Club_____ Sponsor_____

Club Activities Planner

Meeting	Activities
1 ☐	
2 ☐	
3 ☐	
4 ☐	
5 ☐	
6 ☐	
7 ☐	

Special Materials	Upcoming Events

Intent of Fund-Raising

To: The Principal

From: _____

Regarding: Fund-Raising Idea

Fund-Raiser Date & Time _____

In the _____ club, we are interested in having a fund-raiser.

The fund-raising idea is the following:

The reason funds are needed is the following:

This will be our 1st/2nd/3rd/4th/5th fund-raiser for the year.

I hope you can approve this idea. I know the club members will appreciate it.

Approval: Yes	No (See below.)

Bake Sale!

To: Parents

From Sponsor:_____

Your baked goods are needed to support the _____
club. Our proceeds will go to

_____

_____

_____

_____

If you can help, please fill out this bottom portion and send your
baked items to school.

Please have your child deliver donations to

room _____

on the day(s) of

_____

Thanks for your help!

Goods Baked_____

Please return the following dishware: _____

_____

Parent   _____

Student   _____

Community/Business Request for Help

> to: _____
>
> address: _____
>
> phone: _____

From Your Community School

Name of Club Sponsor _____

Name of School _____

Address _____

Phone _____

We are seeking donations for our school. Proceeds will benefit our students in the following ways:

_____

_____

_____

_____

If you can donate any worthwhile items, please contact

_____

at _____

to arrange an official donation.

The best part of donating is helping our students and the community in general. We won't be shy about spreading word-of-mouth advertising for your business.

Thanks for your help!

Sincerely,

_____

Accounting Log

Date	Money Deposited	Money Withdrawn	Balance

Club_____ Sponsor_____

Club Contacts Matrix

Name	Position	Company/ School	Work # Home #	Fax #	Comments

Club_____ Sponsor_____

Club Event Organizer

Clubs/Schools Involved

_____

_____

_____

Event Description _____

Event Date/Times _____

Event Location _____

Equipment Needed	Materials Needed	Personnel Needed

Money Needed to Pay for Event Items $_____	Funds Raised _____ Funds Needed_____	Fund-Raising Ideas